DK SMITHSONIAN
Animals
a visual encyclopedia

THIRD EDITION

DK Delhi
Editor Aman Kumar
Project Art Editor Noopur Dalal
Senior Picture Researcher Sumedha Chopra
Deputy Managing Editor Sreshtha Bhattacharya
Deputy Managing Art Editor Shreya Anand
Managing Editor Kingshuk Ghoshal
Managing Art Editor Govind Mittal
DTP Designers Bimlesh Tiwari, Mohammad Rizwan
DTP Coordinators Jagtar Singh, Vishal Bhatia
Senior Jackets Coordinator Priyanka Sharma Saddi

DK London
Senior Editor Amanda Wyatt
Project Art Editor Joe Lawrence
US Senior Editor Megan Douglass
US Executive Editor Lori Cates Hand
Managing Editor Rachel Fox
Managing Art Editor Owen Peyton Jones
Production Editor Robert Dunn
Senior Production Controller Laura Andrews
Jacket Designer Surabhi Wadhwa-Gandhi
Jacket Design Development Manager Sophia MTT
Publisher Andrew Macintyre
Associate Publishing Director Liz Wheeler
Art Director Karen Self
Publishing Director Jonathan Metcalf

Consultant John Woodward
Fact Checkers Steve Hoffman, Priyanka Lamichhane

FIRST EDITION
Project Editors Carrie Love, Caroline Stamps
Project Art Editor Rachael Smith
Editors Ann Baggaley, Elinor Greenwood, Wendy Horobin,
Cécile Landau, Lorrie Mack, Penny Smith
Designers Sadie Thomas, Clemence De Molliens,
Gemma Fletcher, Joanna Pocock
Picture Researcher Liz Moore

Packaging services supplied by Bookwork

Publishing Manager Bridget Giles
Art Director Rachael Foster
Production Controller Claire Pearson
Production Editor Lucy Sims
Jacket Designer Natalie Godwin
Jacket Editor Mariza O'Keeffe
Jackets Design Development Manager Sophia MTT

Consultants Dr. Mark Fox; Dr. John Friel;
Matthew Robertson; and Eileen Westwig, MS

This American edition, 2024
First American Edition, 2008
Published in the United States by DK Publishing
1745 Broadway, 20th Floor, New York, NY 10019

Copyright © 2008, 2012, 2024 Dorling Kindersley Limited
DK, a Division of Penguin Random House LLC
24 25 26 27 28 10 9 8 7 6 5 4 3 2 1
001–339259–Mar/2024

A catalog record for this book is available from the Library of Congress.
ISBN 978-0-7440-9287-5 (Paperback)
ISBN 978-0-5938-4177-8 (Hardcover)

DK books are available at special discounts when purchased in bulk for
sales promotions, premiums, fund-raising, or educational use. For details, contact:
DK Publishing Special Markets, 1745 Broadway, 20th Floor, New York, NY 10019
SpecialSales@dk.com

Printed and bound in China

www.dk.com

Smithsonian

Established in 1846, the Smithsonian is the world's largest
museum and research complex, dedicated to public
education, national service, and scholarship in the arts,
sciences, and history. It includes 21 museums and
galleries and the National Zoological Park. The total
number of artifacts, works of art, and specimens in the
Smithsonian's collection is estimated at 155.5 million.

MIX
Paper | Supporting
responsible forestry
FSC™ C018179

This book was made with Forest
Stewardship Council™ certified
paper—one small step in DK's
commitment to a sustainable future.
For more information go to
www.dk.com/our-green-pledge

Contents

Foreword

We share our planet with a wonderful array of diverse and fascinating creatures. From the tiniest insect to the mighty blue whale, animals have adapted to fill every niche in the ecosystem. There are so many different types (species), that even after hundreds of years of scientific study, people have still not managed to catalog every species that exists. Even the most familiar animals have aspects of their behavior, lifestyle, or biology that remain to be discovered. However, it is a sad fact that many species will vanish through habitat loss, pollution, and human exploitation before their true value to biodiversity is known.

This comprehensive guide aims to introduce children to the exciting world of animals. All the major groups are represented: mammals, birds, fish, reptiles, amphibians, and invertebrates. Each section introduces the reader to the main characteristics of the groups, families, and species that follow. Individual entries focus on particularly interesting or common species, detailing their habitat, geographic location, relative size, lifespan, and conservation status. Stunning photographs accompany the text, revealing the spectacular colors and fabulous decorations displayed by many animals, as well as insights into their behavior in the wild. From the biggest to the baddest and the beautiful to the bizarre, the wonders of the animal kingdom are revealed here to amaze and inform young minds.

Dr. John P. Friel
Director, Alabama Museum of Natural History
Interim Chair, Department of Biological
Sciences

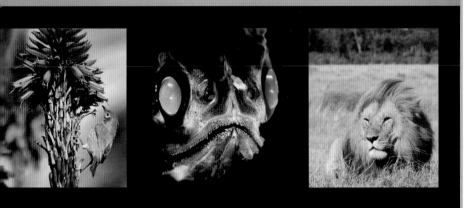

ANIMALS IN DANGER

Many animals face the threat of extinction. An animal is said to be extinct when the last known specimen has died. Scientists monitor how close an animal may be to extinction using a classification system devised by the International Union for the Conservation of Nature (IUCN). Under this system, animals that have been evaluated are put into the following categories:

- **Extinct in the wild:** the animal only exists in captivity or as a naturalized population outside its normal range.
- **Critically endangered:** the animal is facing an extremely high risk of extinction.
- **Endangered:** the animal is facing a very high risk of extinction.

- **Vulnerable:** the animal is facing a high risk of extinction.
- **Near threatened:** the animal is likely to qualify for one of the above categories in the near future, or depends on conservation efforts for its survival.

- **Least concern:** the animal has been assessed but is regarded as widespread and abundant.

- **Data deficient/Not evaluated:** there is not enough information to assess the animal fully or it has not been assessed. Some of these animals, such as earthworms, fall within this category even though they are known to be common. IUCN does not classify animals that are domesticated or farmed, such as cattle, sheep, dromedary camels, goldfish, and household pets.

ANIMAL KINGDOM

Definition: An **animal** is a living being made of many cells that combine to form tissues and organs. All animals get energy by eating plants and other living organisms. Most of them can move from place to place.

What is an *Animal*?

The animal kingdom is a vast collection of weird and wonderful creatures. Members of this group come in many different shapes and sizes, but they are all made up of cells, and they all have nerves and muscles to move and respond to the world around them. Most importantly, all animals eat food to make energy.

ANIMALS

Warm and cold blood Birds and mammals are warm-blooded animals, which means they make their own body heat using the energy from their food. Other animals, such as amphibians, fish, insects, and reptiles, are cold-blooded creatures, which means they cannot make their own body heat. Instead, cold-blooded animals rely on outside sources of heat, such as the warmth of the sun, to raise their body temperature and carry on their daily lives.

VERTEBRATES

are animals with backbones and include amphibians, birds, fish, mammals, and reptiles.

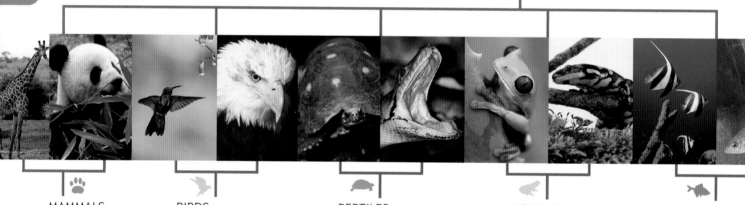

MAMMALS

Mammals have fur and feed their young with milk from the mother's mammary glands.

BIRDS

Birds have feathers and produce young by laying eggs. Most birds move using their wings to fly.

REPTILES

Reptiles have dry skin covered with scales or horny plates. Most produce young by laying eggs.

AMPHIBIANS

Most amphibians spend much of their adult lives on land and breathe air, but return to water to breed.

FISH

Fish have fins and scales and spend of their lives in the water. They breathe using gills.

FOOD CHAINS When

animals eat other animals, the energy in the food passes through a food chain. The first link in the chain is a plant. Plants create food using the energy from the sun. When an animal eats the plant, the energy passes up the chain. The food chain continues as animals eat other animals.

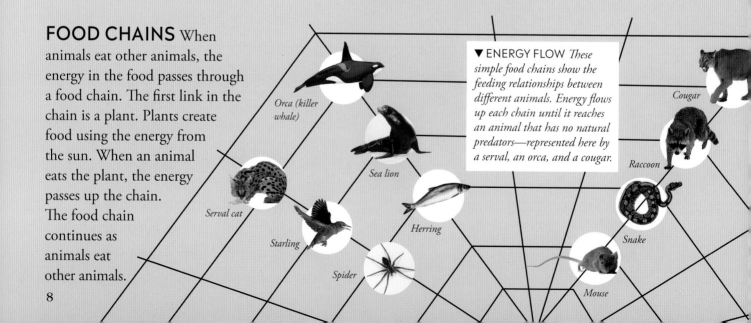

▼ ENERGY FLOW *These simple food chains show the feeding relationships between different animals. Energy flows up each chain until it reaches an animal that has no natural predators—represented here by a serval, an orca, and a cougar.*

Orca (killer whale)

Cougar

Sea lion

Raccoon

Serval cat

Herring

Snake

Starling

Spider

Mouse

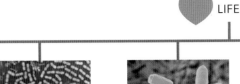 LIFE

BACTERIA ARCHAEA PLANTS FUNGI PROTISTS

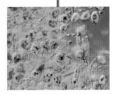

PROTISTS are a group of organisms that include some seaweeds and molds. Many are single-celled.

INVERTEBRATES

make up 95 percent of the animal kingdom. They are animals that do not have a bony skeleton. They include insects, spiders, and many marine creatures such as crabs and starfish.

WORMS
Various unrelated groups.

ARACHNIDS
Scorpions, spiders, ticks, mites.

CRUSTACEANS
Crabs, lobsters, woodlice.

MOLLUSKS
Clams, octopuses, oysters, squid, slugs, snails.

SPONGES

CNIDARIANS
Sea anemones, corals, jellyfish, hydroids.

HORSESHOE CRAB

INSECTS
Butterflies, moths, mosquitoes, flies, dragonflies, beetles.

ECHINODERMS
Starfish, sea urchins, sand dollars.

ANIMAL OVERCOATS

Feathers (left), fur (center), and scales (right).

Animals keep warm and protect their skin and bodies in different ways. Birds are covered with feathers, mammals have coats of fur, while scales or horny plates grow out of the skin of fish and reptiles.

CLASSIFICATION

Scientists organize the living world into groups. Living things of the same species can produce fertile offspring. Related species are grouped into a genus, and genera are grouped into families. This grouping system carries on through order, class, and phylum to kingdom at the top of the classification system. The following shows an example of scientific classification for the lion. The genus name is always written in italics with a capital first letter; the species name is written in italics but does not have a capital first letter.

- **Order:** Carnivora—animals with cheek teeth for slicing meat.

- **Family:** Felidae—includes every type of cat, both large and small.

- **Genus:** *Panthera*—large cats that can roar as well as purr. Includes lions, tigers, panthers.

- **Species:** *leo*—identifies the large cat specifically as a lion.

Animal *behavior*

Anything an animal does is part of its behavior. This ranges from simple things such as eating and keeping clean to more complex activities such as attracting a mate. Some behavior is instinctive, while other behavior develops through experience.

Many animals choose to live and hunt alone and only come together to mate during the breeding season. As soon as the mating takes place, the two sexes part company again.

LIVING TOGETHER

Animals choose to live together for many different reasons. One of the main benefits is safety in numbers. You might think that a group of animals offers a predator a wider choice of prey. In fact, the predator often finds it hard to single out its victim. So for any one animal, the chance of being eaten is less.

Feeding time Animals spend a lot of time looking for food. Some predators hunt alone and rely on speed or stealth to capture prey. Others hunt in groups. Scavengers feed on the remains that other animals leave behind.

▲ LIFE IN THE HERD
Living in a herd offers a better chance of survival for zebras since there are more eyes on the lookout for predators such as lions.

▲ BEE COLONIES
Within a bee colony, one female, called the queen, produces all the young. It's her job, and she is helped by all the bees in the colony.

▲ HOME TO ROOST
During the day, large numbers of bats gather to rest at roosting sites, such as caves. They emerge at dusk to feed.

▲ NESTING SITES
During the breeding season, seabirds such as gannets and gulls make their nests in dense colonies along the coast.

▲ ON THE PROWL
Female lions and their cubs live in groups called prides. Each pride is defended by an adult male. Other males live alone or in groups.

SENDING A MESSAGE

Animals keep in touch in different ways. They may make noisy calls, use body language and other visual cues, or leave scent marks. Animals communicate in these ways for many reasons, such as finding food and finding each other.

◄ SMILE *When a chimpanzee is frightened, it bares its teeth. So what looks like a smile to us is actually a chimpanzee's grin of fear.*

A smile?

◄ BIRD SONG
Birds use a range of melodic songs and calls to "speak" to each other. They use these calls in many ways, perhaps to warn of danger or mark out a territory.

▼ TONGUE TASTER *The snake's forked tongue brings smells and tastes into its mouth. These are then detected in two pits, called "Jacobson's organs," on the roof of its mouth.*

Mangrove snake
Boiga dendrophila

Danger signals

Animals use a range of defensive tactics when they feel threatened. Some rely on their speed to escape from danger, while others puff up their bodies to exaggerate their size and look more dangerous. In some cases, these threats are real.

◄ BROWN BEAR *These bears can be aggressive, especially when a mother is protecting her cubs. Brown bears stand upright to look as threatening as possible, growling and baring their teeth.*

▶ COBRA
When threatened, the Indian cobra spreads its broad hood to look more menacing. This display is usually enough to deter the potential threat.

▶ POISON DART FROG
The bright color of the poison dart frog is a warning to all animals that it contains some deadly poisons.

▶ BUTTERFLY
The large eye spots on the wings of some butterflies and moths may startle predators by resembling the eyes of larger animals.

▶ OPOSSUM
When threatened, the opossum sinks to the ground, bares its teeth, and lolls its tongue to one side in a convincing display of death.

ANIMAL IQ

It is incredibly difficult for people to measure the intelligence of an animal. Some apparently intelligent behavior comes naturally, such as the beaver's ability to build a dam. More reliable examples of animal intelligence are the abilities to learn from experiences and solve problems, but these are relatively rare in the animal world.

▶ TOOLS OF THE TRADE *These chimpanzees are using a thin twig to probe a termite mound for the insects inside. The use of tools is unusual in the animal kingdom.*

◄ MENTAL MAPS *The Eurasian jay buries acorns as a food store for the winter. Rarely do these birds forget the location of the burial sites.*

An ANIMAL'S *life cycle*

The whole of an animal's life has just one purpose: survival of the species. Staying alive long enough to find a mate and produce young is all that really matters. Each species has its own special life cycle that is repeated as one generation follows another.

ANIMAL KINGDOM

GOING COURTING

Some animals mate at any time of year. Others breed only in particular seasons, such as spring and fall. Attracting a mate can mean putting in a lot of effort, especially for the males. Fancy plumage, shows of strength, and mating calls are just some of the ploys animals use.

▶ DISPLAY *The more impressive his tail, the more females a peacock will entice into his harem.*

▶ FROG SONGS *Frogs and toads inflate their throat sacs to make calls to mates.*

▲ LOCKING ANTLERS
These deer are having a wrestling match to decide which one of them wins the females.

▲ BOXING GLOVES
In spring, female hares often fend off excited males by fighting with them in fierce boxing matches.

CARING MOM
This mother orangutan is bringing up her infant without any help from her mate. Over the next 10 years she will teach the youngster survival skills, such as how to live safely in the forests and where to find food.

The way young develop

Most mammals give birth to live young. Animals such as birds, insects, and many reptiles and fish, lay eggs. The time it takes for young to develop independent life, inside the womb or inside an egg, or by passing through larval stages, varies enormously. A small mammal such as a vole is pregnant for two or three weeks, while an elephant's pregnancy lasts about 22 months. Some insects stay at an early stage of development for years.

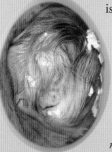

◀ IN THE EGG *An embryo chick may not begin to develop until the parent birds start sitting on the eggs. The growing chick is nourished by the egg yolk.*

▶ IN THE WOMB
At this early stage, a kitten looks much the same as a human embryo. Its body systems will be developed long before birth.

CHILDCARE

Some newborn animals receive lavish childcare. For example, a mother ape carries her young everywhere; an infant kangaroo always has a mother's pouch to shelter in; parent birds feed their nestlings on demand. On the other hand, the young of hares and some deer survive on one short daily visit from their mother, when she shows up to feed them. Often, animals such as insects, fish, and reptiles never meet their parents at all.

▶ A NEST FULL *of chicks is hard work. Many parent birds exhaust themselves feeding their hungry brood.*

▲ PUPS *are ready to be weaned from their mother's milk when they are about three weeks old.*

◀ KING PENGUINS *carry their single egg on their feet, tucked under a warm tummy fold. Both parent birds share the duty.*

◀ YOUNG KANGAROOS *stay in their mother's pouch for six months. They feed from a nipple inside the pouch.*

◀ TADPOLES *know nothing about parents. When they hatch, they must fend for themselves.*

◀ A NEWLY BORN ANTEATER *climbs straight up onto its mother's back. It rides around, clinging to the mother's fur, until it is about one year old.*

A continuing cycle

In some species of animals, mothers and their young stay together as a group for life. Among animals as widely different as lions, monkeys, and killer whales family ties remain unbroken in this way, though the male offspring will leave the group when mature so only one dominant male remains with the females. Other young male and female animals, such as pandas, move on to a largely solitary existence.

▲ ELEPHANT AUNTS
All the females in an elephant herd help a mother look after her calf.

◀ LIFE TIES
The close bond between dolphins and their offspring lasts for life.

WHERE IN THE WORLD?

Habitats are places where animals live and mix with other animals and their surroundings. Most animals can move from place to place, so they have spread to every part of the world. Many thrive in warm, wet tropical forests, while other hardy types live in some of the harshest places on our planet, from arid deserts to the darkest ocean depths.

The following symbols (except Mediterranean-type biomes) are used throughout the book.

 Tropical forest and rainforest

 Temperate forest, including woodland

 Coniferous forest, including woodland

 Mountains, highlands, scree slopes

 Desert and semi-desert

 Open habitats including grassland, scrub, moorland, heathland, savanna, fields

  Rivers, streams, and all flowing water

  Wetlands and all still bodies of water

 Mangrove swamps above or below waterline

 Seas and oceans

  Coastal areas

 Coral reefs and waters immediately around them

 Polar regions, including tundra and icebergs

Mediterranean-type biomes

World habitats

Our planet is home to a range of landscapes and some equally varied weather patterns. Months go by in the desert without a single drop of rain, while rainforests are soaked daily by tropical storms. Little wonder then that Earth supports such an amazing diversity of life.

Wetlands and mangroves

In some wetlands, plants form a thin carpet over the waterlogged soil, while in others stretches of open water mix with patches of dense vegetation. Wetlands are homes for land-based swimmers such as snakes, as well as many insects, fish, and waterbirds. Mangrove swamps (see inset) are flooded with salt water when the tide comes in and left exposed when the water retreats. These swamps contain many fish, and the dense forests provide excellent nesting sites for birds.

Tropic of Cancer

Equator

Tropic of Caprico

Temperate and coniferous forest

In the northern hemisphere, temperate forests of deciduous trees eventually give way to coniferous forests that stretch across the far north, deep inside the Arctic Circle, where the temperatures rarely rise above freezing. Farther south, the temperate forests of evergreen trees have warm summers and mild winters. These forests are home to many different animals. Bears, birds of prey, and wolves live in the coniferous forests of the far north, while deer, lizards, squirrels, and many forest birds are found farther south.

Tundra

The tundra is a vast, cold landscape north of the Arctic Circle. It is so cold that the soil is frozen for most of the year. In the spring, the tundra bursts into life as snow and ice melt. Alpine plants appear, and birds arrive to breed. As the soil starts to freeze again, the plants wither and the birds depart, marking the end of the short summer.

Grassland

Grasslands go by different names in different places. They are prairies in North America, pampas or paramo in South America, steppes in Europe and Asia, and the outback in Australia. The tropical and subtropical grassland of Africa is known as the savanna. In all these areas, grasses are the dominant plants and the main source of food for huge herds of grazing mammals, such as the wildebeest and zebras of Africa. In turn, these grazers are the food for predators such as the big cats and wild dogs.

Arctic Ocean

EUROPE

NORTH AMERICA

ASIA

Atlantic Ocean

Pacific Ocean

AFRICA

ific Ocean

SOUTH AMERICA

Indian Ocean

Atlantic Ocean

AUSTRALIA

DESERT LIFE
The world's deserts are hostile habitats that get very little rain. Many are extremely hot.

ANTARCTICA

Mountain

Few habitats experience such a variation in conditions as the mountains. Lower down the slopes, in the foothills, the conditions usually match that of the surrounding area. Many animals make their home here, including forest birds and large mammals, such as apes, bears, deer, and monkeys. Higher up the slopes, the air gets thinner and the temperature drops rapidly. Only the hardiest animals, such as birds of prey and mountain goats, can cope with the harsh conditions.

Coastal areas

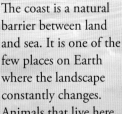

The coast is a natural barrier between land and sea. It is one of the few places on Earth where the landscape constantly changes. Animals that live here must adapt to the rhythm of the tides. Rocky coasts, mudflats, and sandy beaches abound with marine invertebrates and the wading birds that feed on them.

The **rainforest** is warm and wet, creating the perfect conditions for plant growth. This rich vegetation provides the foundations for abundant animal life.

Hot forests

Rainforests enjoy plenty of warmth and moisture. The rainforests that lie on the equator are hot and humid all year round. They are some of the most productive habitats on Earth. The seasonal forests on either side of the equator—the so-called monsoon forests—experience a yearly cycle of rain and sunlight. They are home to a wide variety of animal life.

🏠 TROPICAL RAINFOREST

MEALY PARROT
These large parrots live in pairs or small flocks in the Amazon rainforest, where they feast on the abundant fruits, seeds, and nuts.

TREE DWELLERS
White-faced capuchins live in complex social groups called troops, which patrol the rainforests of Central and South America.

LEAF CUTTERS
Leafcutter ants live in complex colonies in almost every part of the rainforest, from the tallest treetops down to the leaf litter.

NIGHT CAT
The ocelot lives on the floor of the rainforest, where it hunts birds, small mammals, and reptiles under the cover of darkness.

WATER LOVER
The capybara is the largest of all the rodents. It lives in densely forested areas near lakes, rivers, and swamps of the South American rainforest.

Rainforest layers

A tropical rainforest grows in distinct layers. Each layer consists of plants and animals that have adapted to living in that particular part of the rainforest. The top, or emergent, layer consists of the tallest trees. Here it is hot and windy. Below this level is the canopy, a dense layer of branches that is home to most of the forest's animals. The dark understory of shrubs and seedlings is the next level down, followed by the leaf litter on the forest floor, which supports fungi and new plant growth.

HABITATS LARGE AND SMALL

Macrohabitat A typical example of a macrohabitat would be all the regions within a large, complex environment such as a coastal region. For example, the intertidal zone, rocky pools, and sand dunes along the shore would all make up the coastal macrohabitat.

Microhabitat Within each macrohabitat there are many smaller microhabitats. These regions may be no bigger than a small, rotting log within the vast expanse of a rainforest. Each tiny environment harbors animals that may not be found anywhere else in the macrohabitat.

Dry desert heat

The world's deserts are dry, barren habitats that get less than 6 in (15 cm) of rain each year. But weeks without rain are punctuated by brief storms that soak the parched soil and may lead to local flooding. Few living things can cope with these extreme conditions, so deserts are home to a very specialized range of animals and plants.

Life in the cold poles

Earth's deserts and polar regions have one thing in common—very little rainfall. But while many deserts are scorching hot, the polar regions are the coldest places in the world. Only animals that are adapted to survive the very low temperatures can live there. Sea mammals have thick layers of fat under their skin, called blubber, while some fish even have "antifreeze" in their blood.

 DESERT

FOOD TIME *The golden eagle uses its keen sense of sight to hunt animals such as rabbits, hares, squirrels, voles, and mice.*

 POLAR REGIONS

ARCTIC TERN *Arctic terns migrate between the Arctic and Antarctic each year, making full use of the daylight hours at each pole.*

NESTING HOLE *The Gila woodpecker lives in the deserts of the southwestern United States. It builds its nest in holes made in saguaro cacti or mesquite trees.*

POLAR BEAR *Seals are the main food source for these Arctic predators. The polar bear's blubber and thick fur keep it warm underwater and on the ice.*

DESERT CAT *The desert-dwelling bobcat lives in the southerly part of North America, where it hunts birds, hares, rabbits, and other small mammals.*

PENGUIN *These superb swimmers are adapted for a life under water. They use their flipper-like wings to chase fish— a favorite food.*

DEATH RATTLE *The rattle on the end of a rattlesnake's tail gives this venomous snake its name. If threatened, the snake shakes its rattle as a warning to steer clear.*

LEOPARD SEAL *The fearsome leopard seal roams the southern oceans in search of food such as seabirds, smaller seals, and penguins.*

STINGING TAIL *Scorpions have large, hook-shaped stings on the ends of their tails. These act as defensive weapons but can be used to kill prey.*

KRILL *These tiny crustaceans thrive in cold Arctic and Antarctic waters, where they feed on plankton. They are eaten by seals and whales.*

SAVANNA

EYE IN THE SKY
The African white-backed vulture soars high over the vast, open savanna in search of the remains of dead animals.

TREE SNAKE
The boomslang is a highly poisonous tree-dwelling snake that lives in savanna and scrub south of the Sahara Desert.

AFRICAN GIANT
Herds of up to 30 African elephants wander across the savanna in search of food and water holes.

TOP PREDATOR
Female lions hunt together, looking for weak or young zebras and wildebeest in the vast herds that roam the savanna.

DUNG DEALERS
Revolting as it may sound, dung beetles eat poop! They roll the dung into balls and bury them in the soil to feed their young.

URBAN HABITATS

Many animals have chosen to make their homes alongside our own. Towns and cities provide plenty of hiding places for these adaptable animals. The vast amounts of garbage we produce are rich pickings for the hungry scavengers that can cope with the hustle and bustle of city life.

◀ MONKEY PALACE
Rhesus macaques patrol the walls of the Hawa Mahal temple (Palace of the Winds) in Jaipur, India. These monkeys thrive in urban areas and rely on handouts or human garbage. They have become a serious pest in some countries.

CORAL REEF

SEA PIRATES
Frigate birds are famous for stealing food. They attack other seabirds in flight and force them to release their food.

REEF SHARK
The whitetip reef shark is harmless to people. It patrols the reef, searching for food such as crustaceans, octopus, and fish.

SEA TURTLE
The hawksbill turtle uses its narrow beak to forage for sponges, mollusks, and other marine animals among the coral reef.

CLEANER CRAB
The scarlet reef hermit crab is a reef cleaner. Its appetite for hairy and slime algae helps keep the reef clean and tidy.

REEF FISH
With their bold patterns and bright colors, angelfish are some of the most spectacular fish of the coral reef.

FRESH WATER HABITATS

FISHING BIRD
Herons are expert fishing birds. They use their keen sense of sight to pluck fish from below the water's surface.

DRAGONFLIES
These skilled aerial hunters skim over the surface of lakes and rivers, using their big, compound eyes to search for smaller insect prey.

WATER VOLES
These ratlike rodents make burrows in the banks of rivers and streams, where they feed on grasses and other plant material.

WATER LOVERS
Tadpoles spend all their time in the water, but most adult frogs and toads usually live on land, only returning to the water to breed.

PERCH
These freshwater fish live in lakes, ponds and slow-moving streams, where they hunt invertebrates and other small fish.

◄ MOUSE HOUSE
This adaptable rodent, like its relative the rat, has successfully infiltrated urban living. As cute as they look, mice are very troublesome, damaging food stores and spreading disease.

◄ FOX FACTS
The red fox is a common sight in many city centers. Outside the city center, red foxes mainly eat rabbits and hares. Urban foxes raid trash bags for food scraps.

CONSERVATION

It's a hard life living with people, and animals will either adapt to life in the city or die very quickly. Most deaths come from encounters with traffic, especially among nocturnal species. Other hazards include the bright lights, noise, and lack of space.

WHAT'S GOING WRONG?

The greatest threat to animals comes from humans. People are destroying habitats to make room for their own activities. They are poisoning the land, seas, and air with toxic chemicals; they are changing the climate. And, sometimes, the animals that survive all this are killed to meet human demand.

◄ LOGGING *Clearance for timber and land development has destroyed vast areas of forest, with large-scale damage to the environment.*

◄ WARMING *Gases released from burning fossil fuels trap heat in the atmosphere. This warming alters habitats in ways that affect animal survival.*

◄ POLLUTION *The dumping of poisonous chemicals in the oceans is harming marine life and destroying habitats such as coral reefs.*

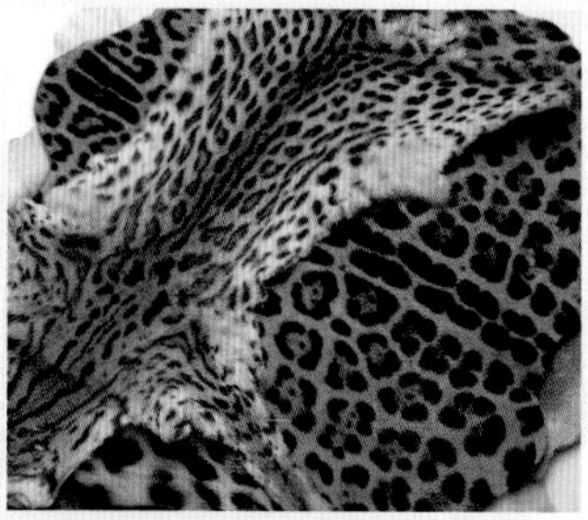

◄ SLAUGHTER *Despite laws that ban trading in animal furs and body parts, the illegal killing of species such as the leopard is difficult to control.*

◄ CAPTURE *Caught wild birds, such as these young African gray parrots, fetch high prices in the exotic bird trade. Many birds die in transit between countries.*

Animals in DANGER

Every year, wonderful animals disappear from Earth—for good. They vanish mostly because their natural habitat has been spoiled or destroyed. When an animal loses its special niche in the world, it will die if it cannot find anywhere else suitable to live. The loss of even the smallest invertebrate can have a huge impact on an ecosystem.

Melting ice Climate warming is melting the Arctic sea ice. Polar bears spend most of the Arctic summer living on the ice, where they hunt seals and mate. Now their habitat is shrinking.

Fewer polar bear cubs are surviving in the Arctic.

GLOBAL CLIMATE

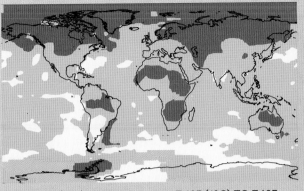

◄ WARMING UP
Based on climate records for the last 60 years, this map shows the rise of surface temperatures worldwide. The pattern of warming is variable and at present the effects are most noticeable in the polar regions.

■ 34°F (1°C) TO 38°F (3.4°C) INCREASE

☐ 32°F (0°C) TO 34°F (1°C) INCREASE

■ 34°F (1°C) TO 36°F (2°C) INCREASE

☐ NO DATA

World weather In the last century, the Earth has warmed up because of human activity. The past eight years have been the warmest recorded years. As temperatures continue to rise, there will be permanent climate changes around the world. Summers are getting hotter and drier. Some types of plants growing in particular areas may die out. Sea levels are rising as the ice caps melt, and more regions will be flooded. Warming is already affecting wildlife habitats both on and in the oceans. Around a million species of animals are threatened by climate change.

Oil and gas exploration in the Arctic pollutes the polar bears' habitat and splits up their hunting grounds. Another hazard is the release of toxic industrial chemicals, carried south by winds and currents. These poisons enter the Arctic food web and are seriously damaging the health not only of polar bears but of the Indigenous peoples.

FACT FILE

■ An estimated 64,585 ft² (6,000 m²) of rainforest are lost every second.

■ The average global sea level rose ¹⁄₁₀ in (0.27 cm) between 2021 and 2022.

■ The world's rarest land mammal is the Javan rhinoceros. Fewer than 80 of these rhinos still survive.

■ One in 8 bird species, 1 in 4 mammal species, and 1 in 3 amphibian species are believed to be currently at risk of extinction.

■ Animals face threats because of trafficking. More than 195,000 pangolins were trafficked in 2019 alone.

WHAT'S BEING DONE?

Around the world, national parks and wildlife reserves help animals by protecting their natural habitats. Breeding rare animals in captivity and releasing them into the wild has also had some success. Animals are further protected by international laws, such as those that place limits on hunting and make it illegal to trade in rare species.

▶ BREEDING
The golden lion tamarin is one of the world's rarest monkeys. Zoo-bred tamarins successfully released into the wild have helped to boost numbers.

▶ PLANNING
American bison, once counted in millions, were hunted almost to extinction. Under a protection plan, small herds are now thriving.

▶ RELOCATION
New Zealand's rare flightless parrot, the kakapo, has been moved to a safer location. This may save the species from being wiped out by predators.

▶ HEALTH CARE
To protect the last few hundred Ethiopian wolves, domestic dogs in nearby areas are vaccinated to prevent the spread of canine diseases.

▶ SANCTUARY
Both the American alligator (front) and the endangered American crocodile (rear) are fully protected while they are in the Everglades National Park.

MAMMALS

Definition: **Mammals** are warm-blooded creatures like humans. They drink milk from their mother when they're first born, and most grow hair and give birth to live young.

What is a MAMMAL?

Mammals are vertebrates that feed their young from the female's mammary glands—these glands give the class its name. Mammals also maintain a constant internal body temperature.

BORN ALIVE

Most mammals give birth to live young—only a few lay eggs. The young of most placental mammals are born fully developed. Newborn marsupials (such as kangaroos) develop further in their mother's pouch.

◄ FEEDING
Because newborn mammals drink milk from their mother, they don't have to wander off and find food.

FACT FILE

There are around 6,400 species of mammals, which are grouped into different families and orders including:

■ **Marsupials**, which give birth to embryos early in their development. The tiny creatures crawl up to the mother's pouch, and continue growing there.

■ **Insectivores**, small mammals that eat insects, spiders, and worms.

■ **Bats**, the only mammals that have true wings and are able to fly.

■ **Rodents**, small mammals with four legs, a long tail, clawed feet, long whiskers, and teeth. There are more species of rodent than any other mammal.

■ **Cetaceans**, such as whales, dolphins, and porpoises. These are aquatic mammals that breathe through lungs.

■ **Carnivores**, animals with sharp meat-slicing teeth. Most carnivores are meat-eaters, but some, such as bears and the giant panda, also eat plants.

■ **Hoofed mammals**, which are known for their speed and strength. Hoofed mammals have long muzzles, grinding teeth, and barrel-shaped bodies.

HAIR

With a few exceptions, mammals have a covering of hair or fur on their body. (Whales and dolphins have no fur.) This helps keep them warm. In cold conditions, each hair will be pulled upright by a tiny erector muscle, trapping a layer of warming air.

▶ SPINY BEAST
The short-nosed echidna is a rare, egg-laying mammal. It has both spines and fur.

Hair

Sweat gland

Sebaceous gland

Erector muscle

Follicle

Blood supply to follicle

BONE STRUCTURE

Mammal skeletons differ from those of other vertebrates—the jaw of mammals is hinged directly to the skull. Also, the lower jaw consists of a single bone. Together, these factors make the jaw extremely efficient at cutting and then chewing food.

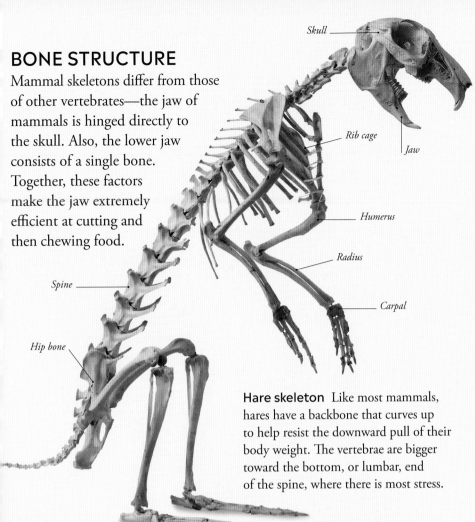

Skull

Rib cage

Jaw

Humerus

Radius

Carpal

Spine

Hip bone

Hare skeleton Like most mammals, hares have a backbone that curves up to help resist the downward pull of their body weight. The vertebrae are bigger toward the bottom, or lumbar, end of the spine, where there is most stress.

Amazing variety

Mammals, which originally developed from prehistoric reptiles, come in all shapes and sizes. They live mostly on land, but they can live in water, too. Some mammals are widely familiar, but other, rarer, species are not as well known.

▲ SLOTHS *live in the rainforest trees of South America. They move slowly, and come down only occasionally to leave droppings.*

▲ ARMADILLOS *are native to South and Central America. They have bony armor that protects them from their enemies.*

▲ THE DUCK-BILLED PLATYPUS *has a furry body, but it lives in water and walks like a reptile. It lays eggs, but its young feed on their mother's milk.*

▶ BOWHEAD WHALES *have no teeth; they feed on the plankton in seawater. Vast quantities of this water are filtered through a tough fringe called baleen, which dangles inside the whale's mouth.*

MONKEY SKULL
Like human jaws, monkeys' jaws are designed to chew rather than tear, since monkeys gather food with their hands.

ELEPHANT SKULL
To grind tough plant fiber, elephants' jaws can move from side to side as well as up and down.

TIGER SKULL
A tiger's jaws anchor huge, sharp teeth for tearing chunks of meat.

▲ JAW ADAPTATIONS
Mammal jaws, like those of all animals, are shaped and constructed to suit the food they eat. Long, thin jaws, for example, are good for probing and nibbling, while short, broad jaws are ideal for grinding plants or cracking bones.

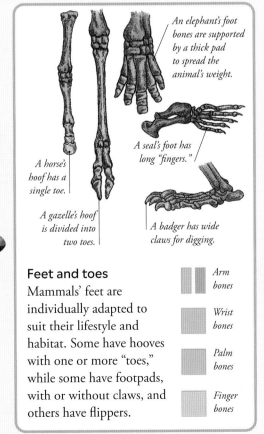

An elephant's foot bones are supported by a thick pad to spread the animal's weight.

A seal's foot has long "fingers."

A horse's hoof has a single toe.

A gazelle's hoof is divided into two toes.

A badger has wide claws for digging.

Feet and toes

Mammals' feet are individually adapted to suit their lifestyle and habitat. Some have hooves with one or more "toes," while some have footpads, with or without claws, and others have flippers.

	Arm bones
	Wrist bones
	Palm bones
	Finger bones

Marsupials

All marsupials give birth to live young which are poorly developed. Most complete their development in a pouch containing teats, from which they drink milk. There are about 350 species of marsupial. Most live in Australia and New Guinea. Some live in the Americas.

LIFE IN A POUCH

When a marsupial is born it makes its way to its mother's pouch where it attaches itself to a teat. It remains firmly attached until it is fully formed and can explore the outside world. Some pouches face up, as in kangaroos, and some face down, as in koalas. Some pouches can hold several babies, but others are a simple flap and the young have to cling tight to their mother's fur.

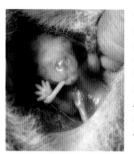

◄ PARMA WALLABY
(Macropus parma) *The tiny newborn wallaby, called a joey, develops in its mother's pouch. It can leave the pouch after about 30 weeks, but is not independent until it is about 40 weeks old.*

Eastern gray kangaroo

Macropus giganteus

- **Length** 5–6 ft (1.5–1.8 m)
- **Weight** 70–132 lb (32–60 kg)
- **Speed** 34 mph (55 kph)
- **Location** Eastern Australia and Tasmania

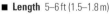

The eastern gray kangaroo is a steely gray color with white underparts, legs, and underside of the tail. Its tail is strong and is **used for balance** while jumping and leaping, and as a prop while standing upright. Females are much smaller than males.

Red kangaroo

Macropus rufus

- **Length** 5 ft (1.6 m)
- **Weight** 200 lb (90 kg)
- **Speed** 30 mph (50 kph)
- **Location** Australia

The red kangaroo is the **largest marsupial**. Males are orange-red in color while the smaller females are blue-gray. Like the gray kangaroo, the red kangaroo **bounds along** on its hind legs. It eats grass shoots, herbs, and leaves.

Northern quoll

Dasyurus hallucatus

- **Length** 12 in (30 cm)
- **Weight** 2 lb (900 g)
- **Location** Australia

Quolls are **carnivorous** marsupials and have many sharp teeth for killing their prey. Northern quolls eat mainly insects, worms, small mammals, and reptiles, but they also like a bit of **honey** and fruit. They are active mostly at night, preferring to sleep during the heat of the day.

Doria's tree kangaroo

Dendrolagus dorianus

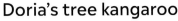

- **Length** 31 in (78 cm)
- **Weight** 32 lb (14.5 kg)
- **Location** New Guinea

Tree kangaroos have **short, broad feet** with long claws, which are useful for gripping as they climb through the trees. They use their long tails to help them **balance on the branches**. Doria's tree kangaroo has dense brown fur, black ears, and a pale brown or cream tail.

Koala

Phascolarctos cinereus

- **Length** 32 in (82 cm)
- **Weight** 33 lb (15 kg)
- **Location** Eastern Australia

Although it is often called a koala bear, the koala is not at all related to the bear. It lives in **eucalyptus trees** and its only food is eucalyptus leaves. It feeds at night and spends all day asleep in a tree. Female koalas have one baby at a time. The baby spends more than six months in its mother's pouch then climbs out and **rides on her back**.

MONOTREME FACT FILE

Monotremes are the only egg-laying mammals. There are five living species: one platypus and four echidnas. As with other mammals, the females produce milk in mammary glands on the belly.

- **Duck-billed platypus** (*Ornithorhynchus anatinus*) live in bank-side burrows in lakes and rivers in Australia. They have a ducklike beak covered with sensitive skin, which they use to find crustaceans and insect larvae on the river bed.

- **Echidnas** have fur, spines, and a beaklike snout. Long-beaked echidnas (*Zaglossus* species) live only in New Guinea. The short-beaked echidna (*Tachyglossus aculeatus*) lives in New Guinea and Australia. They eat ants and termites, which they collect with a sticky tongue.

Duck-billed platypus skull

Long-beaked echidna skull

Duck-billed platypus

Ornithorhynchus anatinus

- **Length** 24 in (60 cm)   - **Weight** 5½ lb (2.5 kg)
- **Location** Eastern Australia and Tasmania

The platypus is well equipped for an **aquatic life**. It has waterproof fur to keep it dry, and dense underfur to keep it warm. It also has webbed feet, which it uses like flippers to propel itself through the water.

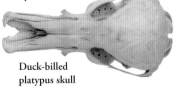

WHY DO THEY GLIDE?

Gliding is a useful method of escaping from predators as well as a quick way to get from tree to tree to find better food. Few mammals can glide. Among them are the sugar glider, shown on the right, and flying lemurs.

Flying lemurs, or colugos, are the world's largest gliding mammals—they are about the size of a domestic cat. Their name is a bit misleading, as they are not actually lemurs and they glide instead of fly! There are two species and they both live in the forests of Southeast Asia. They feed on leaves, flowers, and fruit.

Gliding *mammals*

A few mammals can glide through the trees, but they do not actually fly like birds and bats. They have a membrane of skin on either side of their body, attached between their fore and hind limbs. This skin acts like a sail, allowing the animals to glide down through the air.

Sunda flying lemur
Galeopterus variegatus

Southern flying squirrel
Glaucomys volans

The southern flying squirrel lives in hollow trees, deserted woodpecker holes, and even in bird boxes. It builds a nest out of soft materials such as moss and fur.

Southern flying squirrels live in North and Central America. They look like sugar gliders but they are rodents. Flying squirrels eat lots of different kinds of food including nuts, seeds, fruit, fungi, insects, young birds, and mice. Like other squirrels, they collect and store food for the winter.

Sugar glider
Petaurus breviceps

- **Length** 12 in (30 cm)
- **Tail** 17½ in (44 cm)
- **Weight** 5 oz (150 g)
- **Diet** Sap of the eucalyptus tree, pollen, nectar, and insects
- **Location** Australia, New Guinea, and Indonesia

This animal is a possum and therefore a marsupial, and the female has a pouch. One or two young are born and will remain in the pouch for the first **70 days of life**, before venturing out to explore their world.

PLANNING A PERFECT FLIGHT *A sugar glider is able to make "flights" through the trees of more than 165 ft (50 m). Its long, flat, furry tail is used just like a rudder, to guide it through the air.*

**Look out!
I'm coming down.**
The piece of skin that a glider uses to float through the air is called a patagium. When the animal is gliding, this is stretched taut. When the animal is walking, running, or sitting, the patagium is loose and folded out of the way.

Insect eaters

Many different animals eat insects. Six related families, including moles, hedgehogs, and shrews, are called insectivores because they eat mainly insects. Aardvarks and anteaters specialize in eating ants and termites. They both have long, sticky tongues for sweeping up their prey and powerful claws for digging out the insects' nests.

Out of the way. I'm coming out!
The aardvark has large, upright ears. When it is underground, it folds its ears out of the way. It surfaces at night, and always comes out of its burrow head first.

◄ RUSSIAN DESMAN (Desmana moschata) *A member of the mole family, the desman uses its long, whiskered snout and strong sense of smell to investigate its surroundings.*

▶ AARDVARK (Orycteropus afer) *The "earth pig" spends the day in burrows underground. It comes out at night to find ants and termites.*

WELL-DEVELOPED NOSES

Most insectivores, such as desmans, have poor eyesight but a good sense of smell, with snouts ideal for sniffing out insects. Aardvarks also have a good sense of smell. They have a piglike snout and nostrils surrounded with hair to filter out dust.

FACT FILE

■ **Moles** live in Europe, Asia, and North America. They live in underground tunnels that they dig with their powerful front legs. Their eyesight is poor but they have an acute sense of smell.

■ **Hedgehogs** live only in Europe, Africa, and Asia. They live in many different habitats. Hedgehogs have spines and curl up into prickly balls when danger threatens. They have good hearing.

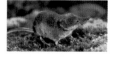

■ **Shrews** live across most parts of the world except Australia and New Zealand and parts of South America. Most have tiny eyes and ears and a long, pointed snout. They have poor vision but good hearing.

◄ ANTEATER
The giant anteater (Myrmecophaga tridactyla) is related to sloths and armadillos. It rips open ant and termite nests with its large claws and collects the ants with its long tongue. It eats up to 30,000 ants in a single day.

Long-eared hedgehog

Hemiechinus auritus

- **Length** 10½ in (27 cm)
- **Weight** 10 oz (280 g)
- **Location** Asia and northern Africa

This hedgehog is found in **dry areas** such as deserts. It is nocturnal and burrows under small bushes during the day, or rests under rocks or in hollows in the ground. It feeds mainly on small invertebrates and insects, which it finds using its **acute senses** of hearing and smell.

Eurasian water shrew

Neomys fodiens

- **Length** 3¾ in (9.5 cm)
- **Weight** ½ oz (14 g)
- **Location** Europe and northern Asia

This shrew has water-repellent fur so it can keep dry. Its tail has a row of bristles, which may help with swimming. The shrew hunts for food underwater, killing insects, small fish, and frogs with a **venomous bite**. It also feeds on land, where it preys on worms, beetles, and grubs.

Streaked tenrec

Hemicentetes semispinosus

- **Length** 6 in (15 cm)
- **Weight** 10 oz (280 g)
- **Location** Madagascar

Tenrecs look a bit like a cross between a shrew and a hedgehog because they have **sharp spines** as well as fur. Their main diet consists of worms and grubs, which they find in grasses or under leaves on the rainforest floor.

European mole

Talpa europaea

- **Length** 6½ in (16 cm)
- **Weight** 4½ oz (125 g)
- **Location** Europe and northern Asia

This mole has fur that can lie at any angle, which means it can go forward and backward in its **tunnels**. As it digs, it pushes up piles of soil as molehills. The mole eats worms and other soil animals that fall into the tunnels, often biting off the head and **storing them** for later.

Russian desman

Desmana moschata

- **Length** 8½ in (21 cm)
- **Weight** 7¾ oz (220 g)
- **Location** Eastern Europe to Central Asia

A desman has a **long tail**—as long as its head and body put together. The tail is flattened from side to side, and the desman uses it as a paddle and **a rudder** to move and steer through water.

Giant anteater

Myrmecophaga tridactyla

- **Length** 4 ft (1.2 m)
- **Weight** 86 lb (39 kg)
- **Location** Central and South America

The giant anteater is mainly gray with black and white markings. It has coarse, long fur and a very **bushy tail**. The anteater walks on the knuckles of its front feet so its **long claws** are kept out of the way. It wanders around its home range like this looking for food, and is active day and night.

Furry epaulet

Buettikofer's epauletted bat
Epomops buettikoferi

Bats

There are two groups of bats, called megabats and microbats. Megabats eat fruit and are often called fruit bats. Most microbats eat insects. Bats usually go looking for food at night. During the day they find somewhere to sleep, or roost, hanging upside down and clinging on with their toes.

▶ SKELETON
This bat's skeleton shows how its arms, legs, and long fingers provide a frame for the wings.

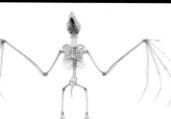

BAT WINGS

Bats are the only mammals that can truly fly, not just glide. Their wings are formed from a double layer of skin stretched between the side of the body and the four long fingers on each hand. The Greek name for bats, *Chiroptera*, means "hand wings."

FACT FILE

■ **Megabats** These bats use their eyes and noses to find their food. They have large eyes so they can see in the dark. Many megabats are found in tropical areas, where there are lots of different fruits to eat. They often feed in groups and fly long distances in search of food.

■ **Microbats** Most microbats eat insects, but some prey on lizards, frogs, or fish. Vampire bats drink fresh blood from animals. Microbats have poor eyesight and find food using echolocation (see page 34). They live in both temperate and tropical areas.

▶ LARGEST
The large flying fox (Pteropus vampyrus) is one of the largest bats with a wingspan of around 5 ft (1.5 m).

◀ SMALLEST
The hog-nosed bat (Craseonycteris thonglongyai) is the smallest bat in the world. It weighs about 1/16 oz (2 g) and is only 1¼ in (3 cm) long.

Size comparison

Large flying fox   Hog-nosed bat

Hammer-headed fruit bat

Hypsignathus monstrosus

   30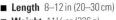

- **Length** 8–12 in (20–30 cm)
- **Weight** 11½ oz (326 g)
- **Wingspan** 35 in (90 cm)
- **Location** Central Africa

This is the largest bat found in Africa. It roosts high in the trees in **tropical forests** to avoid enemies on the ground. These bats are sometimes known as **big-lipped bats** because males have huge lips. They may use these to make their loud honking noises, which can be heard in the forest at night at certain times of the year. The noises attract females to come and hang beside the males on their branch.

Straw-colored fruit bat

Eidolon helvum

  21

- **Length** 7 in (18 cm)
- **Weight** 10 oz (280 g)
- **Wingspan** 30 in (76 cm)
- **Location** Africa

This fruit bat is **widespread** across Africa. It roosts in large colonies of between 100,000 and 1,000,000 individuals. The bats go out at night in small groups to search for food. They **eat mainly fruit** but they do not eat the whole fruit. Instead they suck the juice and spit out the pulp.

Elery's tube-nosed bat

Murina eleryi

 **?**

- **Length** 2½ in (6.5 cm)
- **Weight** ⅛ oz (4 g)
- **Wingspan** 8 in (20 cm)
- **Location** North Vietnam

Elery's tube-nosed bat is a small species with **golden woolly fur**. Its nostrils are located at the end of two tubes that protrude from its nose, which give this type of bat its name. It lives in forests that are home to many other species of bat, and feeds on insects.

Jamaican fruit-eating bat

Artibeus jamaicensis

  10

- **Length** 3½ in (9 cm)
- **Weight** 1½ oz (46 g)
- **Wingspan** 18 in (45 cm)
- **Location** Mexico to Bolivia, Brazil, and Caribbean Islands

This fruit bat roosts in caves and buildings but also **makes "tents"** from leaves. It bites through the midrib of a leaf so that it collapses to form a roof to sleep under. Unlike many other bats, this fruit bat feeds alone.

Comoro black flying fox

Pteropus livingstonii

10

- **Length** 11¾ in (30 cm)
- **Weight** 21 oz (600 g)
- **Wingspan** 5 ft (1.5 m)
- **Location** Comoros Islands

Fruit bats are sometimes called **flying foxes**. The Comoro black flying fox is found on only two islands in the Comoros island chain, off the east coast of Africa. It is **critically endangered** and it is estimated that only around 1,300 individuals exist. These bats roost in small groups called harems and stick together in groups when they go out to look for food.

◄ COLOR
The straw-colored fruit bat gets its name from the color of its neck and back. Its underside is brown or gray.

Listening bats

Most of the bats in the world are microbats. They are smaller than megabats and live on every continent except the Arctic and the Antarctic. Sometimes known as insect-eating bats, they have good hearing that enables them to sense insects flying by. They also use it to avoid obstacles in the dark.

MAMMALS

Gray long-eared bat
Plecotus austriacus

SPECIAL FEATURES

Microbats hunt in the dark, finding insects using a technique called echolocation. Many of these bats have special features to help them. Some have long ears for hearing. Some have a growth on their nose, called a nose-leaf, which focuses sounds.

Echolocation To find moths in the dark, microbats make a rapid series of clicks (shown here by red bars) that get closer together as they approach their prey. The clicks are reflected as echoes, and by listening to these, the bats can pinpoint the moth's position.

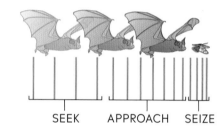

SEEK   APPROACH   SEIZE

Gray long-eared bat
Plecotus austriacus

- **Length** 2 in (5 cm)
- **Weight** ½ oz (14 g)
- **Wingspan** 12 in (30 cm)
- **Location** Central and southern Europe, northern Africa, and southwest Asia

These long-eared bats like to live **near human** settlements, where they can roost in buildings. When they come out to feed, they hunt for moths, flies, and beetles and use their long ears to **listen** for their prey.

Common pipistrelle
Pipistrellus pipistrellus

- **Length** 1½–2 in (3.5–4.5 cm)
- **Weight** ¼–⅛ oz (5–8 g)
- **Wingspan** 7½–10 in (19–25 cm)
- **Location** Europe and East Asia

These bats are found in a wide range of habitats, from **farms and forests to city buildings**, and are among the smallest and most widespread of all bats. They come out to **feed early** (sometimes before sunset) and hunt for moths, gnats, and other small insects— a single bat can eat up to 3,000 insects in one night. The young are born in early summer and leave the roost in August or September.

Townsend's big-eared bat
Corynorhinus townsendii

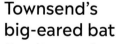

- **Length** 2¾ in (7 cm)
- **Weight** ¾ oz (20 g)
- **Wingspan** 12½ in (30 cm)
- **Location** North America

As their name suggests, these bats have **enormous ears**, which reach to the middle of their body when they are laid flat. The bats go out hunting late in the evening and feed almost entirely on moths. Male Townsend's big-eared bats live on their own, but females form groups when they have their young. These groups, called **nurseries**, contain several hundred animals. They live together for protection.

Got it! This moth will do nicely for supper. The gray long-eared bat has ears almost as long as its head and body put together. These help it detect its insect prey in the darkness.

◀ FOLDED AWAY *When this long-eared bat hibernates, it folds its ears and tucks them under its wings.*

Proboscis bat
Rhynchonycteris naso

- **Length** 1⅜ in (5 cm)
- **Weight** ⅕ oz (5 g)
- **Wingspan** 9⅖ in (24 cm)
- **Location** Central and South America

This species is named for its **long**, **pointed nose**. (A "proboscis" is a long nose.) The bats like to roost head down against the trunks or branches of trees. They are well camouflaged here because their gray-brown speckled fur and small size makes them look a bit like lichen growing on the tree. Small groups of proboscis bats roost together, sometimes spaced out evenly in a vertical line down a tree trunk.

Lesser horseshoe bat
Rhinolophus hipposideros

- **Length** 1½ in (4 cm)
- **Weight** ⅛–⅖ oz (4–10 g)
- **Wingspan** 9 in (23 cm)
- **Location** Europe and northern Africa to west Asia

There are many species of horseshoe bat, and the lesser horseshoe bat is one of the **smallest**. Its body is smaller than a human thumb. Horseshoe bats have a **horseshoe-shaped nose leaf**, which is formed of bare, folded skin. During the day these bats roost in tree holes, chimneys, and caves. They come out at night to hunt for flying insects. In the winter, they hibernate in groups of up to 500 animals.

Vampire bat
Desmodus rotundus

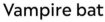

- **Length** 3½ in (9 cm)
- **Weight** 1¾ oz (50 g)
- **Wingspan** 8 in (20 cm)
- **Location** Mexico to South America

The vampire bat is a strong flyer but can also **scuttle along the ground** using its wings as front legs. It is well known for its eating habits. It lands on the ground and moves toward its prey, such as a horse or a cow. It bites away any fur, cuts into the skin, then **licks up the fresh blood**. Its teeth are so sharp that they can cut into the skin easily and the victim hardly notices.

Primates

Humans are primates, as are our closest relatives, the great apes and gibbons. The group also includes all types of monkeys and many less familiar species, including the diverse lemurs of Madagascar and the nocturnal lorises, galagos, and pottos.

PRIMATE FEATURES

Most primates are good climbers and some spend almost their whole lives in trees. They have strong arms and legs and long, grasping fingers and toes for hanging onto branches. Their forward-facing eyes allow them to judge distances accurately—a useful skill when leaping from branch to branch.

FAST LEARNERS Young chimpanzees pick up skills by watching adults, but also by trial and error. It takes a lot of practice to fine-tune methods such as fishing for termites.

I'm ready to go fishing!

Chimpanzees eat many different kinds of food. Ants and termites make a good snack because they contain a lot of protein. To catch them, chimps use stripped twigs or plant stems, which they poke into holes in the termite nest or mound. Only the smartest animals have the ability to make and use tools in this way.

FACT FILE

- The aye-aye has a special long, skinny finger that is perfect for picking insect grubs out of small crevices in tree bark.

- The pads on a tarsier's fingers, toes, palms, and soles provide excellent grip on smooth trunks and branches.

- Chimpanzees are as comfortable moving on the ground as in the trees. Their feet have large, flat soles for walking on.

Madame Berthe's mouse lemur

Microcebus berthae

- **Length** 3½–4⅓ in (9–11 cm)
- **Weight** ⅘–1⅓ oz (24–38 g)
- **Location** Madagascar

This is the world's **smallest primate**. It lives in forests and is active mainly at night, when it scrambles nimbly through the trees, looking for insects, spiders, frogs, and other small animals. It also feeds on honeydew secreted by insects. The long tail is used for balance when climbing. By day, **it sleeps alone** in thick vegetation, unlike some other species of mouse lemurs, which sleep in groups.

Hamadryas baboon

Papio hamadryas

- **Length** 24–30 in (60–75 cm)
- **Height (on four legs)** 28 in (70 cm)
- **Weight** 22–44 lb (10–20 kg)
- **Location** Eastern Africa including Egypt, Ethiopia, Sudan, and Somalia, also in Arabia

Hamadryas baboons spend most of their time at ground level, eating grass and any other plant or animal food they can find. They live in **large groups** called troops. A troop can contain several smaller bands, each led by a large, experienced male. Members of the band show their loyalty by grooming one another's fur.

Bonobo

Pan paniscus

- **Height** 28–32 in (70–83 cm)
- **Weight** 66–132 lb (30–60 kg)
- **Location** Central Africa

These **highly intelligent and social** apes are told apart from chimpanzees by their dark skin and habit of often **walking upright**. Bonobos live in organized groups and are active mainly by day, when they forage for fruits, leaves, and small animals. A large amount of time is spent in social activities such as grooming, cuddling, and mating.

◀ MACAQUE SOCIETY *Most primates live in social groups. Members of the group often groom each other to strengthen the bonds between them and to earn favors.*

Red howler monkey

Alouatta seniculus

- **Length** 18–28¼ in (46–72 cm)
- **Weight** 11–22 lb (5–10 kg)
- **Location** Northern South America

This **tree-dwelling** monkey lives in groups and eats mainly fruit and leaves. Howlers are famous for having one of the **loudest calls** of any animal. They gather each morning for a deafening chorus that lets other groups know their position. Their throaty howls can be heard an incredible 1¾–3 miles (3–5 km) away.

New World, Old World

Monkeys can be either New World monkeys or Old World monkeys. New World monkeys include spider monkeys, squirrel monkeys, and marmosets. Old World monkeys include baboons, macaques, and mandrills. Most of them live in tropical forests.

NOSES AND TAILS

New World monkeys have flat noses and their nostrils are directed outward. The nostrils of Old World monkeys are close together and directed downward. New World monkeys have a fully prehensile tail, but Old World monkeys never do. Old World monkeys are more closely related to apes than New World monkeys.

▶ ACROBATS *Like all spider monkeys, the black spider monkey (Ateles chamek) can swing through the forest canopy incredibly quickly. It uses its long, prehensile tail as a "fifth limb."*

Japanese macaque

Macaca fuscata

- **Length** 18½–23⅜ in (47–60 cm)
- **Tail** 4 in (10 cm)
- **Weight** 31 lb (14 kg)
- **Location** Japan

Japanese macaques **live in groups**, with females usually outnumbering males by about three to one. Females stay in a group for life, and daughters inherit their mother's rank, or position, in the pecking order.

▶ NORTHERN SOULS *Japanese macaques live farther north than any other primate (not counting humans). They grow a thick coat to help them cope with the cold winters. Sometimes the monkeys bathe in hot springs to keep warm.*

FACT FILE

- New World monkeys are found from Mexico down through Central America to Argentina.
- Old World monkeys can be found in most of Africa and southern and eastern Asia.

The numbers show where the featured monkeys are found.

Chacma baboon

Papio ursinus

- **Length** 32 in (82 cm)
- **Tail** 33 in (84 cm)
- **Weight** 66 lb (30 kg)
- **Location** Southern Africa

This is the **largest baboon** and it spends most of its time on the ground. Males are twice as big as females and have two large canine teeth. The baboons eat a variety of food—fruit, nuts, grass, roots, insects, and other small animals. At night, they **sleep in a tree** or on a cliff, using one of several chosen spots in their territory.

Golden lion tamarin

Leontopithecus rosalia

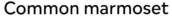

- **Length** 10 in (25 cm)
- **Tail** 14½ in (37 cm)
- **Weight** 28 oz (800 g)
- **Location** Eastern South America

These monkeys are **rare** because their habitat has almost vanished and many of them are captured and sold as pets. Tamarins live in small troops in which only one dominant pair breeds. They look for food during the day, using their **long, thin fingers** to find grubs in crevices and tree bark. At night, they often sleep in a hole in a tree.

Kipunji

Rungwecebus kipunji

- **Length** 35½ in (90 cm)
- **Tail** 43½ in (110 cm)
- **Weight** 35 lb (16 kg)
- **Location** Tanzania

This **rare monkey** is found in a small area in Tanzania and numbers around 1,100 individuals. It is brownish gray in color and **has a distinctive crest** on top of its head. Although shy and secretive, adult kipunjis emit a loud "honk-bark" noise to communicate with members of their group.

Common marmoset

Callithrix jacchus

- **Length** 10 in (25 cm)
- **Tail** 14 in (35 cm)
- **Weight** 12 oz (350 g)
- **Location** Brazil

Common marmosets are unusual among primates because they have **clawlike nails** instead of true nails. They use these to help them cling vertically to tree trunks and run on all fours along branches. These marmosets **eat tree sap** as well as fruit and insects.

Mandrill

Mandrillus sphinx

- **Length** 32 in (81 cm)
- **Tail** 3½ in (9 cm)
- **Weight** 82 lb (37 kg)
- **Location** Western central Africa

Mandrills are easily recognized by the **bright red and blue nose**. Males are much larger than females and are the largest monkeys in the world. These monkeys **live in mixed groups** containing one dominant male, and can form troops of up to 250 animals. They spend most of their time on the ground looking for fruits, seeds, eggs, and small mammals.

Common squirrel monkey

Saimiri sciureus

- **Length** 12½ in (32 cm)
- **Tail** 16½ in (42 cm)
- **Weight** 34 oz (950 g)
- **Location** Western to central South America

Squirrel monkeys **form large troops**, sometimes containing more than 200 individuals. They eat a wide range of food including fruit, nuts, berries, leaves, seeds, flowers, insects, and small animals.

Brown capuchin

Cebus brunneus

- **Length** 17 in (42 cm)
- **Tail** 19 in (49 cm)
- **Weight** 10 lb (4.5 kg)
- **Location** Northern, central and eastern South America

These intelligent monkeys eat mostly fruit, but they also eat nuts, eggs, insects, and other small animals. They are known to **use tools**, such as stones, to crack open hard nuts. Groups of up to 20 animals **leap and climb** through the trees, and the young often come down to the ground to play.

MOM AND BABY *A female gelada's main job is to care for her young. She carries, grooms, nurses, and protects her offspring until they are independent enough to find their own food, usually when they are around 12 to 18 months old.*

The *unique* gelada

The gelada's ancestors roamed over the whole of Africa, but the modern-day gelada is found only in the grassy highlands of Ethiopia and is the only grass-eating primate. Geladas nibble away at blades of grass, as well as stems, seeds, and roots. All this munching can take up a lot of time: these monkeys spend up to 60 percent of their day eating—more than any other monkey.

Gelada

Theropithecus gelada

- **Length** 28–29 in (70–74 cm)
- **Tail** 11⅘–19⅜ in (30–50 cm)
- **Weight** 44 lb (20 kg)
- **Location** Ethiopia

The gelada is a close cousin of the baboon and is sometimes known as a gelada baboon. **Both males and females have a triangular patch of bright pink skin** on their chest, outlined with white hairs. This is why this species of monkey is sometimes called the pink-chested gelada. The male has a thick mane that hangs halfway down his back and a much longer tail than the female, with a dense tuft of hairs at its tip.

COMING TO BLOWS

Gelada males rarely fight, but when they do they can be quite vicious, tearing at each other's flesh with their long, pointed canine teeth. Fortunately, most conflicts are resolved long before this happens. Angry stares and slapping the ground to warn off an aggressor are usually all it takes to restore peace.

Safety in numbers Geladas are not very territorial, so separate families often graze together. Troops of up to 400 individuals are common. Each family in the troop is made up of an adult male, his "harem" of three to five females, and their young. Grooming each other helps the adults to bond, but it is the close friendships of the females that hold the family together.

My baby likes to ride on my back.
From about three months old, young geladas ride on their mother's back just like a jockey rides a horse. Females usually have one baby at a time and only four or five in a lifetime. But they spend a lot of time and energy caring for them.

Apes

An ape is not a monkey! Apes do not have a tail, but most monkeys do. Apes are able to swing from branches using their hands and feet, but monkeys cannot. There are two families of apes—the lesser apes (gibbons) and the great apes (orangutans, gorillas, and chimpanzees).

LIVING IN THE TREES

Apes are found mainly in tropical forests and are largely vegetarian. Like most primates, they are good climbers and their long arms and grasping hands are ideal for swinging through the trees. All great apes are on the endangered species list because their forest homes are being cut down.

FAST FACTS

■ **Great apes** There are six species of great ape: two species of orangutan; two species of gorilla; the chimpanzee; and the bonobo, or pygmy chimpanzee. They are known for their intelligence and the ability to hold things in their hands.

■ **Lesser apes** There are 14 species of lesser ape, or gibbon. They have long arms and use their hands like hooks to swing from branch to branch. This way of moving is called brachiation. The apes can travel through the trees at about 9 mph (15 kph).

O *Orangutan*   G *Great apes*   L *Lesser apes*

■ **Distribution** The orangutan lives in forests only on the islands of Sumatra and Borneo in Indonesia and Malaysia. Other great apes live in forests in western and central Africa. Lesser apes live in southern and Southeast Asia.

We can stay up here all day. Orangutans spend most of their time in the trees. They have longer arms and more flexible joints than other great apes, so they can swing through the branches with ease.

▲ INFANT APE *Female orangutans give birth in a treetop. The young ape clings to its mother as she clambers around and stays with her until it is about eight years old.*

▶ GRASPING HANDS *All apes can move their thumbs around to touch their fingers, like humans. These are called opposable thumbs. This means they can pick up and hold things.*

Western gorilla

Gorilla gorilla

  50

- **Height** 6 ft (1.8 m)
- **Weight** 397 lb (180 kg)
- **Location** Central Africa

Gorillas are the **largest** great apes. They may look fierce, but they are shy and peaceful unless threatened. Males are more aggressive than females and show off their strength by standing up and **beating their chests** with their fists. Gorillas walk on all fours with their hands curled over so their knuckles touch the ground. The animals live in small groups in forests, where they eat mainly plant stems, leaves, and berries.

Bornean orangutan

Pongo pygmaeus

  50

- **Height** 4½ ft (1.4 m)
- **Weight** 175 lb (80 kg)
- **Location** Borneo

The orangutan's **bright red** fur makes it easy to recognize. The name orangutan is a Malay word meaning "**man of the forest**," and this great ape spends most of its time on its own in the treetops. During the day, it looks for food, such as fruit, leaves, and honey, or sometimes small lizards and baby birds. At night, it sleeps on a platform, which it makes by weaving branches together.

Siamang

Symphalangus syndactylus

    30

- **Height** 35 in (90 cm)
- **Weight** 33 lb (15 kg)
- **Location** Southeast Asia

The siamang is the largest gibbon and it has an amazingly **loud voice**. Males and females sometimes "sing" together. The female's voice is like a bark but the male's voice is more like a **scream**. Their duet can be heard more than ½ mile (1 km) away.

White-handed gibbon

Hylobates lar

   25

- **Height** 25 in (65 cm)
- **Weight** 12 lb (5.5 kg)
- **Location** South and Southeast Asia

This gibbon hardly ever comes down to the forest floor. It stays up in the trees, moving through its territory in the forest by **swinging** from branch to branch. A male and female usually **stay together** for their whole lives. They live with their young, which leave the family to find partners when they are ready.

Chimpanzee

Pan troglodytes

   60

- **Height** 3 ft (1 m)
- **Weight** 132 lb (60 kg)
- **Location** West to central Africa

The chimpanzee is one of the **most intelligent** of all animals. It is one of very few animals to use **tools**, using stones to crack nuts and sticks to get ants and termites out of their nests. It strips off the bark with its teeth, then pokes the stick into the ants' nests to make them swarm onto the stick. It then pulls the stick out and wipes it between its lips to eat the ants. Chimps live in groups of up to 120 animals, and a young chimp will stay with its mother for up to 10 years.

Crested gibbon

Nomascus concolor

   25

- **Height** 21⅜ in (55 cm)
- **Weight** 20 lb (9 kg)
- **Location** Southeast Asia

Young crested gibbons are born with yellow fur, but they gradually **change color** as they grow older. Males become black with white cheeks, while females turn brown or gray. Crested gibbons live in **family groups**, but they may join other families to feed at a good spot. They eat buds, young leaves, and fruit.

Prosimian *primates*

What is a prosimian? The word means "before monkeys," and this group of animals is the most primitive of all primates. Like monkeys and apes, they are adapted for life in trees, with grasping hands and feet. Prosimians include lemurs, bush babies, and lorises.

I like to dance and leap.
Verreaux's sifaka (*Propithecus verreauxi*) is a species of lemur that spends a lot of time on the ground as well as in trees. It takes great strides and springs through the air at speed as if it were dancing. Babies have to hold on tight!

▲ LONG FINGER *The aye-aye (Daubentonia madagascariensis) lives in Madagascar. It taps on trees with its long middle finger then listens for insects moving under the bark. If anything is there, it rips off the bark with its teeth and hooks out the insects with its finger.*

HITCHING A RIDE
When they are old enough, young Verreaux's sifakas ride piggyback style on their mother. Younger infants cling to their mother's belly where they are safer.

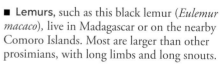

FACT FILE

■ **Lemurs**, such as this black lemur (*Eulemur macaco*), live in Madagascar or on the nearby Comoro Islands. Most are larger than other prosimians, with long limbs and long snouts.

■ **Bush babies** (or galagos), such as this lesser bush baby (*Galago senegalensis*), live south of the Sahara in Africa and on nearby islands. They have a bushy tail and a childlike cry.

■ **Lorises**, such as this red slender loris (*Loris tardigradus*), are found in southeast and southern Asia. The related pottos live in central and western Africa. They move hand-over-hand, always gripping a branch, never leaping.

Thick-tailed bush baby

Otolemur crassicaudatus

- **Length** 16 in (40 cm)
- **Tail** 19 in (49 cm)
- **Weight** 4½ lb (2 kg)
- **Location** Central, eastern, and southern Africa

This is the **largest bush baby**. It is nocturnal and has huge ears and eyes to help it find insects in the dark. It catches its prey by hand in a split second. It also scrapes up gum and sap from trees with its teeth.

Ring-tailed lemur

Lemur catta

- **Length** 18 in (46 cm)
- **Tail** 24 in (62 cm)
- **Weight** 7¾ lb (3.5 kg)
- **Location** Southern Madagascar

Unlike most lemurs, ring-tailed lemurs are **active during the day** and feed on the ground. They gather flowers, fruits, and leaves with their hands. They are **sociable** and form groups of up to 25 animals with the females in charge.

Lesser bush baby

Galago senegalensis

- **Length** 6 in (16 cm)
- **Tail** 9 in (23 cm)
- **Weight** 9 oz (250 g)
- **Location** Western to eastern Africa

With its large ears and eyes, and bushy tail, this animal is a perfect example of a bush baby. It can leap as far as 16½ ft (5 m) using its **long back legs**. As well as having keen senses of smell, hearing, and sight, the lesser bush baby has a **good sense of touch**. It can even catch flying insects in its hands!

Golden angwantibo

Arctocebus aureus

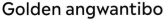

- **Length** 12 in (30 cm)
- **Tail** ½ in (1 cm)
- **Weight** 17 oz (475 g)
- **Location** Western Africa

The angwantibo is nocturnal and largely solitary. It has **unusual hands** with two long fingers and two shorter fingers (one is hardly more than a fleshy pad). It is a **good climber**, moving slowly through the trees, looking for insects to eat, and picking them off twigs and leaves. It also eats fruit.

White-footed sportive lemur

Lepilemur leucopus

- **Length** 12 in (30 cm)
- **Tail** 10 in (25 cm)
- **Weight** 21 oz (600 g)
- **Location** Southern Madagascar

This species of lemur **eats mostly leaves**. It moves through the forest by leaping between tree trunks rather than from branch to branch, and has large pads on its fingers and toes to help it cling on tight. A female and her young form small groups. **Each male lives in a separate area,** but it overlaps with territories of one or more females.

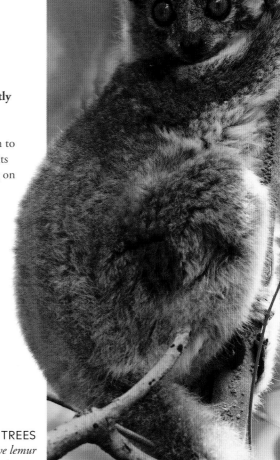

LIFE IN TREES

The white-footed sportive lemur spends most of its time in trees and looks for food at night.

Rodents

Rodents are found worldwide, except Antarctica, and can be divided into three groups—squirrel-like rodents, cavy-like rodents, and mouselike rodents. They get their name from the Latin word *rodere*, which means "to gnaw." All rodents gnaw food and other things with their long front teeth.

▲ BABIES *The world's largest rodent, the capybara, usually has one litter a year, with five young. Most smaller rodents have more offspring. A house mouse can have up to 120 babies a year (in separate litters)!*

FACT FILE

■ **Squirrel-like rodents** have long whiskers and a furry tail. There are a variety of squirrel-like species with different lifestyles, living in lots of different habitats worldwide.

■ **Cavy-like rodents** are found in Africa, the Americas, and Asia. Most species have a large head, sturdy body, short tail, and slender legs. The cavy is the ancestor of the guinea pig.

■ **Mouselike rodents** have a pointed face and long whiskers. Most species are small and nocturnal. They are found worldwide.

HUGE INCISORS *All rodents have four large front teeth called incisors, which never stop growing and always stay sharp. This is the skull of a paca (Agouti paca), a cavy-like rodent from South America.*

GOOD SENSES

Most rodents have excellent senses of smell and hearing. They also have sensitive whiskers. They use their senses to find their way around, find food, and also to be alert to predators. Nocturnal species, such as the dormouse, have large eyes for seeing in the dark.

I need to eat a lot!

The dormouse hibernates from October through April. Before it curls up in its nest, it eats enough to almost double its weight. It then has enough body fat to live on during the winter.

TREE DWELLER *The dormouse (Muscardinus avellanarius) lives in trees. It sleeps during the day in a nest made from grasses and strips of bark woven together. It comes out at night to feed, mainly on flowers, fruits, and nuts.*

Brown rat

Rattus norvegicus

- **Length** 11 in (28 cm)
- **Weight** 20 oz (575 g)
- **Location** Worldwide, except polar regions

This **intelligent** mammal eats almost anything, and can survive in almost any habitat. It lives in huge groups near humans because food is easy to find there. Wild brown rats are **not liked** by humans because they spread disease and eat food stores.

Long-tailed field mouse

Apodemus sylvaticus

- **Length** 4 in (11 cm)
- **Weight** 1 oz (30 g)
- **Location** Western Europe to western and central Asia

The fast and agile field mouse lives mainly in woods and fields, but can be found in **most habitats** that are not too wet. Its food changes with the seasons—seeds in winter, buds in spring, caterpillars and grubs in summer, and fruit and fungi in the fall. Most field mice live in an **underground burrow**, which gets passed on from generation to generation.

Long-tailed chinchilla

Chinchilla lanigera

- **Length** 15 in (38 cm)
- **Weight** 28 oz (800 g)
- **Location** Southwest South America

The chinchilla is often kept as a **pet**, but some wild chinchillas still live in the Andes mountains. They have **thick, soft fur**, which keeps them warm during the cold nights. They are very active at twilight and at night.

Eastern chipmunk

Tamias striatus

- **Length** 6½ in (16.5 cm)
- **Weight** 4 oz (125 g)
- **Location** Southeastern Canada to central and eastern US

This **bold**, inquisitive animal is a popular visitor to picnic sites, and is not afraid of people. It normally eats **seeds, berries, and nuts** but this mischievous creature also likes sandwiches!

Mongolian jird

Meriones unguiculatus

- **Length** 5 in (12.5 cm)
- **Weight** 2 oz (60 g)
- **Location** Eastern Asia

Wild jirds live in hot, **dry places** and eat mainly seeds. They get most of the water they need from their food. Like many other desert mammals, jirds have **furry feet** to keep them cool on the hot ground. They have a burrow underground where they shelter from the hot sun, store food, and have their young.

Cape porcupine

Hystrix africaeaustralis

- **Length** 31 in (80 cm)
- **Weight** 44 lb (20 kg)
- **Location** Central to southern Africa

The most noticeable thing about this rodent are the **long spines** that grow in its fur. The spines, called quills, cover the porcupine's back and sides. Shorter ones grow on its tail. These spines come out easily, and if a predator gets one stuck in its nose, it hurts!

Southern viscacha

Lagidium viscacia

- **Length** 16 in (40 cm)
- **Weight** 6½ lb (3 kg)
- **Location** Western South America

With its soft, **woolly coat** and large ears, the viscacha looks a bit like a rabbit, but it is related to the chinchilla. It lives in groups of about 50 animals among rocks in the Andes mountains. Males do **sentry-duty** at the entrance to the burrow and warn the others if there is a threat.

A *world* of rodents

Rodentia is the largest group of mammals, with more than 2,200 species. Because of their huge numbers, rodents are of great significance to humans. Several make good pets, others help shape the environment, but some cause damage and spread disease.

Common vole
Microtus arvalis

Northeast African spiny mouse
Acomys cahirinus

Naked mole rat
Heterocephalus glaber

Long-tailed field mouse
Apodemus sylvaticus

Malagasy giant rat
Hypogeomys antimena

House mouse
Mus musculus

Eastern gray squirrel
Sciurus carolinensis

Golden hamster
Mesocricetus auratus

Domestic guinea pig
Cavia porcellus

Northern flying squirrel
Glaucomys sabrinus

Brown rat
Rattus norvegicus

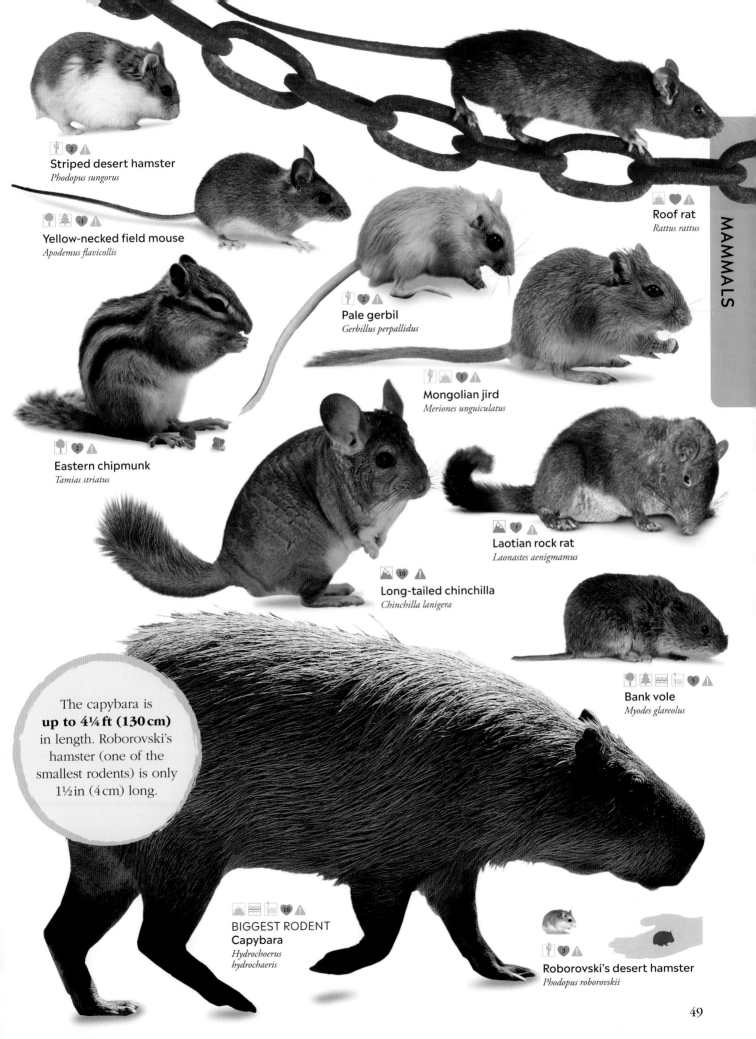

Striped desert hamster
Phodopus sungorus

Yellow-necked field mouse
Apodemus flavicollis

Roof rat
Rattus rattus

Pale gerbil
Gerbillus perpallidus

Eastern chipmunk
Tamias striatus

Mongolian jird
Meriones unguiculatus

Laotian rock rat
Laonastes aenigmamus

Long-tailed chinchilla
Chinchilla lanigera

Bank vole
Myodes glareolus

The capybara is
up to 4¼ft (130 cm)
in length. Roborovski's
hamster (one of the
smallest rodents) is only
1½in (4 cm) long.

BIGGEST RODENT
Capybara
Hydrochoerus hydrochaeris

Roborovski's desert hamster
Phodopus roborovskii

49

Beaver *engineers*

An American beaver can fell a tree by gnawing through the trunk! Once it has felled enough trees, branches are dragged to dam a stream. Why? The dam creates a lake, in the middle of which a beaver family builds its home: a lodge. Underwater entrances provide protection from land predators. It's a fantastic piece of engineering.

I've just got to finish this part.
Beavers start to build a dam in the summer. Families work together to push branches into position, before covering them with mud and stones. The task must be done before winter, when they retreat into the dark protection of the lodge.

American beaver

Castor canadensis

- ■ **Length** 35 in (88 cm)
- ■ **Weight** 57 lb (26 kg)
- ■ **Location** Canada and US

Beavers eat leaves, twigs, and bark. In the fall, they fell small trees, cut them into logs, and store them near their lodge so they have a **supply of bark**. They live in family groups, with males and females pairing up for life.

▲ BUILT TO LAST *Beaver dams and lodges are strong and last for several years. In fact, they are usually abandoned only because the beavers have exhausted local supplies of food. After a few years, a new family may move in and repair an old dam and lodge, giving it a new lease on life.*

▲ FEAT OF ENGINEERING *Beaver dams are about 10 ft (3 m) high. They can be more than 1,640 ft (500 m) long, depending on the size of the stream the beavers are trying to block. They alter the landscape in a big way.*

BEAVER TEETH

Beavers have strong upper incisors for gnawing wood. These teeth are orange. They are about ⅕ in (5 mm) wide and up to 1 in (25 mm) long. As with all rodents, these teeth never stop growing, so the beaver can go on cutting down trees as long as necessary.

> **FIT FOR LIFE**
> *The beaver is well-adapted for its water-based life. It has thick, waterproof fur; a large, flat tail that can act as a rudder; and large, webbed hind feet.*

Whales and dolphins

Whales and dolphins look like big fish; most adults have no hair, and they have flippers instead of arms or legs, yet they are mammals. They breathe air with their lungs and suckle their young with milk. They even have belly buttons!

◀ *Whales close their blowhole when under water. As they surface they release a spout of air—a blow—before taking another breath.*

BLOWHOLES

No whale, dolphin, or porpoise can breathe under water. They breathe air—but not through a nose and not through their mouth. They use a hole (or two holes) on the top of their heads called a "blowhole."

▶ *Whales and dolphins choose when they want to take a breath. This means they cannot go to sleep. Instead, they shut down half their brain at a time, resting one half, then the other.*

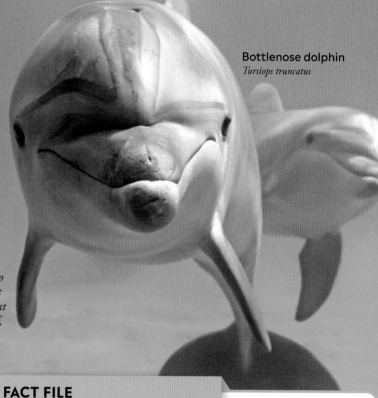

Bottlenose dolphin
Tursiops truncatus

FACT FILE

Size comparison

Toothed whale

Baleen whale

■ **Number of species:** 90, of which 14 are baleen whales and 76 are toothed whales. The largest is the blue whale; the smallest is Hector's dolphin.

■ **Toothed whales** include dolphins and porpoises as well as the killer whale and sperm whale. They have sharp teeth for catching slippery prey, such as fish or squid. Toothed whales have one blowhole.

■ **Baleen whales** filter feed by straining mouthfuls of water through fringed plates of flexible baleen that hang from their upper jaws. Baleen whales have two blowholes.

■ **Distribution** At least one type of whale lives in every ocean. Many species have a wide range, living in both tropical and temperate waters.

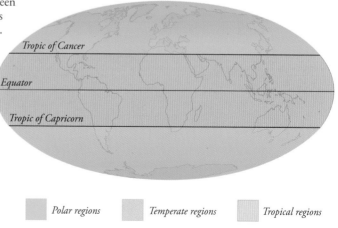

Tropic of Cancer

Equator

Tropic of Capricorn

Polar regions Temperate regions Tropical regions

Blue whale

Balaenoptera musculus

  90

- **Length** 66–98 ft (20–30 m)
- **Weight** 220,000–352,740 lb (100,000–160,000 kg)
- **Diet** Krill
- **Location** Worldwide (except Mediterranean, Baltic, Red Sea, and Arabian Gulf)

The blue whale is Earth's **biggest animal**, and can weigh as much as 35 elephants. It can swallow thousands of krill (a shrimplike animal) in one enormous gulp, and its song is the loudest noise made by any animal.

Northern right whale

Eubalaena glacialis

70

- **Length** 43–56 ft (13–17 m)
- **Weight** 198,416 lb (90,000 kg)
- **Diet** Plankton
- **Location** Temperate and near-polar waters worldwide

One of the **most endangered** of all the big whales, this ocean cruiser feeds on plankton near the surface and doesn't tend to dive down. This makes potentially fatal collisions with ships a danger for the whale.

Gray whale

Eschrichtius robustus

 60

- **Length** 43–49 ft (13–15 m)
- **Weight** 30,865–77,162 lb (14,000–35,000 kg)
- **Diet** Marine invertebrates
- **Location** North Pacific (temperate and tropical)

The gray whale has an unusual feeding habit (in addition to filter feeding). It scoops up huge mouthfuls of mud and filters out starfish, crabs, and worms. It **travels the farthest** of any mammal—migrating from the Arctic to winter in Mexico.

Common dolphin

Delphinus delphis

   20

- **Length** 7½–8½ ft (2.3–2.6 m)
- **Weight** 175 lb (80 kg)
- **Diet** Fish and squid
- **Location** Temperate and tropical waters worldwide

Common dolphins are both **social** and chatty. Their whistles and squeaks as they leap, tumble, and ride the waves can be heard from nearby boats. They travel in big groups, sometimes with thousands of members.

Bottlenose dolphin

Tursiops truncatus

50

- **Length** 6¼–13 ft (1.9–4 m)
- **Weight** 1,100 lb (500 kg)
- **Diet** Fish, mollusks, and crustaceans
- **Location** Worldwide (except polar regions)

The bottlenose is **found everywhere** except the chilly waters around the poles. It can leap high out of the water—up to 16 feet (5 meters)—and likes to land with a splash. It eats a wide variety of foods, from soft squid to crunchy crabs.

Amazon river dolphin

Inia geoffrensis

30

- **Length** 6½–8½ ft (2–2.6 m)
- **Weight** 220–350 lb (100–160 kg)
- **Diet** Fish, crabs, and river turtles
- **Location** South America (Amazon and Orinoco basins)

This slow-moving, **small-eyed** river dolphin uses its long beak to poke around the riverbed for fish and crabs that may be hiding in the mud. It makes short dives lasting just one or two minutes. It usually lives alone or in pairs.

Narwhal

Monodon monoceros

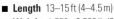   50

- **Length** 13–15 ft (4–4.5 m)
- **Weight** 1,750–3,500 lb (800–1,600 kg)
- **Diet** Fish, mollusks, and crustaceans
- **Location** Arctic Ocean

The narwhal **lives farther north** than any other mammal, among ice-floes in Arctic waters. The male grows a long tusk (the female doesn't have one), which he uses like a sword to "fence" with rival males. Their powerful lips and tongues are used to "suck" prey into their mouths.

Dall's porpoise

Phocoenoides dalli

17

- **Length** 7¼–7¾ ft (2.2–2.4 m)
- **Weight** 375–440 lb (170–200 kg)
- **Diet** Fish and squid
- **Location** North Pacific (temperate and tropical)

A friendly and curious animal, Dall's porpoise is known to surface close to boats and playfully "bow ride" at high speeds. And porpoises can really move! They zip along at 35 mph (55 kph), making them the **fastest** of all the whales, dolphins, and porpoises.

Killer whale

Orcinus orca

80

- **Length** 30 ft (9 m)
- **Weight** 22,000 lb (10,000 kg)
- **Diet** Varied, but can include fish, marine mammals, turtles, and birds
- **Location** Worldwide

These intelligent and sociable whales are **built for hunting**. They are stocky, powerful, fast, and have an awesome set of teeth. They eat a wide assortment of prey, including other whales.

Hector's beaked whale

Mesoplodon hectori

- **Length** 13 ft (4 m)
- **Weight** 2,200 lb (1,000 kg)
- **Location** Temperate waters in the southern hemisphere

This is **one of the smallest** of the beaked whales, and has a relatively short beak. This species lives in deep waters and is **rarely seen**. It feeds on deep-water squid and fish, which it catches by sucking them in with sea water.

Bowhead whale

Balaena mysticetus

- **Length** 65 ft (19.8 m)
- **Weight** 220,460 lb (100,000 kg)
- **Location** Arctic and sub-Arctic

The bowhead whale gets its name from its strongly curved, or "bowed," upper jaws. Its **huge head** accounts for about one-third of its total weight and it has the longest baleen of any whale. The plates can reach 15 ft (4.6 m) long. This whale has a layer of blubber under its skin, which can be 10–20 in (25–50 cm) thick. The blubber keeps it warm in the **icy cold** waters of the Arctic Ocean.

Sperm whale

Physeter macrocephalus

- **Length** 66 ft (20 m)
- **Weight** 125,700 lb (57,000 kg)
- **Location** Worldwide

This is the largest toothed whale and the world's **largest hunter**. Bulls (males) are twice as big as the cows (females). Cows form mixed groups with their young. Young bulls often form groups, but become **more solitary** as adults.

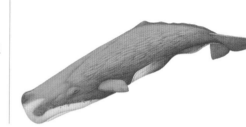

We have been hunted by humans for our oil.

Sperm whales have waxy oil in their head. This helps them control their buoyancy and may focus sound when they are using echolocation. The sperm whale has been hunted by humans for its oil and other body parts and it is a threatened species.

DEEP DIVERS

The sperm whale can stay underwater for nearly two hours. It is probably the deepest diver of all whales and may travel 9,800 ft (3,000 m) below the surface. When whales go underwater, their heart rate slows, while blood flow to the skin is stopped so it can flow to the vital organs for longer.

Beluga whale

Delphinapterus leucas

- **Length** 10–18 ft (3–5.5 m)
- **Weight** 1,540–3,530 lb (700–1,600 kg)
- **Location** Arctic Ocean

The beluga is the only white-skinned whale, and is closely related to the narwhal. Belugas are well known for their high-pitched sounds. They spend the winter hunting in open water away from the polar pack ice. Large groups often wait for the Arctic ice to crack up or melt during late spring. As ice melts and new passages open up, the whales are able to swim to new feeding areas.

Harbor porpoise

Phocoena phocoena

- **Length** 6 ft (1.83 m)
- **Weight** 200 lb (90 kg)
- **Location** North Pacific, North Atlantic, and Black Sea

Also known as the **common porpoise**, this porpoise is numerous in the areas where it lives. It likes shallow seas and stays near the coast for most of the time. Sometimes it **swims into harbors**, which is how it gets its name. It feeds on fish and shellfish on the seabed, gripping its prey in its teeth.

Sei whale

Balaenoptera borealis

- **Length** 52 ft (16 m)
- **Weight** 88,185 lb (40,000 kg)
- **Location** Worldwide except Mediterranean, Baltic, Red Sea, and Arabian Gulf

The sei whale is a **baleen whale**. It eats a variety of food, from plankton to small squid and fish. These whales usually swim in groups of up to **five animals**. They do not dive more than 1,000 ft (300 m) and stay underwater for no more than 20 minutes.

TAIL SPIN *The sperm whale lifts its tail high into the air before making a dive. This helps it get into position. The powerful tail then propels the whale through the water.*

A *world* of whales

There are 90 different species of whales and dolphins. These range in size from Hector's dolphin, which can reach 5 ft (1.5 m) in length, to the world's largest animal—the blue whale. This enormous creature can grow up to 98 ft (30 m) long. It is so heavy that on land its internal organs would be crushed by its great weight.

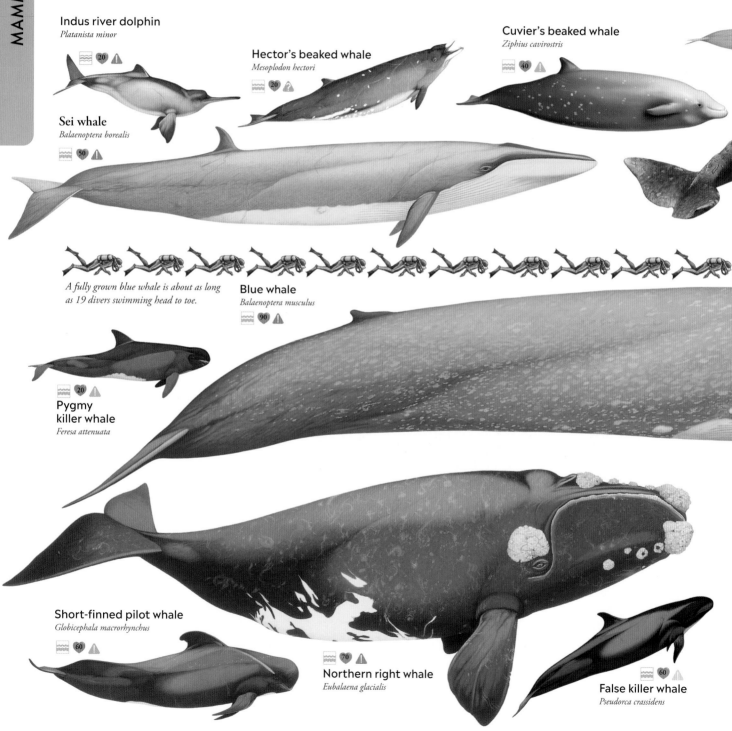

Indus river dolphin
Platanista minor

Hector's beaked whale
Mesoplodon hectori

Cuvier's beaked whale
Ziphius cavirostris

Sei whale
Balaenoptera borealis

A fully grown blue whale is about as long as 19 divers swimming head to toe.

Blue whale
Balaenoptera musculus

Pygmy killer whale
Feresa attenuata

Short-finned pilot whale
Globicephala macrorhynchus

Northern right whale
Eubalaena glacialis

False killer whale
Pseudorca crassidens

Beluga
Delphinapterus leucas

Northern right whale dolphin
Lissodelphis borealis

Atlantic spotted dolphin
Stenella frontalis

Chilean dolphin
Cephalorhynchus eutropia

Harbor porpoise
Phocoena phocoena

Bottlenose dolphin
Tursiops truncatus

Killer whale
Orcinus orca

Gray whale
Eschrichtius robustus

Humpback whale
Megaptera novaeangliae

Sperm whale
Physeter macrocephalus

Hector's dolphin
Cephalorhynchus hectori

This dolphin is found off
the coast of New Zealand.
It is incredibly rare.

Common dolphin
Delphinus delphis

Dall's porpoise
Phocoenoides dalli

Shepherd's beaked whale
Tasmacetus shepherdi

Spinner dolphin
Stenella longirostris

Narwhal
Monodon monoceros

Mother and calf

A humpback female usually gives birth to a single calf, and will feed and protect it for the first year. The calf suckles its mother's milk until it is about six months old, when it can begin to catch fish itself. The calf grows rapidly, doubling its length in the first year.

Humpback whale

Megaptera novaeangliae

- **Length** 46 ft (16 m)
- **Weight** 66,000 lb (30,000 kg)
- **Diet** Small fish and krill
- **Location** Worldwide except Mediterranean, Baltic, Red Sea, and Arabian Gulf

This whale's enormous flippers can be up to one-third the length of its body. It is a **baleen whale**, and feeds by filtering fish from the water through its long baleen plates.

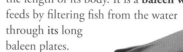

SINGING

Humpbacks are noisy whales, and male humpback whales actually sing. It's not known why they sing, but it may be to attract a female and warn off a rival male. It also may help them detect other whales. Each song can last for about 30 minutes.

◄ FISHING *Small groups of humpbacks join together to encircle fish, trapping them in blown "nets" of bubbles. It's an effective technique.*

MIGRATION

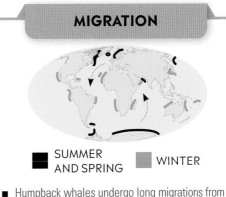

■ SUMMER AND SPRING   ■ WINTER

■ Humpback whales undergo long migrations from cold summer waters near the poles, which are rich feeding grounds, to warmer tropical or subtropical waters in the winter, where females calve and males seek mates.

Dolphin communication

Dolphins are sociable animals and live together in groups called pods. Pods vary in size from just a few dolphins to more than one thousand. The dolphins communicate with each other in a "language" of whistles, clicks, and cries. This enables them to recognize, locate, and help each other.

Quick! Someone's in trouble. When dolphins recognize a distress call they will follow it in search of a lost friend or relative. If a dolphin is sick, others will help push it to the surface so it can breathe.

TEAMWORK *Pods, such as this one of common dolphins* (Delphinus delphis)*, are larger where there are lots of fish. Dolphins cooperate with each other to catch the fish.*

DOLPHIN SPEAK

Communication in dolphins is still being investigated, but scientists think that dolphins have a complex system of language. They respond to each other's whistles and clicks, and make noises when playing, hunting, or when predators are near. They make lots of different sounds.

Look at me Bottlenose dolphins *(Tursiops truncatus)* are probably the most friendly dolphins. They even communicate with humans, sometimes coming inshore to ask for food. They often appear near boats and swimmers.

The dolphin listens to the sounds bouncing off prey. The nearer the prey, the more quickly the echoes come back.

▲ FINDING PREY *Dolphins find their food using a technique called echolocation. They send out sounds, which bounce back off their prey and tell them exactly where it is.*

CONSERVATION

Some dolphins are hunted by humans for their flesh and many are eaten by killer whales and big sharks. Thousands more are caught in commercial fishing nets, which is greatly reducing dolphin numbers. Some nets are now designed to be "dolphin friendly."

Dogs

Dogs and foxes belong to the family Canidae and are part of a group of meat-eating mammals called carnivores. They are hunters, with excellent senses for tracking prey, strong legs for running, and sharp teeth for biting.

Red fox
Vulpes vulpes

All pet dogs—even small dogs such as terriers and chihuahuas—are descended from the gray wolf. Dogs were first domesticated about 12,000 years ago. They were bred to protect and herd livestock, such as sheep, from as early as 1,000 BCE. They reached Australia about 4,000 years ago. The Australian dingo *(above)* is descended from these, but now lives in the wild.

Arctic fox

Vulpes lagopus

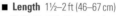

- **Length** 1½–2 ft (46–67 cm)
- **Tail** 10–17 in (25–43 cm)
- **Weight** 4½–20 lb (2–9 kg)
- **Location** Arctic

This small fox is perfectly suited to its freezing home. The Arctic fox has a thick fur coat, **the warmest fur of any mammal.** This snugness is helped by its clever body-temperature control and layers of insulating fat. It preys on smaller mammals, such as lemmings and Arctic hares. Arctic fox males and females both care for their litter of pups, usually in a den that can house several generations of foxes.

▶ SUMMER COAT *An Arctic fox has a darker, thinner coat in the summer to blend in with the landscape.*

African wild dog

Lycaon pictus

- **Length** 2½–3½ ft (76–112 cm)
- **Tail** 12–18 in (30–45 cm)
- **Weight** 33–77 lb (15–35 kg)
- **Location** Africa

The Latin name for this dog means "painted wolf" and comes from its striking **patterned coat.** The African wild dog lives in packs of about 10 individuals. All the adults help care for the young, but only one pair breeds. The pack **hunts together** and brings down animals as large as wildebeest and zebra. This dog is endangered because of habitat loss and diseases such as rabies.

◀ WILD PACK *Male African wild dogs will stay with their family pack. This is unusual for social pack mammals.*

We are red fox cubs.

The red fox can have up to 12 cubs in a litter. They are born underground in a den and don't leave there until they are about four or five weeks old. Both parents look after the cubs.

▼ GOOD PRACTICE
When fox cubs come out of their den, they tumble around together and play-fight. This helps them learn the skills they will need for hunting when they are adults.

Coyote
Canis latrans

    15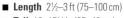

- **Length** 2½–3 ft (75–100 cm)
- **Tail** 10–15½ in (25–40 cm)
- **Weight** 15–46 lb (7–21 kg)
- **Location** North America to northern central America

The coyote is well-known for **its howl**, which can be heard at night, echoing across the landscape. Coyotes howl to tell neighboring coyotes where they are and where their territory is. These dogs usually go looking for food on their own. They **eat almost anything**—snakes, mice, fruit, and dead animals. They will also search through garbage to find something tasty to eat. The female gives birth to her puppies in the safety of a burrow and the male brings them food.

Gray wolf
Canis lupus

    16

- **Length** 4¼–6½ ft (150–200 cm)
- **Tail** 14–22 in (35–56 cm)
- **Weight** 44–130 lb (20–60 kg)
- **Location** North America, eastern Europe, and Asia

The **largest member of the dog family**, the gray wolf used to live all over the northern hemisphere. Now it is only found in remote areas. Wolves **live in packs** containing a pair of adults and several generations of their young. The pack has a strict order of seniority and all the wolves know where they stand in the pecking order.

Golden jackal
Canis aureus

 10

- **Height** 2¼–3⅓ ft (70–105 cm)
- **Tail** 8–12 in (20–30 cm)
- **Weight** 15–33 lb (7–15 kg)
- **Location** North and eastern Africa to southeast Europe and Asia

A pair of golden jackals live together **for life** and share the task of looking after their puppies. When the puppies grow up, one or two will usually stay with their parents for a year to help take care of the next litter. They hunt small animals, as well as scavenge carcasses, such as a lion's leftovers. Sometimes, they **bury pieces of meat** to hide them from other animals.

Born for the cold!

It's a strange fact, but one of a polar bear's biggest problems can be keeping cool. They have the most northerly range of any bear and so live surrounded by ice and snow. Hollow hairs, black skin, and a thick layer of blubber all contribute to storing the sun's heat. It's an efficient system, but these enormous bears can overheat in warmer weather.

POLAR BEARS *roll in the snow to cool down. Their fur acts as a natural insulator, but they can overheat at temperatures above 50°F (10°C).*

I'm safer with mom.
Young polar bears are born in snow dens. After emerging, they stay with their mother for the first 2½ years.

Polar bear
Ursus maritimus

- **Height** 7–11 ft (2–3.4 m)
- **Weight** 880–1,500 lb (400–680 kg)
- **Speed** 6 mph (10 kph) swimming speed
- **Location** Arctic and N. Canada

The male polar bear is the **largest animal** in the order **Carnivora** (carnivores), though at birth a cub weighs little more than a bag of sugar. The bears' main food is ringed seals, but they will also prey on walruses, belugas, narwhals, and seabirds. They will eat carrion, too.

CONSERVATION

The polar bear population, estimated at just over 20,000, is under threat because of climate change. In Northern Canada, more and more ice melts each spring, and polar bears are being forced farther inland before they have built up their fat stores by eating seal pups.

AT HOME ON THE ICE
Polar bears live in the Arctic at the edge of the ice shelf. Non-retractable claws help them grip the ice, digging in like ice picks as the animal walks. It's a bit like having built-in running spikes!

▲ PAW PADDLES *Polar bears use their front paws to paddle through water, and they can hold their breath for up to two minutes. But, as the Arctic ice melts due to climate change, bears are having to swim greater distances between ice floes. Sometimes they get exhausted and drown.*

Bears

There are eight species of bears. Bears are large meat-eaters, but eat lots of other things, too. The giant panda is almost exclusively vegetarian. Bears can move fast if they have to and can stand upright, making themselves look even bigger.

DON'T SURPRISE A BEAR

Bears have a good sense of smell but not such good eyesight and hearing. This means that they can be taken by surprise, and then they can be dangerous. They have large, strong paws with long claws, and can kill another animal with one blow.

◀ WINTER SLEEP *Bears that live where it gets cold go to sleep through the winter in a cave, hollow tree, or a den they dig themselves. Cubs are born in late winter and come out of their den in the spring.*

BROWN BEAR CUB

◀ CANINE TOOTH *Bears have powerful jaws and teeth for eating different kinds of food. Canines, such as this brown bear's tooth, tear into meat, but bears also have teeth for grinding plant material.*

CONSERVATION

Most species of bear are endangered. They are hunted for their gall bladders, which are used in traditional Chinese medicine. Their habitat is also being destroyed as people cut down the trees to make room for their own homes and farms, or for logging.

FACT FILE

■ Bears can be found in Europe, Asia, North America, and parts of South America. They live in all sorts of habitat, from ice floes in the Arctic (*see page 64 for the polar bear*) to grasslands, deserts, and mountains—but most of them live in forests in the northern hemisphere. They all like to be within easy reach of water, for drinking and for food (such as fish).

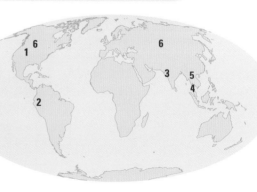

The numbers show where the featured bears are found.

American black bear

Ursus americanus

- **Length** 6 ft (1.8 m)
- **Weight** 660 lb (300 kg)
- **Location** North America

The American black bear is the **smallest** North American bear and the most common. It is an **excellent climber** and will climb up a tree if it is scared. Mother black bears teach their cubs to climb at an early age. Black bears are intelligent animals and have learned to live in a variety of habitats. Most of them hibernate during the winter, depending on what the weather is like in their area and how much food is available.

Spectacled bear

Tremarctos ornatus

- **Length** 6½ ft (2 m)
- **Weight** 390 lb (175 kg)
- **Location** Western South America

The **pale fur** around this bear's eyes give it its name. This is the only bear that lives in South America. It spends most of its time in trees, **sleeping or eating**. It bends branches down so it can reach the fruit more easily.

Sun bear

Helarctos malayanus

- **Length** 4½ ft (1.4 m)
- **Weight** 145 lb (65 kg)
- **Location** Southeast Asia

This bear has a **long tongue** for licking grubs and honey from holes. It also lets ants crawl over its paws then licks them off. The bear has unusually **loose skin**. If it is grabbed by a tiger, it can turn around in its skin and bite back!

Sloth bear

Melursus ursinus

- **Length** 6 ft (1.8 m)
- **Weight** 320 lb (145 kg)
- **Location** Southern Asia

A sloth bear loves to eat ants and termites. It tears open their nests, then forms its mouth into a tube and **sucks up** the insects—very noisily! It can even **close its nostrils** to stop ants from crawling up its nose.

Asiatic black bear

Ursus thibetanus

- **Length** 6 ft (1.8 m)
- **Weight** 88–440 lb (40–200 kg)
- **Location** Eastern, southern, and southeast Asia

The Asiatic black bear is often called the **moon bear** because of the white crescent of fur on its chest. It is a good climber and spends a lot of time in trees where it eats fruits and nuts. It also takes **honey** from bees' nests. This bear feeds mostly at night but will come out during the day if there is no danger.

Brown bear

Ursus arctos

- **Length** 10 ft (3 m)
- **Weight** 1,720 lb (780 kg)
- **Location** Northern North America, northern Europe, and northern Asia

There are several different kinds of brown bear, which live in different places. The **Kodiak bear** is the largest. It lives on Kodiak Island in Alaska. The grizzly bear lives in North America. It is called the **grizzly bear** because its fur is tipped with paler fur which makes it look "grizzled" or as if it is going gray. Brown bears are not good climbers and prefer to stay on the ground. They eat almost anything (including other bears) and often catch salmon as the fish migrate up rivers.

Saving *giant* pandas

The giant panda is one of the world's rarest animals. There are probably only about 1,800 left in the wild. Pandas rely on bamboo for their survival. However, more than half of the bamboo forests in central and western China where they live have disappeared since 1974.

We were bred in captivity.

More than 600 pandas live in zoos or nature reserves, but only about a third of the cubs that are born in captivity survive more than six months.

MOTHER LOVE *By the time a giant panda cub is four months old, it is really energetic, running along behind its mother and climbing trees. Mother pandas often wrestle and roll around with their playful infants.*

Giant panda

Ailuropoda melanoleuca

   27

- **Length** 5–6⅗ ft (1.5–2 m)
- **Weight** 155–350 lb (70–160 kg)
- **Location** Central China

The giant panda's **black and white coat pattern** does not appear until it is a few weeks old. At birth, the cub is a tiny pink creature, barely 3 in (8 cm) long, covered in white hairs. It will develop a thick, oily fur coat to keep it warm in the subzero winters of central China. Adults have strong jaws and teeth, essential for chewing the 84 lb (38 kg) of bamboo they need to eat daily to stay healthy.

▲ SPECIAL "THUMB" *Pandas have a bony lump on each front paw. They can move these false "thumbs," and use them with their toes to help them get a firm grip on a bamboo stem, while they nibble away at the juicy green shoots.*

▶ FEMALE PANDAS *usually give birth to one or two blind, helpless cubs, but often only one will survive as they need so much care from the mother. A cub stays with its mother for up to three years.*

CONSERVATION

Bamboo forests in China are being cleared by farmers, destroying the panda's main source of food. Poachers also kill pandas for their fur. To save these special bears from extinction, the Chinese government has set up more than 50 special panda reservations.

Cats

All cats are specialized for eating meat. Helped by their acute senses of hearing and sight, supple muscles, and sharp teeth and claws, they are all excellent hunters. Each cat hunts according to its size, strength, speed, and stamina.

CUDDLY CATS

Although they are expert hunters and killers, cats are some of the most loved animals. Their round faces, bright eyes, and beautiful soft fur make them look cute and cuddly. Unfortunately their beauty has come at a cost, because many cats are hunted for their fur.

▲ ADAPTABLE CAT
The puma (Puma concolor) is found in large parts of North, Central, and South America and can live in many different habitats. It has a variety of common names, such as cougar and mountain lion.

CONSERVATION

Poachers, livestock farmers, and roadkills all threaten the survival of wild cats. The destruction of their habitats makes their situation worse. Several species of cat have become extinct and many are now endangered. Conservationists are keeping a constant watch on their populations and are trying to discourage poaching.

FACT FILE

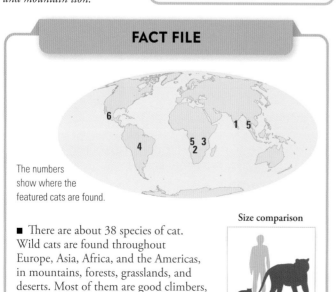

The numbers show where the featured cats are found.

■ There are about 38 species of cat. Wild cats are found throughout Europe, Asia, Africa, and the Americas, in mountains, forests, grasslands, and deserts. Most of them are good climbers, and several are excellent swimmers.

Size comparison

My thick fur keeps me well insulated.
The Siberian tiger grows a long coat to keep it warm in the cold winters. The coat also becomes paler to help it blend into the snow.

▶ ENDANGERED *The Siberian tiger (Panthera tigris altaica) is the largest living cat. The species is critically endangered and is rarely seen in the wild.*

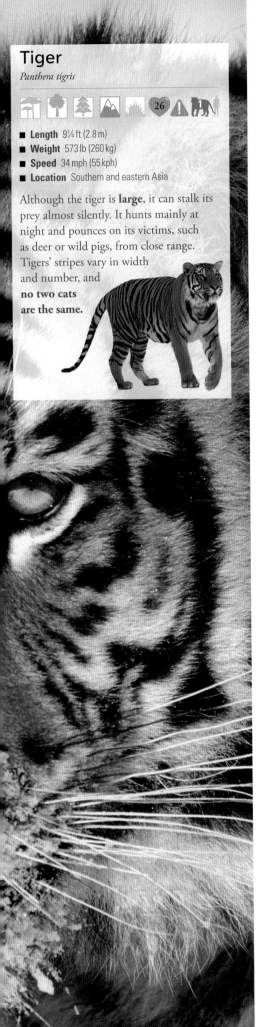

Tiger

Panthera tigris

- **Length** 9¼ ft (2.8 m)
- **Weight** 573 lb (260 kg)
- **Speed** 34 mph (55 kph)
- **Location** Southern and eastern Asia

Although the tiger is **large**, it can stalk its prey almost silently. It hunts mainly at night and pounces on its victims, such as deer or wild pigs, from close range. Tigers' stripes vary in width and number, and **no two cats are the same.**

Caracal

Caracal caracal

- **Length** 36 in (91 cm)
- **Weight** 42 lb (19 kg)
- **Speed** 34 mph (55 kph)
- **Location** Africa and western and southwestern Asia

The caracal has long legs and is known for the way it can **spring up** into the air and catch low-flying birds in its front paws. It also eats other animals, such as rodents, hares, and even small antelopes. This cat lives mostly on the ground, but **can climb well**.

Cheetah

Acinonyx jubatus

- **Length** 5 ft (1.5 m)
- **Weight** 159 lb (72 kg)
- **Speed** 62 mph (100 kph)
- **Location** Africa and western Asia

The cheetah is **famous for its speed**. It is the fastest land animal, but can run at top speed for only 10 to 20 seconds. Cheetahs are **sociable** cats. The young stay with their mother for up to two years. Brothers may stay together longer.

Ocelot

Leopardus pardalis

- **Length** 3 ft (1 m)
- **Weight** 35 lb (16 kg)
- **Location** Southern US to central and South America

This **solitary cat** is very adaptable. It lives in a variety of habitats and eats lots of different food. Its favorite food is small rodents, but it will also eat lizards, fish, birds, snakes, and even turtles. Its spotted coat has led to it being one of the **most hunted** species of cat and it is now endangered.

Leopard

Panthera pardus

- **Length** 6¼ ft (1.9 m)
- **Weight** 200 lb (90 kg)
- **Location** Africa and southern Asia

The leopard relies on **stealth** rather than speed to catch its prey. It can kill larger and heavier animals, such as wildebeest and antelopes. All leopards are spotted, even the black panther, shown here, which is a leopard with **dark skin and fur**.

Bobcat

Lynx rufus

- **Length** 3⅗ ft (1.1 m)
- **Weight** 34 lb (15.5 kg)
- **Location** Southern Canada, US, and Mexico

This is the most common wild cat in North America. It gets its name from its short, **"bobbed" tail**. The bobcat hunts mainly rabbits and hares, but will also eat rodents, bats, birds, deer, and carrion when its favorite food is scarce. It is a solitary, **secretive** animal and does most of its hunting at dawn and dusk.

Lion *teamwork*

Lions are the only cats that live and hunt in groups. These groups are called prides and contain between 4 and 35 animals. By working together, they can take down animals larger than themselves. Female lions do most of the work.

WORKING TOGETHER
The female members of a pride team up to hunt large animals such as zebra, antelopes, and buffalo. After stalking to within 100 ft (30 m), they fan out to encircle their prey.

Lion

Panthera leo

- **Length** 5½–8¼ ft (1.7–2.5 m)
- **Weight** 330–550 lb (150–250 kg)
- **Location** Africa (south of the Sahara) and south Asia (Gir Forest, west India)

Lions are the most sociable of all big cats, which makes them **great teamworkers**. Most live in Africa, where their coloring blends in well with the dry, grassy plains, making it **hard for prey to spot them** approaching. The smaller Asiatic lion (*Panthera leo persica*) lives in the Gir Forest in India.

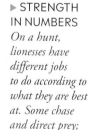

▶ STRENGTH IN NUMBERS
On a hunt, lionesses have different jobs to do according to what they are best at. Some chase and direct prey; others ambush and kill.

**Shush!
Take it slowly.**
Female lions are sleek
and powerful. They do
not have a mane like males,
because it would impede them
as they hunt. They creep up
silently on their prey, before
swiftly moving in
for the kill.

▶ ME FIRST!
*After a successful kill
by the females, the
male arrives to take
his share. Although
he hasn't done any
of the work, he is
always allowed to
feed first. His role
in the pride is to
defend territory,
which he does by
pacing around,
roaring, and leaving
his scent on trees.*

Who is the scavenger?
A male lion that does not have
any females to hunt for him
may take food from other
hunters, such as hyenas. He
will wait for a pack of hyenas
to do all the hard work of a
kill, and then bully them away
to enjoy the feast himself. Once
he is full, vultures will usually
dive in to strip any remaining
meat from the carcass.

A *world* of cats

Wild cats range in size from the black-footed cat, about the size of a small pet cat, to the tiger, whose body can be the length of a small car. But all cats are accomplished hunters, and all species move and hunt in similar ways, stalking their prey with stealth and patience.

Cheetah
Acinonyx jubatus

Bobcat
Lynx rufus

Lion
Panthera leo

Wild cat
Felis silvestris

Jungle cat
Felis chaus

Sand cat
Felis margarita

Black panther
These cats are either leopards (Panthera pardus) or jaguars (Panthera onca) that have black fur.

Canadian lynx
Lynx canadensis

Caracal
Caracal caracal

Ocelot
Leopardus pardalis

LARGEST CAT
Tiger
Panthera tigris

A tiger hunts largely at night, but its coat provides effective camouflage during the day.

SMALLEST CAT
Black-footed cat
Felis nigripes

Serval
Leptailurus serval

Domestic cat
Felis catus

Fishing cat
Prionailurus viverrinus

Playing *to survive*

Playing is a good way to learn. When young mammals tumble around together and chase each other, they are picking up hunting and fighting skills, which will be vital for their survival in later life. They learn coordination and control and gain experience of situations which will help them when they have to fend for themselves.

TAKING OVER *Young male lions leave their family when they reach adulthood, and wait until they are strong enough to fight for leadership of their own pride. Once in charge, they tolerate their own cubs, but kill those of the previous leader.*

GAINING EXPERIENCE

Lion cubs tumble, prowl, and pounce around. As well as enjoying themselves and learning useful skills, they are establishing their position in the "pecking order" within their family. They also discover—in a controlled, safe environment—what risks they can take and what could happen if they put themselves in unnecessary danger.

▶ GONE FISHING
Bear cubs learn from their mother by following her and copying what she does. An important lesson for brown bear cubs is fishing. They watch their mother while she fishes for salmon, then imitate her until they know how to catch fish for themselves.

Retract those claws, kids. They're sharp!

Like most cats, lions can retract their claws. When play-fighting, cubs keep in their claws and do not expose their teeth. In a real hunt, lions kill their prey by leaping on it and biting into the neck.

Learning the ropes Young tiger cubs love to wrestle with each other and with adults. In this way they learn how to test another animal's strength without the risk of being injured if they get it wrong. This playful form of fighting is also a good opportunity for the cubs to practice their suffocating grip on each other.

FACT FILE

■ Young lions do not become independent until they are at least 16 months old. Females stay with their pride, while the males leave.

■ Tiger cubs start to take part in hunting expeditions when they are about five to six months old. They stay with their mother until they are 18 months to three years old.

■ Brown bear cubs remain with their mother for two to four years. Once they have left, the mother usually starts a new family.

Weasels and *their relatives*

Weasels belong to a family of animals called mustelids. Their relatives include otters, badgers, and martens. Many mustelids are small but they are strong and can be fierce hunters. They live in a variety of habitats everywhere except Australia, New Zealand, and Antarctica.

WEASEL SKULL

▲ HUNTER'S HEAD *A weasel's head is little wider than its neck, which allows it to get through small holes. Like other meat-eaters, it has very sharp canine teeth. It kills its prey of voles and mice with a quick bite to the back of the neck.*

European pine marten
Martes martes

COMMON FEATURES

Most mustelids have a long, flexible body; short legs; and a long tail. They have five toes on each foot with nonretractable, curved claws. They have an acute sense of smell, which they use for hunting. Many of these animals, especially the sable, have been hunted by humans for their soft, thick fur.

FACT FILE

■ **Terrestrial, or land-based, mustelids** include the weasel, the black-footed ferret, and the stoat.

■ **Arboreal, or tree-based, mustelids** include the European pine marten and the American marten.

■ **Semiaquatic mustelids** include the European mink and the American mink. They live near water.

■ **Fully aquatic mustelids** include the giant otter, sea otter, and river otters. They spend most of their time in water.

■ **Burrowing mustelids** include the European badger, honey badger, and the wolverine. They live in burrows.

▶ AGILE HUNTER *The European pine marten is an excellent climber and often hunts for prey in trees. But it hunts mainly on the ground, feeding on small rodents, birds, insects, and fruit.*

Least weasel

Mustela nivalis

- **Length** 9½ in (24 cm)
- **Weight** 9 oz (250 g)
- **Location** North America and Europe to northern, central, and eastern Asia

The least weasel is the **smallest** mustelid. It is small enough to chase mice into their burrows, but can kill a rabbit up to ten times its own weight. It must eat one-third of its body weight every day, and so it hunts **day and night**.

European badger

Meles meles

- **Length** 35 in (90 cm)
- **Weight** 75 lb (34 kg)
- **Location** Europe to eastern Asia

Unlike most mustelids, the European badger lives in groups. It has a burrow called a **sett**, which is a system of tunnels and chambers. It hunts at night and **eats a varied diet**, from worms to small birds.

European polecat

Mustela putorius

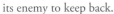

- **Length** 20 in (50 cm)
- **Weight** 3 lb (1.5 kg)
- **Location** Europe

This animal is probably the ancestor of the pet ferret. It **swims well** and can catch fish to eat, but it prefers to eat small mammals, reptiles, and birds. If it is threatened, the polecat **produces a strong smell** to persuade its enemy to keep back.

Wolverine

Gulo gulo

- **Length** 41 in (105 cm)
- **Weight** 55 lb (25 kg)
- **Location** Canada, northwest US, and northern Europe to northern and eastern Asia

This bearlike creature is a **fierce** predator and has strong jaws for crushing bones. It is also called **the glutton**— a word used for a greedy person!

Giant otter

Pteronura brasiliensis

- **Length** 4½ ft (1.4 m)
- **Weight** 70 lb (32 kg)
- **Location** Northern and central South America

The giant otter is the **largest** mustelid in terms of length. It feeds mainly on fish and crabs, which it catches with its mouth. Groups of up to 10 otters live in **dens** or burrows beside a river.

▼ POWERFUL SWIMMER
The paws and feet of the giant otter are fully webbed, which helps them dive down to catch slow-moving fish that live on the riverbed.

At home *with sea otters*

This is the only species of otter that spends its whole life
at sea. Its food includes fish, crabs, mollusks, and sea urchins,
and it has strong teeth for crushing the shells. A social animal,
the sea otter lives in groups called rafts, separated
into male and female rafts.

Sea otter

Enhydra lutris

- **Length** 4¼ ft (1.3 m)
- **Weight** 62 lb (28 kg)
- **Location** North Pacific ocean

Unlike most sea mammals, the sea otter does not have blubber under its skin to keep it warm. **Thick fur** traps a layer of air so the otter's skin never gets wet. In fact, a sea otter has more hairs on a fingernail-size patch of its skin than a person has on their head!

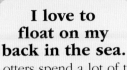

I love to float on my back in the sea.

Sea otters spend a lot of time floating on their back with their paws out of the water. They eat and sleep on their back, and mother sea otters nurse their pups while floating on the surface.

SAFELY STOWED *Sea otters are found in beds of giant kelp, a type of seaweed. They often use the kelp to anchor themselves while they sleep. Mothers also wrap their pups in kelp to keep them safe while they go fishing.*

▲ USING TOOLS *The sea otter has learned to use tools to open shellfish and sea urchins. While floating on its back, it cracks open the shell on a rock it carries on its tummy.*

PROTECTED SPECIES

Once hunted for its fur, the sea otter nearly became extinct in some areas. It is now a protected species and its numbers are increasing in certain places. Efforts are being made to relocate it to other areas.

▲ UNDERWATER *This excellent swimmer has a strong, flat tail that it uses as a rudder and flipper-like hind feet. It dives to forage for food on the seabed and its large lungs allow it to stay under the water for several minutes.*

Civets *and relatives*

These catlike animals belong to four families. There are about 70 species, and they include civets, mongooses, and genets. They are all very different—many are fierce predators, some are solitary, while others work together in social colonies.

▲ SKULL AND JAW
This is an Egyptian mongoose skull (Herpestes ichneumon). *The long face is typical of animals in these families, which, though related to cats and hyenas, have more snap to their bite, with up to 40 teeth.*

BODY PARTS

Civets and their relatives have a long body, short legs, and a long tail. They have thick coats, often marked with spots or stripes. They have scent glands under their tail, and if an enemy comes too close, some will spray a nasty-smelling liquid.

I'm a tree climber.
The spotted genet is an excellent climber. It hunts for birds at night when they are roosting and not likely to escape. It also forages for eggs, rodents, insects, and small reptiles.

CATLIKE *The large spotted genet (*Genetta tigrina*) looks a bit like a cat. But its snout is more pointed and it can only partly retract its claws when they are not being used.*

FACT FILE

■ The spotted linsang (*Prionodon pardicolor*) of southeast Asia uses its tail to balance and brake as it climbs.

■ The binturong (*Arctictis binturong*) of southeast Asia is one of only a few carnivores with a prehensile tail.

■ The fossa (*Cryptoprocta ferox*) is the largest carnivore to live on the island of Madagascar.

The numbers show where the featured animals are found.

Yellow mongoose

Cynictis penicillata

- **Length** 13 in (33 cm)
- **Tail** 10 in (25 cm)
- **Weight** 29 oz (800 g)
- **Location** Southern Africa

The yellow mongoose is sometimes called the **red meerkat**, and it often shares burrows with meerkats. It lives in colonies containing **one breeding pair** and up to 20 of their young and other relatives.

Striped civet

Fossa fossana

- **Length** 18 in (45 cm)
- **Tail** 10 in (25 cm)
- **Weight** 4½ lb (2 kg)
- **Location** Madagascar

This **shy, nocturnal** civet hunts for small animals on the forest floor. It can store fat in its tail as **preparation** for winter when food may be scarce.

Meerkat

Suricata suricatta

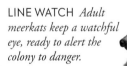

- **Length** 14 in (35 cm)
- **Tail** 10 in (25 cm)
- **Weight** 35 oz (975 g)
- **Location** Southern Africa

Meerkats live in burrows. They often take over old burrows of ground squirrels, which they enlarge by digging with their long front claws. Their claws are also useful for finding insects, spiders, roots, and bulbs to eat. **These sociable creatures form colonies** of up to 30 animals. While the colony is searching for food, some **act as lookouts** and warn if a predator is nearby. The colony then dives for cover.

LINE WATCH *Adult meerkats keep a watchful eye, ready to alert the colony to danger.*

Banded mongoose

Mungos mungo

- **Length** 18 in (45 cm)
- **Tail** 9 in (23 cm)
- **Weight** 5½ lb (2.5 kg)
- **Location** Africa

Mongooses eat lots of different foods, from termites to bird eggs, but they are known for the way they **attack snakes.** Their thick fur helps protect them from being bitten, and they are **partially immune to venomous snake bites**.

Dwarf mongoose

Helogale parvula

- **Length** 11 in (28 cm)
- **Tail** 7½ in (19 cm)
- **Weight** 12 oz (350 g)
- **Location** Eastern and southern Africa

As its name suggests, this is the **smallest mongoose.** It forms packs of 2 to 20 animals that live and feed together—on insects, lizards, snakes, birds, eggs, and mice. Female dwarf mongooses have up to six young, and the **whole pack helps** take care of them.

Seals and sea lions

These sea mammals belong to a group of animals called pinnipeds. They spend most of their time at sea and cannot move around so well on land. They haul themselves out onto rocky or sandy beaches to breed. All species have fur and long whiskers.

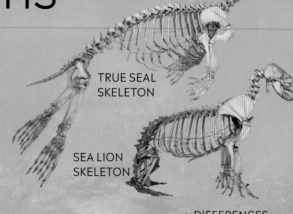

TRUE SEAL SKELETON

SEA LION SKELETON

▲ DIFFERENCES
A true seal's back flippers point backward. Sea lions and fur seals can rotate their back flippers forward for moving on land.

▲ COLONY *During the breeding season, several thousand brown fur seals come on shore and form colonies.*

WATER MAMMALS

Seals and sea lions have a layer of blubber under the skin, which keeps them warm. They have flippers, instead of legs, and can close their ears and nostrils when they dive. Their large eyes help them see well underwater.

Northern elephant seal
Mirounga angustirostris

SWIMMERS *Seals and sea lions have streamlined bodies and powerful flippers for swimming. In water, they are agile and graceful.*

FACT FILE

■ **Number of species:** There are 33 species of pinniped in three families. There are 18 true seals, 14 eared seals (sea lions and fur seals), and one walrus (*see pp.86–87*).
■ **Key features:** They are all carnivorous. Seals and sea lions feed mainly on fish and small crustaceans called krill.

True seals have no external ears. They include the bearded seal (*Erignathus barbatus*), top left, the gray seal, and the harbor seal. Eared seals have small external ears. They include the Californian sea lion (*Zalophus californianus*), bottom left, and the brown fur seal.

Californian sea lion

Zalophus californianus

- **Length** 7¾ ft (2.4 m)
- **Weight** 860 lb (390 kg)
- **Location** West coast of North America

Like all sea lions, Californian sea lions can **support themselves** on their front flippers on land. They are fast swimmers, reaching speeds of 25 mph (40 kph). They are **playful** animals and can sometimes be seen surfing and leaping out of the water.

Steller's sea lion

Eumetopias jubatus

- **Length** 11 ft (3.5 m)
- **Weight** 2,425 lb (1,100 kg)
- **Location** North Pacific coast

This is the **largest** sea lion, and a male might weigh three times as much as a female. Males are aggressive and fight each other for mates. This species is **in danger** because it has been hunted and its food is decreasing due to overfishing.

Gray seal

Halichoerus grypus

- **Length** 8¼ ft (2.5 m)
- **Weight** 680 lb (310 kg)
- **Location** North Atlantic and Baltic Sea

Gray seal pups are born with soft, **white fur**. They shed this within three weeks and grow a gray coat. The Latin name for this seal means "hook-nosed sea pig" and the male particularly has a long, **hooked nose**.

Harbor seal

Phoca vitulina

- **Length** 6¼ ft (1.9 m)
- **Weight** 375 lb (170 kg)
- **Location** North Atlantic and North Pacific coasts

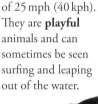

Also known as the common seal, the harbor seal is the **most widespread** pinniped. Harbor seals do not gather in such large groups as other seals although they do rest on rocky shores, mud flats, and sandy beaches. They do not travel more than about 12 miles (20 km) away from the shore.

Southern elephant seal

Mirounga leonina

- **Length** 20 ft (6 m)
- **Weight** 770–8,820 lb (350–4,000 kg)
- **Location** Southern Ocean

Male southern elephant seals are four or five times the weight of the females. The males have a **huge nose**, which looks a bit like an elephant's trunk. When they are fighting for females during the breeding season, they **inflate** their nose and roar at their rivals.

Antarctic fur seal

Arctocephalus gazella

- **Length** 5½ ft (1.7 m)
- **Weight** 286 lb (130 kg)
- **Location** Antarctic and subantarctic waters

Fur seals have a layer of **soft underfur** as well as the short fur that most seals have. This keeps them dry and warm. Male seals arrive first at the breeding ground on a rocky island, and **fight for territory**. When the females arrive, about five females join each male.

OFTEN SEEN
The Antarctic fur seal is one of the most common fur seals.

Brown fur seal

Arctocephalus pusillus

- **Length** 7½ ft (2.3 m)
- **Weight** 794 lb (360 kg)
- **Location** Southern Africa, southeast Australia, and Tasmania

Brown fur seals spend most of the time at sea, but they do not swim far from land. Mother fur seals spend several days at sea, feeding, and **return to their pups regularly** to feed them. The pups **play together** while their mothers are away.

Walrus

Odobenus rosmarus

- **Length** 12 ft (3.6 m)
- **Weight** 4,400 lb (2,000 kg)
- **Location** Arctic waters

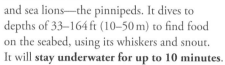

The walrus belongs to the same order of animals as seals and sea lions—the pinnipeds. It dives to depths of 33–164 ft (10–50 m) to find food on the seabed, using its whiskers and snout. It will **stay underwater for up to 10 minutes**.

USEFUL TUSKS

The walrus is the only member of the pinnipeds to have tusks, which can grow to nearly 3 ft (1 m) long on males. They are basically overgrown canines. The males use their tusks as weapons when they compete for territory during the breeding season.

Sunbathing When walruses lie in sunlight their skin turns pink, as if they were sunburned. This is because the arteries that take blood to the skin's surface expand. Blood flows to the skin cells and absorbs heat from the sun. This is one way in which walruses keep warm.

▲ SAFETY IN NUMBERS *Mother walruses are protective of their young. In fact, all the adults help protect the pups from predators. They swim in a tight group, keeping the pups carefully guarded in the middle.*

I am the *walrus*

The walrus lives in Arctic waters. It is hunted by killer whales so it prefers shallower waters and comes ashore to breed. Walruses are social animals and gather on land and on ice floes in large herds containing hundreds of animals. Space can get very tight!

ICE MAN *This walrus is resting on pack ice in northeast Canada. Its thick skin and blubber keep it warm. It can also contract the blood vessels close to its skin to reduce heat loss.*

Look! I have my own ice picks!
Both male and female walruses have tusks. They are useful for helping to haul the walrus out of the water and onto the ice— they are purpose-built ice axes!

Elephants

These giant animals are the largest living land mammals. With their long, mobile trunks; curved, white tusks; and large, flapping ears, elephants are instantly recognizable. But what many do not know is that there are three different elephant species—one living in Asia and two in Africa.

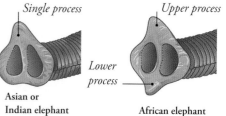

FACT FILE

- **Family:** Elephantidae
- **Number of species:** Three
- **Key features:** Distinctive trunk used as a "fifth limb"; upper incisors elongated into large, curved tusks in bulls; large, fan-shaped ears; thick, wrinkly skin.

Single process

Upper process

Lower process

Asian or
Indian elephant

African elephant

SAY HELLO *Elephants often greet each other by standing close and twining their long trunks. The sense of touch is extremely important in elephant society.*

Asian elephant
Elephas maximus

- **Head–body length** 18–21 ft (5.5–6.4 m)
- **Shoulder height** 8–10 ft (2.5–3 m)
- **Weight** Males 12,000 lb (5,400 kg); females 6,000 lb (2,700 kg)
- **Location** Southern and Southeast Asia

The Asian elephant is smaller than its African cousins. Only the males have visible tusks. The Asian elephant population is **rapidly declining**. There may be fewer than 60,000 individuals in the world, including captive animals.

The Asian elephant has smaller ears than its African cousin.

African bush elephant
Loxodonta africana

- **Head–body length** 18–24½ ft (5.5–7.5 m)
- **Shoulder height** 8–13 ft (2.4–4 m)
- **Weight** Males 14,000 lb (6,300 kg); females 7,700 lb (3,500 kg)
- **Location** Africa (South of the Sahara Desert)

The African bush elephant is the **world's largest land mammal**. These giants roam the African savanna, foraging for bark, branches, leaves, and grasses. A single adult needs to eat around 350 lb (160 kg) of food a day.

Pygmy elephant
Loxodonta cyclotis pumilio

- **Head–body length** 8–9¼ ft (2.4–2.8 m)
- **Weight** 4,000–7,000 lb (1,800–3,200 kg)
- **Location** Congo Basin of central Africa

Some zoologists think that these small elephants are a separate species, but they are **forest elephants** whose size may be a result of environmental pressures such as **restricted food**.

African forest elephant
Loxodonta cyclotis

- **Head–body length** 18–24½ ft (5.5–7.5 m)
- **Shoulder height** 5¼–9¼ ft (1.6–2.8 m)
- **Weights** Males 13,228 lb (6,000 kg); females 6,000 lb (2,700 kg)
- **Location** Central and western Africa

These elephants are smaller than their savanna relatives, and their ears are more rounded. The tusks are generally straighter than those of the bush elephant and **point downward**, which may be an adaptation to help them move through the dense lowland jungle. Sometimes they wander along the edges of the forest, where they come into contact with bush elephants.

The African forest elephant has yellow tusks.

Elephant family

Elephants have long held our fascination. These giant mammals have the biggest brains in the animal world. Since their intelligence is combined with great strength, it is no surprise that we have harnessed them as working animals. Humans are the elephant's worst enemy because of the ivory trade and competition for land.

I won't let you out of my sight.
Female elephants are called cows and their babies are calves. It is not only the mother that looks after her calf. Every cow in the family unit plays a part in helping to bring up the young elephants.

FAMILY LIFE
Females live in family units made up of related cows and their young offspring. A cow and her calf are rarely more than a trunk's length apart.

▲ LONG REACH *Elephants can stand on their hind legs to reach high branches for tasty fresh green leaves.*

▲ PRECIOUS WATER *A water hole in the middle of the African savanna attracts animals from far and wide. Hot and thirsty elephants love to cool down in water holes.*

CONSERVATION

All elephant species are endangered. In parts of Asia and Africa, people compete with elephants for land. But the real damage was done before the 1989 worldwide ivory ban, when elephants were hunted for their tusks. The sale of ivory is now strictly controlled in most countries, and seized tusks have been publicly burned, but poachers still supply a criminal market.

Dugongs and *manatees*

Manatees and dugongs are the only existing animals in the order of mammals called sirenians. They have a flat tail, paddlelike front limbs, but no hind limbs. They are the only marine mammals that feed purely on plants. An adult manatee will often eat up to nine percent of its body weight per day.

I'm not in a hurry.
Manatees are large, slow-moving creatures. Their bodies contain a lot of gas, given off by all the plants they eat. This could make them rise to the surface, but they have heavy bones to help them stay underwater.

TOTALLY AQUATIC

Sirenians spend their whole life in water and never come on land. Manatees make long dives and can stay underwater for up to 15 minutes before they have to come to the surface to breathe. The dugong dives for only about one minute.

MANATEES *have tough skin, which can be up to 2 in (5 cm) thick. Underneath is a thinner layer of blubber. Because manatees live in warm water, they do not need lots of blubber.*

West Indian manatee

Trichechus manatus

- **Length** 15 ft (4.5 m)
- **Weight** 1,320 lb (600 kg)
- **Location** Southeast US to northeast South America, and Caribbean

Manatees live in **shallow water** near the coast, and in nearby rivers and freshwater lagoons. Females have only **one calf** every two years. Mother and calf often "mouth" each other to help keep the bond between them.

MAMMALS

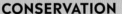

CONSERVATION

There are only about 130,000 sirenians left in the world. In the past they were hunted for their meat, skin, and oil. Now, many manatees are injured or killed by boat propellers because they often sleep near the surface of the water and are difficult to see.

▲ DUGONG
The end of a dugong's tail is crescent-shaped, or fluked, a bit like a whale's tail. It flaps it up and down to propel itself through the water and also steers with it.

▲ MANATEE
A manatee's tail is rounded and looks a bit like a beaver's tail. The manatee flaps it only about 30 times a minute to swim.

Grazers Sirenians such as the dugong (*Dugong dugon*) graze on the seabed. They use their flexible upper lip to collect sea grasses and other plants, then crush the food between horny plates on their mouth. Finally, they grind it between their teeth before swallowing.

Horses, asses, and zebras

There are four types of horse—Przewalski's horse, asses, zebras, and domestic horses (including ponies). They are called "odd-toed" animals because they have one toe on each foot. In the wild, they live out in the open where they can keep an eye out for predators.

CONSERVATION

Przewalski's horse is rare. Most are now found in zoos, but several attempts have been made to reintroduce the horse into the wild in Mongolia. The African wild ass and Grevy's zebra are also in danger of extinction due to hunting and loss of habitat.

RUNNING WILD

There are many herds of horses and ponies living in the wild. Most are descended from domestic horses. They include the mustangs of North America, the brumbies of Australia, and the white horses of the Camargue in France. Many breeds of pony live wild in Britain.

▼ ROUND UP *Many herds of wild mustangs in the US are rounded up every year. The horses are gathered into corrals. Some are kept and domesticated for riding. The rest are returned into the wild.*

FACT FILE

■ **Horses** All domestic and semi-wild horses and ponies are the same species. Przewalski's horse is a different species. It is the only truly wild horse.

■ **Zebras** The three species of zebra are Grevy's zebra, the plains zebra, and the mountain zebra. Stripe patterns differ between species and even individuals within a species.

■ **Asses** The Asian wild ass, or onager; the kiang; and the African wild ass are the three species of wild ass. The African wild ass is the ancestor of the domestic donkey.

▼ MIXTURES *A zebra/donkey cross is called a zedonk (right). A male donkey and female horse produce a mule (below right). A male horse and female donkey produce a hinny (below left).*

African wild ass

Equus africanus

- **Height** 4¼ ft (1.3 m)
- **Weight** 510 lb (230 kg)
- **Speed** 45 mph (70 kph)
- **Location** Eastern Africa

The African wild ass lives in **hot, dry, rocky deserts**, where it eats almost any plant material it can find, from grass to thorny bushes. It can go without water for several days. The wild ass **lives in herds** of up to 50 individuals.

Plains zebra

Equus quagga

- **Height** 4¼ ft (1.3 m)
- **Weight** 850 lb (385 kg)
- **Speed** 34 mph (55 kph)
- **Location** Eastern and southern Africa

Also known as the common or Burchell's zebra, the plains zebra is the only zebra with **stripes under its belly**. It is widespread, and herds containing several hundred animals are a common sight. The herds are made up of many family groups.

MAMMALS

Przewalski's horse

Equus ferus

- **Height** 4½ ft (1.4 m)
- **Weight** 660 lb (300 kg)
- **Speed** 37 mph (60 kph)
- **Location** Mongolia

In the 1880s, these wild horses were found in Mongolia by **an explorer**. A few were taken to Europe to save the species. There are now small herds living both in **zoos** and in the wild.

Donkey

Equus asinus africanus

- **Height** 4 ft (1.2 m)
- **Weight** 573 lb (260 kg)
- **Speed** 30 mph (50 kph)
- **Location** Kept domestically worldwide

Domestic donkeys are often kept as working animals or as pets. They are strong and can **carry heavy loads** over great distances with little food and water. Donkey **breeds vary in size** from miniature (less than 36 in [90 cm] high) to the French Poitou (up to 5 ft [1.5 m] high).

Mountain zebra

Equus zebra

- **Height** 4¼ ft (1.3 m)
- **Weight** 860 lb (390 kg)
- **Speed** 34 mph (55 kph)
- **Location** South Africa

This zebra is a good climber and has **hard, pointed hoofs** to help it clamber up the steep, rocky slopes where it lives. Another difference between this and other zebras is that it has a fold of skin, called a **dewlap**, just under its throat.

Grevy's zebra

Equus grevyi

- **Height** 5 ft (1.5 m)
- **Weight** 990 lb (450 kg)
- **Speed** 40 mph (64 kph)
- **Location** Eastern Africa

This is the **largest species** of zebra. It is not as social as the other zebras and does not form permanent herds. Female Grevy's zebras and their foals **roam freely**, looking for grass and other plants to eat. But they stay within the territory of their dominant male.

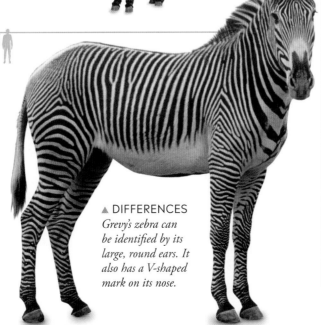

▲ DIFFERENCES
Grevy's zebra can be identified by its large, round ears. It also has a V-shaped mark on its nose.

Mustang

Equus caballus

- **Height** 4½–5 ft (1.4–1.5 m)
- **Weight** 700–1,000 lb (317–454 kg)
- **Speed** 40 mph (64 kph)
- **Location** Wild in North America

The mustang is descended from Spanish horses taken to the Americas in the 1500s. It is the same species as all **domestic horses** and ponies and comes in many different colors. This one is described as **bright bay**.

Giraffe and okapi

Most people will have heard of a giraffe, but not so many know about the giraffe's smaller relative, the okapi. Both live in Africa, but they are found in different places. Giraffes roam the savanna and open woodlands in small herds. Okapis live alone and hide away in tropical rainforests.

My spots are the perfect camouflage.

Different subspecies of giraffe have different skin patterns. Some have clear, chestnut patches (above, left). Others have black patches (above, center), and some have small, blurry patches of yellow (above, right).

HORNY HEAD *Giraffes have small horns, called ossicones, covered with skin. Baby giraffes are born with soft horns that turn hard as they grow older.*

Giraffe

Giraffa camelopardalis

- **Height** 18 ft (5.5 m)
- **Weight** 4,200 lb (1,900 kg)
- **Speed** 35 mph (56 kph)
- **Location** East Africa

Giraffes use their long, **dark tongues** and thin, mobile lips to pick off leaves and shoots from the treetops. The taller male giraffes eat the leaves from higher up the tree to **avoid competing** with the females.

NECK LOCK

The giraffe is the tallest animal in the world thanks to its long neck. The bulls (males) use their necks to compete for the attention of the cows (females). In a display called "necking," the bulls lock necks and often clash heads. The winner earns the right to mate with the cows.

◀ TALL ORDER
The front legs of a giraffe are much longer than its back legs. So the giraffe spreads its front legs apart to drink at a water hole. The front legs are very strong. Giraffes use them to kick predators. One blow can kill a lion.

▶ STRIPED SKIN
With striking black-and-white stripes across its legs and rump, the okapi looks more like a zebra than a giraffe. Like giraffes, okapis have long necks and browse on soft twigs, leaves, and juicy shoots. Okapis are shy and the stripes help them hide in the rainforests of central Africa. In fact, they are so shy they weren't scientifically recorded until 1901!

Rhinoceroses

There are five species of rhinoceros living in the savannas of Africa or the swampy grasslands of Asia. They are large, heavy animals—only elephants and hippos are bigger. They have poor eyesight but make up for this with good senses of hearing and smell. Not all live in the wild—the black and the white rhinoceros are now only found in sanctuaries.

All rhinoceroses like to wallow in mud. This cools them and protects their skin. Black rhinos look black because of mud dried on their skin.

RHINO HORNS

Rhinos have one or two horns, depending on the species. The horns are made of hairlike material called keratin, not bone—in fact, the same material that your hair and nails are made of. The horns are "perched" on top of the skull rather than being part of it.

▼ TWO HORNS
The white rhinoceros has two horns. The front horn is longer than the back horn and used for digging for water and plants.

I'm staying close to mom.
Young rhinoceroses are called calves. A female white rhinoceros usually has one calf every two to four years. The calf can run beside its mother after only three days.

Indian rhinoceros
Rhinoceros unicornis

- **Length** 12½ ft (3.8 m)
- **Weight** 4,850 lb (2,200 kg)
- **Location** Nepal and northern India

The **largest** of the Asian rhinoceroses, the Indian rhino has only one horn. It eats trees and shrubs, but feeds out in the open, not in forests. Its **hairless** skin has lots of small lumps and hangs down in heavy folds. This makes the rhino look as if it is wearing armor.

CONSERVATION

All five species of rhinoceros are threatened. There are fewer than 80 Javan rhinos left in the world and the black rhinoceros is disappearing faster than any other mammal. Rhinos are in danger because they are killed for their horns. Rhino horn is used in China as a drug. In the Middle East, horns are carved to make dagger handles. Removing the horns to deter poaching has failed to stop their decline and is no longer practiced.

White rhinoceros
Ceratotherium simum

- **Length** 13 ft (4 m)
- **Weight** 5,070 lb (2,300 kg)
- **Location** East and southern Africa

The white rhinoceros is not really white, but gray. Its name comes from the Afrikaans word *weit* meaning "wide." This refers to its **wide, straight mouth** which is ideal for eating grass.

Javan rhinoceros
Rhinoceros sondaicus

- **Length** 11½ ft (3.5 m)
- **Weight** 3,090 lb (1,400 kg)
- **Location** Java (Indonesia)

This rhino has only one horn, and some females have no horn at all. Like the Indian rhino, it has **no hair** except on its ears and the tip of its tail. This is one of the **rarest** large mammals in the world.

Sumatran rhinoceros
Dicerorhinus sumatrensis

- **Length** 10½ ft (3.2 m)
- **Weight** 1,764 lb (800 kg)
- **Location** South and Southeast Asia

This is the **smallest** rhinoceros. It is also the **hairiest** because it is covered with coarse, bristly hair. The Sumatran rhino lives in forests on hillsides, where it feeds on twigs, leaves, and fruits. It has two horns. The front one can grow to 35 in (90 cm) long.

Black rhinoceros
Diceros bicornis

- **Length** 10 ft (3 m)
- **Weight** 2,870 lb (1,300 kg)
- **Location** East and southern Africa

Unlike the white rhino, the black rhino feeds on trees and shrubs. It has a **pointed upper lip** which it can curl around twigs and shoots and pull them into its mouth to be bitten off. The rhino is sometimes called the hook-lipped rhinoceros. It is more aggressive than the white rhino and may charge without warning. Like other rhinos, it can run surprisingly **fast for its size**—25 mph (40 kph) in short bursts, which is the same as an Olympic sprinter!

Battling hippos

The hippopotamus is one of Africa's largest mammals. It is also one of the continent's most dangerous animals. Males can weigh more than 6,800 lb (3,048 kg). They are also quick tempered and, when roused, can be lethal. Never get too close to a hippo.

▼ BARING THEIR TEETH
Hippos have enormous heads, with huge jaws. On the lower jaw are two daggerlike teeth. These razor-sharp fangs may be as long as 12 in (30 cm) and can be deadly in a fight.

I'm boss here. Challenge me and you'll be sorry!
Male hippos often fight over territory. If roaring and splashing fail to drive off a rival, a bloody battle may break out. This could last for hours, and even end with the loser's death.

Hippopotamus
Hippopotamus amphibius

- **Height** 5 ft (1.5 m)
- **Length** 16½ ft (5 m)
- **Weight** 6,600–9,900 lb (3,000–4500 kg)
- **Location** Africa

Hippos **cannot sweat** to control their body temperature, so they spend their day **wallowing** in rivers and streams to keep cool. They are also protected from the baking sun by an oily red liquid that oozes out from special glands in their skin. At night, they leave the water to graze on grass, wandering up to 3 miles (5 km) to find food.

▲ UNDERWATER *Hippos have webbed feet that allow them to spread their weight when they put their feet down. This helps them walk along riverbeds. They can stay underwater for up to five minutes.*

▲ KEEPING WATCH *A hippo's eyes, nostrils, and ears are on top of its head. This means that it can breathe and watch for any trouble while almost totally submerged in water. Hippos can close off their nostrils and ears when underwater.*

SURPRISE KILLERS
Hippos are thought to kill more people in Africa than any other wild animal. A hippo may appear to be unconcerned by nearby humans, but can attack very suddenly if it feels threatened. Hippos are known to wade under small boats, tip the occupants into the water and then attack with their huge, knifelike teeth.

Dromedary
Camelus dromedarius

   40

- **Height** 6–7½ ft (1.8–2.3 m)
- **Weight** 1,500 lb (690 kg)
- **Speed** 40 mph (65 kph)
- **Location** Northern and eastern Africa and western and southern Asia

This single-humped camel has been **domesticated** for centuries. It eats a wide variety of plants, even salty ones, and scavenges on bones and dry carcasses.

▲ THIRSTY CREATURE
Smaller than camels and dromedaries, vicuñas are not suited to dry conditions—they need water every day. Living high in the Andes in South America, they were once hunted so widely for their fur that they nearly became extinct.

▲ ANCIENT HELPER
Native to the Andes, llamas were domesticated there thousands of years ago. Kept by Indigenous peoples (and now bred all over the world) for their wool, their meat, and their skin, llamas also make excellent pack animals because they're sure-footed on rough, hilly ground.

Camels *and* relatives

If an animal has a split upper lip, one or two humps, long legs, and an unusual, rocking walk, then it's a camel. Camels and their relatives walk this way because they move both their left legs together, then both their right legs together, in a special gait known as "pacing." Some species, such as llamas, are domesticated, while others, such as vicuñas, are wild.

DESERT BEAST *The dromedary is perfectly adapted to desert life: its broad feet make it stable on shifting ground, its long lashes keep sand out of its eyes, and its nostrils close tight during dust storms. It has been used to carry loads for more than 4,000 years.*

FACT FILE

- Bactrian camels have two humps. In winter, they grow a woolly brown coat, which they shed in spring. There are still a few wild bactrian camels in eastern Asia.

- Camels' feet have two large, equally sized toes with a wide, cushioned pad underneath. This pad makes the animal particularly stable by spreading its weight evenly across the whole foot.

**I can survive
for days and days
without any water.**
Dromedaries can not only drink
more than 13 gallons (50 liters)
of water at a time, they can also
store it; this allows them to survive
for long periods without drinking.
To conserve water, they produce
very small amounts of sweat
and urine.

◄ CAMEL HUMPS *are full
of fat, which the animals store
to provide them with an energy
source when food is in short supply.*

Deer

With more than 50 species, deer can be found in most parts of the world. They are herbivorous and live in a range of habitats. Their most striking feature is their antlers, which grow on nearly all adult males.

▲ NEW PASTURES
In North America, reindeer are called caribou. In the fall, they form large herds of up to 500,000 animals and migrate slowly southward to escape the extreme cold. In spring, they gather together again and migrate back northward.

Reindeer

Rangifer tarandus

15

- **Height** 4 ft (1.2 m)
- **Weight** 660 lb (300 kg)
- **Speed** 37–50 mph (60–80 kph)
- **Location** N. North America, Greenland, and N. Europe to E. Asia

Reindeer have an extremely **thick coat** to keep them warm in the cold of the far north. Their feet are furry, to give them grip on icy ground, and broad, to spread their weight and stop them sinking into the snow. Reindeer eat grass, leaves, and twigs, and also lichen, a mosslike plant. The female is the **only female deer to have antlers**.

White-tailed deer

Odocoileus virginianus

10

- **Height** 3 ft (1 m)
- **Weight** 474 lb (215 kg)
- **Speed** 40 mph (64 kph)
- **Location** S. Canada to N. South America

When the white-tailed deer is alarmed, it runs to safety with its long, bushy tail held up in the air. The **tail is white underneath**, and as the deer runs, the flashes of white warn other members of the herd of danger. This deer eats a variety of plant material, which is why it is able to survive in different **forest habitats**.

FACT FILE

■ True deer belong to the family Cervidae. The two other families of deer are chevrotains (Tragulidae) and musk deer (Moschidae).

■ Many young deer are born with white spots to hide them from predators. They curl up and keep still in long vegetation.

■ Antlers are made of solid bone. They are shed after the rut in the fall and grow again in the spring, usually getting larger each year.

■ When antlers first grow they are covered with skin called velvet. This gradually rubs off in time for the rut.

■ Deer walk on two toes. A scent gland between the toes leaves a smell on the ground for other deer to follow.

■ Deer are native to Asia, Africa, the Americas, and Europe and have been introduced to Australia and New Zealand.

MAMMALS

◀ MOOSE (OR ELK) RUT *At the start of the breeding season, also known as the rut, male deer compete for the right to breed with the females. They bellow at each other and lock antlers to test each other's strength.*

Moose (also called Elk)

Alces alces

- ■ **Height** 7½ ft (2.3 m)
- ■ **Weight** 1,820 lb (825 kg)
- ■ **Speed** 35 mph (55 kph)
- ■ **Location** Alaska, Canada, and N. Europe to N. and E. Asia

This is the **largest deer** and its antlers can span up to 6½ ft (2 m). Moose eat twigs and bark and in summer often **wade into rivers** and lakes to eat water plants.

Reeves's muntjac

Muntiacus reevesi

- ■ **Height** 22 in (55 cm)
- ■ **Weight** 40 lb (18 kg)
- ■ **Location** Eastern Asia

Male muntjacs have short, pointed antlers and **two short tusks**. They live mainly on their own. These deer are often called barking deer because they make loud, **bark-like calls** when they are alarmed and also during the breeding season.

Indian spotted chevrotain

Moschiola meminna

- ■ **Height** 14 in (35 cm)
- ■ **Weight** 6½ lb (3 kg)
- ■ **Location** S. Asia

Chevrotains are also known as **mouse deer**. They are not true deer and belong to a different animal family. They do not have antlers, but they do have two small tusks that point downward. These tiny animals are **nocturnal** and prefer to live alone.

105

Cattle and antelope

All these hoofed animals belong to the same family—the bovids. Some of them are huge and hairy; others are slim and delicate. The members of this group that have long, slender legs (such as springbok and impala) are known generally as "antelopes."

▶ SURVIVORS
Excessive hunting in earlier centuries wiped out American bison in their millions. The remaining wild herds live mainly in protected areas, such as Yellowstone National Park in Wyoming.

FACT FILE

Horny heads All species in this family have pointed horns, which usually appear on both males and females. Horns do not branch like antlers, but they are often shaped in fantastic twists and spirals. A horn has a bony core covered by a sheath of tough material called keratin.

■ The desert-dwelling oryx has straight, ringed horns that can be 5 ft (1.5 m) in length.

■ Each of the topi's horns forms the shape of an "L." They are heavily ridged and point backward.

■ The Asian water buffalo has the widest horn span of this group. It can reach 6½ ft (2 m) across.

■ Only male impalas have horns. These horns are ringed and lyre-shaped, and have heavy ridges.

American bison

Bison bison

20

- ■ **Height** 5–6½ ft (1.5–2 m)
- ■ **Weight** 770–2,200 lb (350–1,000 kg)
- ■ **Location** North America

Bison are also sometimes called American buffalo. These huge animals roam in groups, spending the greater part of their day grazing and ruminating. The cows (females) form herds with their calves under the leadership of a dominant female. The bulls (males) live in separate herds and usually approach the cows only in the mating season. Rival bulls competing for cows **fight one another** in fierce head-to-head clashes.

▲ WRAPPED UP
The bison's range extends to mountain areas, where the winters can be bitterly cold. With its massively thick coat and shaggy mane, the bison stays warm even when the temperature drops below zero.

Springbok

Antidorcas marsupialis

- **Height** 2¼–3 ft (70–87 cm)
- **Weight** 66–106 lb (30–48 kg)
- **Location** Southern Africa

When a springbok is frightened, or just excited, it bounces up and down on stiff legs. This leaping, called **"pronking,"** can lift the springbok as much as 10 ft (3 m) straight upward. A frightened springbok may also open a skin fold on its back to reveal a **crest of white hairs**.

Impala

Aepyceros melampus

- **Height** 3 ft (90 cm)
- **Weight** 88–143 lb (40–65 kg)
- **Location** East and southern Africa

These small antelopes are very **agile**. They can leap high and run fast to escape predators such as leopards. A **scent released from glands** above their hind feet is thought to help a group of impala stay in touch with each other.

Wild yak

Bos mutus

- **Height** 6½ ft (2 m)
- **Weight** Up to 2,200 lb (1,000 kg)
- **Location** South and east Asia

Domesticated yaks are common in Asia, but wild yaks are **rare**. These hardy animals live in the icy, high-altitude steppes, and can survive on mosses and lichens. For protection against the cold they have a **double coat**. This has a dense underlayer and long top hairs.

Musk ox

Ovibos moschatus

- **Height** 4–5 ft (1.2–1.5 m)
- **Weight** 440–900 lb (200–410 kg)
- **Location** North America and Greenland

Musk oxen are found only in Arctic regions. They live in herds of one male with a group of females. If a herd is threatened by predators such as bears or wolves, the musk oxen form **a defensive circle**, sheltering any young in the center.

Wildebeest *migration*

The wildebeest is a member of the cattle family. Huge herds roam the plains of eastern and southern Africa. In Tanzania's Serengeti National Park, more than a million wildebeest migrate with the seasons, moving from open grasslands to wooded savanna to find fresh grass.

DANGEROUS JOURNEY
Migrating wildebeest will travel hundreds of miles to find fresh grass. At river crossings they are vulnerable to attacks from crocodiles, which lie in wait for them.

Serengeti wildebeest
Connochaetes taurinus

- **Length** 5–8 ft (1.5–2.4 m)
- **Weight** 264–606 lb (120–275 kg)
- **Speed** 50 mph (80 kph)
- **Location** Eastern and southern Africa

The Serengeti wildebeest, or brindled gnu, can have **horns up to 31 in** (80 cm) long. Every spring, just before the calves are born, wildebeest seek out the richest pastures. This helps the females produce milk for their calves that is full of health-giving nutrients.

▲ *Migrating wildebeest can form herds more than a quarter of a million strong.*

▲ *In Serengeti National Park, in Tanzania, the line of migrating wildebeest can be more than 25 miles (40 km) long.*

▲ *Wildebeest calves are born during the rainy season. They can stand and run within minutes of birth. Calves need to keep up with the herd, or they could end up as dinner for a hungry lion.*

BIRDS

Definition: **Birds** are warm-blooded, egg-laying animals, most of which are able to fly. Their features include feathers, powerful wings, and hollow bones.

What is a BIRD?

Birds are warm-blooded vertebrates, but they differ from other vertebrates in having feathered wings and bills instead of toothed jaws. Most can fly, and their bodies are specially adapted for this purpose.

Wing feather

Contour feathers

Blue-and-yellow macaw
Ara ararauna

Tail feather

FACT FILE

There are almost 10,000 species of birds. They can loosely be split into groups of similar birds, including the following:

■ **Flightless birds**, such as ostriches, rheas, emus, and penguins.

■ **Waterbirds**, such as swans, ducks, and geese, live on coasts, estuaries, or riverbanks.

■ **Waders, gulls, and auks** live close to the coast and in wetlands.

■ **Birds of prey**, such as falcons, vultures, and eagles, are expert predators.

■ **Owls**, unlike birds of prey, are well adapted for hunting at night.

■ **Fruit and nectar eaters**, such as toucans and parrots.

■ **Passerines, perching birds, or songbirds**, the largest group of birds.

FEATHERS

Feathers are formed from the same material as mammal hair—keratin—and they play an important role in protecting a bird from water and temperature changes. Flying birds have four different types of feathers: down, contour, tail, and wing.

▲ **DOWN FEATHERS** *are soft and form a warm underlayer.*

▲ **CONTOUR FEATHERS** *are small and provide a smooth covering over the body.*

▲ **TAIL FEATHERS** *can be very elaborate. They are used for flying, steering, and display.*

▲ **WING FEATHERS** *are the flight feathers. They are long and rigid, providing the lift required for flight.*

LIVING DINOSAURS

Scientists have shown that birds are living dinosaurs, descended from small, feathered hunters such as *Velociraptor* that ran around on two legs.

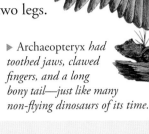

◄ *One of the earliest known birds was Archaeopteryx, which appeared about 150 million years ago.*

Fossilized Archaeopteryx

▶ *Archaeopteryx had toothed jaws, clawed fingers, and a long bony tail—just like many non-flying dinosaurs of its time.*

Nests Most birds build nests in which to lay their eggs. Nests are made from a huge variety of materials.

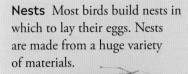

WOVEN GRASS NEST

Eggs and young Birds lay eggs, which hatch as chicks. These chicks are dependent on their parents for food and protection.

CHICK HATCHING

Preening Birds frequently clean and tidy their feathers to keep them in good condition. They waterproof the feathers with oil that they take from a gland at the base of the tail.

FEATHER CARE

BONES FILLED WITH AIR

A bird's skeleton is lightweight, which helps keep its body weight low for flying. In fact, many birds have feathers that weigh more than their skeleton!

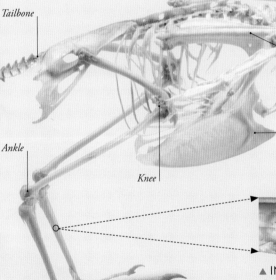

Skull

Eye socket

Bill

Neck

Tailbone

Wing

Ankle

Knee

Keel, a wide breast bone. This is the anchor for the flight muscles.

Foot

▲ INSIDE A BONE *A bird's skeleton is designed to save weight. It is largely composed of hollow bones with inner strengthening struts, as shown in this magnified picture.*

THE SHAPE OF A BILL

▲ **FINCHES** *are seed eaters and have a strong, cone-shaped bill that is ideal for breaking seeds open.*

▲ **HUMMINGBIRDS** *have long, narrow bills just perfect for extracting nectar from flowers.*

▲ **PARROTS** *have powerful bills, with a sharp hook to break into nuts and peel back fruit skins.*

▲ **HERONS** *have a long, strong, pointed bill to catch fish. They don't spear the fish, but catch it in the bill.*

▲ **EAGLES** *have sharp, hooked bills, which help them tear up the prey they grasp in their talons.*

A *world* of birds

There are about 10,000 species of bird with a huge variety of size, color, and habitat. They all have wings and feathers, but not all of them can fly. Flightless birds include the ostrich, which runs fast on powerful legs. Penguins use their wings as flippers to speed through the water.

North Islan brown kiwi
Apteryx mantelli

Blue-and-yellow macaw
Ara ararauna

Red crossbill
Loxia curvirostra

Toco toucan
Ramphastos toco

Yellow-fronted woodpecker
Melanerpes flavifrons

Red-billed hornbill
Tockus erythrorhynchus

Inca tern
Larosterna inca

Masked lapwing
Vanellus miles

Greater flamingo
Phoenicopterus roseus

Dalmatian pelican
Pelecanus crispus

Wattled jacana
Jacana jacana

Humboldt penguin
Spheniscus humboldti

Eurasian golden plover
Pluvialis apricaria

Chukar
Alectoris chukar

Diederik cuckoo
Chrysococcyx caprius

Common nightingale
Luscinia megarhynchos

Common peafo
Pavo cristatus

Budgerigar
Melopsittacus undulatus

Red-tailed hawk
Buteo jamaicensis

Barn owl
Tyto alba

Laughing kookaburra
Dacelo novaeguineae

Fire-tufted barbet
Psilopogon pyrolophus

Bearded reedling
Panurus biarmicus

European robin
Erithacus rubecula

Scarlet ibis
Eudocimus ruber

Southern crested caracara
Caracara plancus

Swallow-tailed manakin
Chiroxiphia caudata

Mallard
Anas platyrhynchos

White helmet-shrike
Prionops plumatus

LARGEST BIRD
Ostrich
Struthio camelus

SMALLEST BIRD
Bee hummingbird
Mellisuga helenae

Gray crowned crane
Balearica regulorum

King penguin
Aptenodytes patagonicus

The ostrich can be up to 9 ft (280 cm) tall. The **male bee hummingbird** is only 2¼ in (6 cm) long.

Birds of a *feather*

Not all birds can fly. These big birds are too heavy and they have small wings. Instead, they race across open countryside on their strong legs. But how can you tell an emu from an ostrich or a rhea from an emu? For a start, they come from different parts of the world.

I am the largest bird.

Ostriches are the world's largest birds. They are also unlike other birds in having just two toes on each foot. The legs are powerful and are used for defense to kick out at a predator if necessary.

OSTRICHES PREFER *to live in groups and are rarely found on their own. In common with rheas and emus, the male bird usually cares for the eggs and chicks.*

Ostrich

Struthio camelus

- **Height** 5⅗–9 ft (1.7–2.8 m)
- **Weight** 198–286⅗ lb (90–130 kg)
- **Speed** 40 mph (70 kph)
- **Location** W. to E. Africa (south of the Sahara) and southern Africa

This is the **world's largest and heaviest bird**—it is also the fastest runner. Powerful legs help propel it forward by up to 16 ft (5 m) at a time, and once it begins to run it can keep going for about 30 minutes. It feeds on plants (from which it gets water), insects, and lizards. Small stones are swallowed to help digestion.

Common rhea

Rhea americana

- **Height** 3–5 ft (1–1.5 m)
- **Weight** 33–66 lb (15–30 kg)
- **Speed** 37 mph (60 kph)
- **Location** South America

The rhea is **also known as the American ostrich** because it looks similar to the ostrich, but the rhea is actually about half the size. Rheas live in groups of about six individuals. They eat broad-leafed plants, seeds, fruit, insects, lizards, and small snakes. A male bird mates with up to 12 females, then builds one nest for all of the eggs.

The male takes care of the eggs and then the newly hatched young. He will charge at anything that goes near, including the mothers.

Emu

Dromaius novaehollandiae

  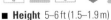

- **Height** 5–6 ft (1.5–1.9 m)
- **Weight** 66–121 lb (30–55 kg)
- **Speed** 30 mph (50 kph) with a 10-ft (3-m) stride
- **Location** Australia

Australia's biggest bird, the emu has drooping, fur-like feathers and **small wings**. It is named after the Portuguese word *ema*, meaning "large bird." Flocks may contain dozens of birds. It will eat berries, seeds, and insects, and will peck seeds from animal droppings.

Birds of prey

Most of these meat-eating birds are skilled hunters, although vultures leave the killing to others, then feast on their leftovers. A bird's prey depends on its size. Some species target insects and worms; others can tackle a lamb or a young deer.

▶ FOOD PASS *Male kestrels hunt for food, but the females carry it home. The female flies up to the male so he can drop his prey into her open beak. Then she flies off to feed their young.*

Family groups

There are more than 300 different species of birds of prey (also called raptors). They are divided into five groups or families:

- Eagles, hawks, kites, harriers, and Old World vultures
- Condors and New World vultures
- Ospreys
- Falcons
- **Secretary bird** This family is unusual as it has just one member.

▶ STOOPING *Peregrine falcons spot their prey from high in the sky, then dive down on it in a "stoop." They reach speeds of up to 199 mph (320 kph) when stooping.*

FACT FILE

- **Key features:** Most have a large head and large eyes with excellent vision. (It is thought that they can see four times as much detail as a human!) Many also have a keen sense of smell and very good hearing. Almost all have a powerful, hooked bill and strong feet, with sharp talons that they use to kill.
- **Size:** The smallest, the falconets of southeast Asia, are about the size of a sparrow. Condors weigh up to 27 lb (12.25 kg) with a wingspan of more than 10 ft (3 m).

Size comparison

Peregrine falcon
Falco peregrinus

- **Length** 13–20 in (34–50 cm)
- **Weight** 1–3¼ lb (0.5–1.5 kg)
- **Diet** Other birds
- **Location** Worldwide (except Antarctica)

The peregrine is **one of the fastest moving animals** on earth and one of the largest falcons. Females are almost twice the size of males, but both sexes are swift, efficient killers, chasing and swooping down on their prey. They are popular birds for falconry.

Golden eagle

Aquila chrysaetos

    30

- **Length** 29½–35 in (75–90 cm)
- **Weight** 6½–14 lb (3–6.5 kg)
- **Diet** Birds, reptiles, and small mammals
- **Location** Europe, North America, Asia, and North Africa

An impressive wingspan of 7½ ft (2.3 m) helps this bulky bird soar elegantly across the sky, ready to swoop down on any prey it spots. It is often seen from a distance, but close encounters are rare. Its name comes from the **golden-brown feathers** around its neck.

Broad wings

Large talons

White-backed vulture

Gyps africanus

    20

- **Length** 37 in (94 cm)
- **Weight** 8¾–15 lb (4–7 kg)
- **Diet** Freshly dead animals (carrion)
- **Location** Central and southern Africa

Despite it size, this large bird **can be rather timid** compared with other scavengers. It will wait for others to open up a fresh carcass and is often pushed to one side when jostling for a share of the meat.

Secretary bird

Sagittarius serpentarius

   15

- **Length** 4–5 ft (1.3–1.5 m)
- **Weight** 5½–10 lb (2.5 kg–4.5 kg)
- **Diet** Snakes, insects, and small rodents
- **Location** Central and southern Africa

Unlike any other bird of prey, this one has amazingly long legs. It **runs very fast** and chases its prey, which it stamps on when caught, digging in with its sharp talons.

Northern goshawk

Accipiter gentilis

   20

- **Length** 19–24⅖ in (48–62 cm)
- **Weight** 2¼–3¼ lb (1–1.5 kg)
- **Diet** Birds, reptiles, and small mammals
- **Location** Europe, North America, Mexico, and Asia

This bird is a **bold and cunning** hunter. Often, it sits well hidden in a tree, ready to pounce on any unsuspecting prey that is passing by. It will happily tackle a large crow or a hare.

Osprey

Pandion haliaetus

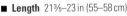 30

- **Length** 21⅜–23 in (55–58 cm)
- **Weight** 3¼–4½ lb (1.5–2 kg)
- **Diet** Fish
- **Location** Worldwide (except Antarctica)

This bird is **well adapted for catching fish.** It hovers patiently over lakes and rivers, waiting for a fish to swim close to the surface. Then it plunges in at lightning speed and grasps its prey firmly with its sharp claws. Talons that can move to grip both sides of the fish and small spines on the soles of the bird's feet help it hold on to its catch.

Andean condor

Vultur gryphus

 50

- **Length** 3¼–4¼ ft (1–1.3 m)
- **Weight** 24¼–33 lb (11–15 kg)
- **Diet** Freshly dead animals (carrion)
- **Location** W. South America

This huge black vulture has the **largest wings** of any bird. It can soar on rising air currents for hours, constantly on the lookout for freshly killed meat left by hunters and other animals. Deer and cattle are its favorite foods. Males are bigger than females, unlike most birds of prey, and have a fleshy comb along the top of their head.

Crested caracara

Caracara plancus

   9

- **Length** 19½–23 in (49–59 cm)
- **Weight** 1¾–3¼ lb (0.8–1.5 kg)
- **Diet** Freshly dead animals (carrion), insects, and small birds
- **Location** Southern United States, Central America, and South America

Caracaras feast mainly on the leftovers other animals leave behind. But they will also **steal food** from other birds, raid nests, and peck at passing insects.

Bald eagle

Haliaeetus leucocephalus

- **Length** 28–38 in (71–96 cm)
- **Weight** 6½–14 lb (3–6.5 kg)
- **Diet** Fish, carrion, small animals, and birds
- **Location** North America

The bald eagle is a large bird of prey, with a wingspan of up to 8 ft (2.5 m). It is known for its white head and neck, brown body, and white tail feathers, but this plumage does not develop until the bird is about five years old. **Females are larger than males.**

▲ NESTING *Bald eagles pair up for life, building a large nest in a tree or on the ground, which they will return to year after year, adding material each time. They will lay between one and three eggs a year, with both male and female tending them, but usually not all the chicks will survive.*

▲ FIGHTING FOR FOOD *Bald eagles will fight others for their food; it is sometimes easier to steal another bird's catch than hunt for their own. This happens more in winter, when food can be scarce.*

Bald eagle

This eagle is named after its white head, though it is not bald: the head and neck are feathered. It is famous for being the national bird of the US (since 1782), and it has been protected in North America since 1940. Its Latin name means "sea eagle."

TIME FOR FISHING

The bald eagle is built to fish. Its keen eyesight allows it to spot fish—the eagle's eyes have a bony ridge just above them to shade out the sun. Once grasped, a fish has no chance; a hind talon on each foot pierces the fish's body, while it is held securely by long front talons. It is a killer grip!

▲ BALD EAGLES *can lift about half their body weight. If a fish is heavier, a bird will swim with it to shore, using its immense wings as oars. However, occasionally a fish proves so large it is able to pull an eagle underwater, drowning the bird.*

Silent owls

This group of birds have mastered the skill of night hunting. Especially soft feathers mean they can swoop down almost silently on their unsuspecting prey, while hooked beaks and sharp talons help them catch and kill very quickly.

▲ CARE *Owls are attentive parents. Between one and five young are cared for in a cavity or tree hole, with the male bringing food and the female staying nearby.*

AN OWL'S SKULL

This diagram of an owl's skull shows how large the eye sockets are. Large eyes help the owl to see at night. However, an owl cannot move its eyes in their sockets. If it needs to look to the side, it has to turn its whole head—and thanks to a very flexible neck, it can even look directly behind itself.

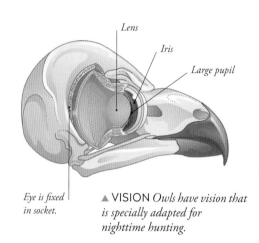

Lens

Iris

Large pupil

Eye is fixed in socket.

▲ VISION *Owls have vision that is specially adapted for nighttime hunting.*

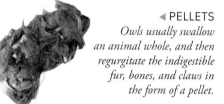

◀ PELLETS
Owls usually swallow an animal whole, and then regurgitate the indigestible fur, bones, and claws in the form of a pellet.

▼ FLIGHT *An owl flies fairly low—and silently.*

FACT FILE

■ **Number of species:** More than 200.
■ **Key features:** Sharp talons, hooked bill, head that can swivel around, large eyes, soft plumage. Swallow prey whole and produce pellets containing the indigestible parts.
■ **Size:** The largest is the Eagle owl (*Bubo bubo*) at up to 28 in (70 cm) in length. The smallest is the Elf owl (*Micrathene whitneyi*) at less than 6 in (15 cm) long.

Size comparison

Snowy owl

Bubo scandiacus

  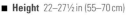 10

- **Height** 22–27½ in (55–70 cm)
- **Weight** 2¼–5½ lb (1–2.5 kg)
- **Diet** Lemmings, rabbits, hares, and waterfowl
- **Location** Polar regions

This owl **lives farther north** than any other owl. Long, thick feathers extend over the bill and the toes, keeping the owl incredibly well insulated.

Spectacled owl

Pulsatrix perspicillata

  30

- **Height** 17–20½ in (43–52 cm)
- **Weight** 16–35 oz (450–1,000 g)
- **Diet** Small mammals, insects, and crabs
- **Location** Southern Mexico to Central South America

With the **ring of white feathers** around its eyes, it's easy to see where this owl gets its name. It usually makes its home in dense rainforest.

Great horned owl

Bubo virginianus

     28

- **Height** 20–23½ in (50–60 cm)
- **Weight** 1½–5½ lb (675–2,500 g)
- **Diet** Small mammals, insects, reptiles, amphibians, and birds
- **Location** North, Central, and South America

This owl has an **instantly recognizable hoot**. It will choose a favorite perch, and when it spots its prey, it will swoop silently down to snatch it up. Females lay between one and five eggs, and both the male and female will care for the young for at least six weeks after hatching. It is the largest American owl.

Pel's fishing owl

Scotopelia peli

- **Height** 22–25 in (55–63 cm)
- **Weight** 4½–5½ lb (2–2.5 kg)
- **Diet** Fish and frogs
- **Location** Africa

As its name suggests, **this owl feeds on fish**, in addition to frogs and any other freshwater animals that it can catch. It helps an animal to live near its food source, so the fishing owl's nest is always found in a tree hole at the edges of lakes, rivers, swamps, and marshes. Long, curved talons help it grasp and hold on to its usually slippery prey.

Barn owl

Tyto alba

 2

- **Height** 11½–17 in (29–44 cm)
- **Weight** 11–23 oz (300–650 g)
- **Diet** Small rodents
- **Location** North, Central, and South America, Europe, Asia, Africa, and Australia

This owl is the **most widespread** of all owls, and is found on all continents apart from Antarctica. It nests in a hollow tree, or an abandoned building. It has a shriek rather than a hoot.

Southern boobook

Ninox boobook

- **Height** 12–14 in (30–35 cm)
- **Weight** 5–13 oz (146–360 g)
- **Diet** Insects, small mammals, and birds
- **Location** Australia (including Tasmania), S. New Guinea, Indonesia

This owl is **named for its cry**, a distinctive two-syllable "boo book." It is Australia's smallest owl, and often hunts by snatching flying insects from the air.

Common scops owl

Otus scops

7

- **Height** 6½–8 in (16–20 cm)
- **Weight** 2⅛–4¾ oz (60–135 g)
- **Diet** Insects, spiders, worms, bats, and small birds
- **Location** Europe to C. Asia, Africa

When motionless, this owl is hard to spot as its plumage helps it vanish against a background of tree bark. It will even sway, if surprised, to imitate a branch moving in the wind! **Its call is a low whistle**, not a hoot.

Game birds

The birds in this group usually live on the ground in a wide variety of habitats. Wild game birds, such as grouse and pheasants, have long been a food source for humans and hunted for sport, while their domestic relatives, such as chickens, are a valuable source of meat and eggs.

◄ SHORT SPRINT *A ring-necked pheasant launches into flight to escape from a predator. The strong flight muscles can support short bursts of speed but are useless for longer distances.*

FACT FILE

■ Number of species: Around 290
■ Key features: Game birds are mainly ground-dwellers. The cocks (males) of many species have spectacular plumage or brightly colored patches of bare skin, while the hens (females) are usually very dull in color. The cocks perform elaborate courtship displays to attract hens. Many game birds use camouflage to escape detection by predators.

The numbers show where the birds featured on the next page are found.

FEATHER FAN *A peacock fans out his train of feathers to attract a peahen during courtship. He shakes the fan of erect feathers during the display to add to the effect.*

Common peafowl

Pavo cristatus

Shimmering blue neck and breast.

- **Length** 6–7½ ft (1.8–2.3 m)
- **Weight** 8¾–13 lb (4–6 kg)
- **Diet** Fruit, seeds, insects, and snakes
- **Location** Parts of South Asia

Few can mistake the spectacular sight of a male peafowl (the peacock) displaying his long **train of "tail" feathers**. Each feather extends from the bird's back, not the tail, and ends with a **colorful "eye."**

Long train of "tail" feathers.

▲ THE EYES HAVE IT *Female peafowl look at the number of eyes on peacocks' tails when choosing mates—the more, the better.*

Willow ptarmigan

Lagopus lagopus

- **Length** About 15 in (38 cm)
- **Weight** 20–25 oz (550–700 g)
- **Diet** Mosses, lichens, and berries; chicks also eat insects
- **Location** Northern areas of northern hemisphere

These are hardy game birds, with **feathery legs** to insulate them from the cold winter. Most of these birds turn from reddish brown to white in winter as camouflage, but willow ptarmigan from Scotland (known as red grouse) are an exception.

Temminck's tragopan

Tragopan temminckii

- **Length** 25 in (64 cm)
- **Weight** 2–3½ lb (980–1,600 g)
- **Diet** Plants and insects
- **Location** Central and Southeast Asia

During courtship, the cock **inflates his blue and red throat wattle**, which looks like a brightly colored bib. If this show of strength impresses a hen, the pair will mate. The cock **mates with lots of hens** but plays no part in rearing his young.

Gunnison sage-grouse

Centrocercus minimus

- **Length** 12⅗–22 in (32–56 cm)
- **Weight** 2–5¼ lb (1–2.5 kg)
- **Diet** Plants and insects
- **Location** Utah and Colorado

A male sage-grouse has two yellow air sacs on its chest that it uses to make **popping sounds** during courtship. He also makes **swishing noises** by brushing his wings against his stiff, white chest feathers.

Common pheasant

Phasianus colchicus

- **Length** Up to 36 in (90 cm)
- **Weight** 1¾–4½ lb (0.75–2 kg)
- **Diet** Plants, insects, and small vertebrates
- **Location** Native to Asia

As one of the **most hunted** game birds, the common pheasant has been introduced to many countries. Typical of the game birds, the cock is much brighter than the hen, with **distinctive red wattles** on the face to attract hens during courtship.

Red jungle-fowl

Gallus gallus

- **Length** Up to 27½ in (70 cm)
- **Weight** 1–3¼ lb (0.5–1.5 kg)
- **Diet** Mainly seeds and small insects
- **Location** Southern Asia

The domestic **chicken is the descendant** of the red jungle-fowl, which lives around forests and the edges of villages.

Malleefowl

Leipoa ocellata

- **Length** 24 in (60 cm)
- **Weight** 4½ lb (2 kg)
- **Diet** Buds, fruits, seeds, and the odd insect and spider
- **Location** Southern Australia

▶ EGG COMPOST *If the eggs get too cold, the malleefowl adds more mud and vegetation to its homemade incubator.*

Malleefowl are unusual because they **do not sit on their eggs** to keep them warm. Like other megapodes, these birds build a **natural incubator**, laying their eggs in a pile of mud and rotting plant matter. The heat given off by the incubator keeps the eggs warm.

Seabirds and shorebirds

The birds of sea and shore live in or near the world's oceans. Seabirds spend most of their lives at sea but return to shore to breed. They are strong fliers, and some can dive into the sea to catch fish. Shorebirds live along the coast. Many have long legs and probing bills to forage beneath the sand and mud for crustaceans, mollusks, and marine worms.

FACT FILE

- ■ **Number of species:** Around 379
- ■ **Key features:** These birds are usually plain with bright body parts such as eyes or legs. Their bills come in many shapes and sizes, from long, slender bills used to probe in the mud, to short, compact bills for stabbing at prey. They may have salt glands to expel the excess salt from seawater.

The numbers show where the featured animals are found.

Ivory gull

Pagophila eburnea

- ■ **Length** 16–17 in (40–43 cm)
- ■ **Weight** 16–25 oz (450–700 g)
- ■ **Diet** Fish, marine invertebrates, small mammals, and carrion
- ■ **Location** High Arctic, from Canada and Greenland to northern Europe and Russia

Like all gulls, the ivory gull is a **scavenger**. It feeds on the remains left behind by predators such as polar bears. Little else is known about this bird since it lives on the edge of the pack ice deep within the Arctic Circle.

FEEDING FRENZY *Every May, horseshoe crabs lay their eggs on the shores of the Delaware Bay. The eggs are a feast for hungry shorebirds such as laughing gulls.*

Herring gull
Larus argentatus

    30+

- **Length** 22–26 in (55–66 cm)
- **Weight** 1¾–3¼ lb (0.8–1.5 kg)
- **Diet** Fish, invertebrates, small birds, eggs, carrion, and human garbage
- **Location** Northern hemisphere

These large, noisy gulls are a common sight along coastal regions, but they are also **found farther inland**, where they scavenge on garbage dumps and in city centers.

Brown skua
Catharacta antarctica

 11+

- **Length** About 24 in (60 cm)
- **Weight** 3½–4¼ lb (1.6–1.9 kg)
- **Diet** Fish, marine invertebrates, small seabirds and their chicks, eggs, and carrion
- **Location** Antarctic and subantarctic zones around the Southern Ocean

In summer, brown skuas breed in sheltered rocky areas on the many islands of the Southern Ocean. The breeding pair **defend their nest fiercely**, flying at the heads of intruders with claws outstretched. The birds fly north in winter, spending a lot of time at sea.

Ringed plover
Charadrius hiaticula

 6+

- **Length** 7–8 in (17–20 cm)
- **Weight** About 2¼ oz (60 g)
- **Diet** Mainly marine invertebrates
- **Location** Breeds in Arctic and northern temperate zones; many migrate to Africa and Asia for the winter

Ringed plovers are small, plump wading birds that **forage for food on beaches**, fields and tidal flats. As these birds tap their feet on the loose sand or mud, tiny marine worms and other invertebrates rise to the surface to be eaten.

Avocet
Recurvirostra avosetta

 20+

- **Length** 16–18 in (40–45 cm)
- **Weight** 9–10 oz (260–290 g)
- **Diet** Insects and crustaceans
- **Location** Europe, Africa, and Asia

When feeding, the distinctive avocet sweeps its **slender, upturned bill** from side to side through the water. Many avocets winter in southern Africa and Asia and then migrate north in the summer to breed.

Common oystercatcher
Haematopus ostralegus

 30+

- **Length** About 17 in (42 cm)
- **Weight** About 19 oz (540 g)
- **Diet** Marine worms and shellfish
- **Location** Europe, Africa, and Asia

Shellfish such as mussels are a favorite food for these striking birds, but they do **eat oysters** when they find them. They use their bright bills to prize the two halves of the shell apart and stab at the soft parts inside.

Guillemot
Uria aalge

 20

- **Length** 15–18½ in (38–46 cm)
- **Weight** 2–2¼ lb (0.9–1 kg)
- **Diet** Fish and marine invertebrates
- **Location** Across the northern hemisphere as far south as Mexico and North Africa

These **expert divers** can descend to depths of 130 ft (40 m) or more when fishing. Common guillemots gather in **huge breeding colonies** on rocky cliffs and sea stacks. Three weeks after hatching, the chicks leave their nesting ledge and fly out to sea.

Atlantic puffin
Fratercula arctica

 20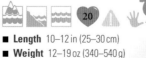

- **Length** 10–12 in (25–30 cm)
- **Weight** 12–19 oz (340–540 g)
- **Diet** Mainly small fish
- **Location** High Arctic to the Mediterranean, depending on the season

The **large, colorful bill** of the Atlantic puffin can hold a vast number of small fish such as capelin and sprat. When feeding, these striking seabirds gather in large groups, called rafts, a few miles offshore.

Penguins

These flightless birds are found only in the seas and cold currents of the southern hemisphere. Penguins are fast, graceful swimmers, but on land they waddle awkwardly. To speed up a long journey over snow and ice, penguins sometimes toboggan on their bellies.

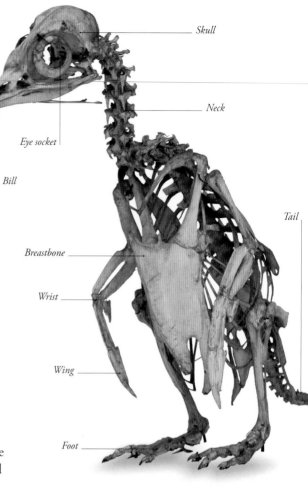

PENGUIN SKELETON

Skull

Neck

Eye socket

Bill

Tail

Breastbone

Wrist

Wing

Foot

LIVING IN COLONIES

Penguins spend a lot of their lives in water hunting for food. However, most species come on land in the warmer months to live in colonies and breed. Colonies can be made up of hundreds of thousands of birds. Penguins communicate by calls and visual displays when they are gathered in large groups.

Anatomy Penguins have plump bodies, short legs, and webbed feet. Their coat of dense feathers repels water and traps in body heat. Penguins have a thick layer of fat, called blubber, which insulates them from cold weather. Their wing bones are flattened to form flippers and solid to increase strength.

King penguin
Aptenodytes patagonicus

FACT FILE

- Number of species: 17–20
- Key features: Live in colonies; fast swimmers.
- Diet: Fish, krill, and squid
- Largest: Emperor penguin, up to 45 in (115 cm) in height.
- Smallest: Little penguin, up to 18 in (45 cm) in height.

Little and emperor penguins

The numbers show where the featured animals are found.

DIVING *Penguins can dive down to about 951 ft (290 m), flapping their wings to provide power. Some species can swim at speeds of 9 mph (14 kph).*

Emperor penguin

Aptenodytes forsteri

   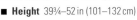

- **Height** 39¾–52 in (101–132 cm)
- **Weight** 55–99 lb (25–45 kg)
- **Location** Southern Ocean and Antarctica

Emperor penguins are the only penguins to breed during the harsh Antarctic winter. After laying her single egg, the female goes back to the sea to hunt for food. Her **male partner cares for the egg for two months**, holding it on his feet beneath a flap of belly skin. All the males huddle together in a group to keep warm during winter storms. The females return to feed the chicks when they hatch.

FLUFFY *The gray down of emperor chicks is not waterproof, so they cannot go in the sea.*

African penguin

Spheniscus demersus

   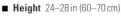

- **Height** 24–28 in (60–70 cm)
- **Weight** 4⅖–11 lb (2–5 kg)
- **Location** Namibia and southwestern coast of Africa

This penguin **breeds in Africa**, coming ashore to nest in **burrows**. Over-fishing and oil spills have caused a shortage of food for the African penguin.

Galápagos penguin

Spheniscus mendiculus

- **Height** 19–20¾ in (48–53 cm)
- **Weight** 4½–5 lb (2–2.5 kg)
- **Location** Galápagos Islands and Isabela Island

Galápagos penguins are **among the rarest** species of penguin. They live the farthest north of any penguin species, and because of this they struggle to keep cool. To help heat escape from their bodies, they **hold out their wings**.

Royal penguin

Eudyptes schlegeli

- **Height** 28 in (70 cm)
- **Weight** 13 lb (6 kg)
- **Location** Macquarie Island and nearby islands south of New Zealand

This is one of several species of penguins known as **crested penguins**, which have plumes on their head. A **female royal penguin lays two eggs**. The first egg, which is small, is kicked out of the nest. The reason for this is unknown.

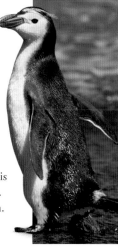

Humboldt penguin

Spheniscus humboldti

  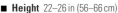

- **Height** 22–26 in (56–66 cm)
- **Weight** 10–11 lb (4.5–5 kg)
- **Location** Peru and northern Chile

Like all penguins, Humboldt penguins are very **sociable**. Their nesting burrows are always close together and the birds usually hunt in a group. Over-fishing in the area has reduced the Humboldt penguins' food supply and caused a **decline in their numbers**.

Little penguin

Eudyptula minor

- **Height** 14–17 in (36–43 cm)
- **Weight** 2¼ lb (1 kg)
- **Location** Southern and southeastern Australia, New Zealand, Tasman Sea, and Southern Ocean

This is the **smallest** penguin and the only one that stays offshore in the daytime. Most little penguins live in **sand or soil burrows**, but some make their homes among fallen rocks or under houses and sheds.

Gentoo penguin

Pygoscelis papua

- **Height** 30–35 in (75–90 cm)
- **Weight** 10–19 lb (4.5–8.5 kg)
- **Location** Subantarctic islands

No other penguin can swim as **fast underwater** as a gentoo penguin. These birds make their nests from stones and twigs piled up in a circular shape. They guard their property jealously. Arguments frequently break out in a gentoo colony because one bird has stolen a pebble from another's nest. The **chicks are cared for by both parents**.

The *wandering* albatross

The wandering albatross is the world's largest seabird, with an incredible wingspan that can reach 11 ft (3.5 m). Albatrosses spend much of their long lives soaring over the sea, on journeys that cover thousands of miles. They come on land to breed.

BIRDS

GROWTH *Albatrosses take about nine years to mature into adults, before they seek a mate. They will pair up for life.*

Ready to fly.
A wandering albatross
has amazing powers of flight.
Albatrosses have been observed
following ships across oceans
without stopping to rest.
One bird traveled
3,700 miles (6,000 km)
in 12 days.

Wandering albatross
Diomedea exulans

- **Length** 3½ ft (1.1 m)
- **Weight** 13–28 lb (5.9–12.7 kg)
- **Diet** Fish and squid
- **Location** Circumpolar around Antarctica

Although the wandering albatross has a large wingspan, each wing is just 9 in (23 cm) at its widest point. **Long, narrow wings** allow the bird to soar on air currents with ease.

CONSERVATION

Several species of albatross are under threat. Many have been accidentally killed when caught on baited hooks set out for fish, while others have lost eggs to foxes or rats. Efforts are now being made to protect them.

▲ NESTING *An albatross lays a single 4-in- (10-cm-) long egg in a nest made from mud, grass, and moss. Parents take it in turns to sit on the egg and will then feed the chick for the first nine months of its life. Albatrosses breed slowly, laying perhaps one egg every second year, so their success depends on the survival of these individual chicks.*

131

Pelicans and relatives

These large birds include boobies, cormorants, gannets, and frigate birds as well as the pelicans. Pelicans and their relatives are the only birds with webbing between all four toes, so most are strong swimmers. They all eat fish, but they catch their food in different ways.

Brown pelican

Pelecanus occidentalis

20+

- **Length** 3¼–5 ft (1–1.5 m)
- **Weight** Up to 12 lb (5.5 kg)
- **Diet** Mainly fish
- **Location** Caribbean and the Americas

This is the **smallest of the eight pelicans**, and it is the only one that dives after fish. It plunges headfirst, mouth wide open, scooping up fish in its large throat pouch. The weight of the catch can often prevent the pelican from flying.

PELICAN PLUNGE *With wings folded back, these brown pelicans are ready to plunge into the sea to catch their next meal.*

FACT FILE

- **Number of species:** 67
- **Key features:** Four webbed toes on each foot; diving species have small or closed nostrils (some breathe through their mouths); nest in large colonies.
- **Distribution:** Found near coastal waters of most seas and oceans; also found around inland waters.
- **Diet:** Mainly fish but some will eat crustaceans, mollusks, and other marine invertebrates.

The numbers show where the featured birds are found.

Blue-footed booby

Sula nebouxii

  20+

- **Length** 31–33 in (80–85 cm)
- **Weight** 3¼ lb (1.5 kg)
- **Diet** Fish and squid
- **Location** Mexico to northern South America and the Galápagos Islands

The **bright blue feet** that give this bird its name play a part in the male's mating dance. He struts in front of the female, raising each foot in turn. She tucks her head under her wing as a sign of approval.

Red-billed tropic bird

Phaethon aethereus

 15+ 3

- **Length** 35⅖–41¼ in (90–105 cm)
- **Weight** 21–29 oz (600–825 g)
- **Diet** Fish and squid
- **Location** Tropical waters of the Atlantic, eastern Pacific, and northern Indian oceans

These small seabirds spend most of their lives hundreds of miles from land, **flying high above the ocean**. Red-billed tropic birds come to land to breed, usually on remote tropical islands. The female lays a single egg on a rocky cliff ledge or directly on the ground. Although they are poor swimmers, these birds plunge-dive from great heights to catch their prey. They are especially fond of flying fish.

STREAM AND SCREAM *These birds flick their tail streamers and make screaming calls in a spectacular, but noisy, aerial courtship display.*

Brown booby

Sula leucogaster

  25+ 4

- **Length** 25–33½ in (64–85 cm)
- **Weight** 1½–3¼ lb (0.7–1.5 kg)
- **Diet** Fish and squid
- **Location** Tropical Pacific, Atlantic, and Indian oceans

The brown booby is **an expert diver**, plunging into the ocean from heights of 100 ft (30 m). The streamlined shape of the bird helps it cut through the water to catch its prey. Brown boobies also skim the surface of the ocean, picking off flying fish as they leap from the water.

Great cormorant

Phalacrocorax carbo

   15 5

- **Length** 31–39 in (80–100 cm)
- **Weight** Up to 8 lb (3.5 kg)
- **Diet** Mainly fish
- **Location** Eastern North America, Greenland, Eurasia, central to southern Africa, and Australasia

Great cormorants are sleek and streamlined—the **ideal shape for diving and swimming**. These common coastal seabirds can dive to considerable depths, but they often fish in shallow water.

Galápagos cormorant

Phalacrocorax harrisi

 ? 6

- **Length** 39 in (100 cm)
- **Weight** 5½–9 lb (2.5–4 kg)
- **Diet** Mainly fish
- **Location** Galápagos Islands

The Galápagos cormorant lives on the islands of Fernandina and Isabela on the western shores of the Galápagos. This bird has **lost the ability to fly**. Instead, it uses its powerful legs and webbed feet to swim after squid, octopus, eels, and various small fish.

Northern gannet

Morus bassanus

 25+ 7

- **Length** 34¼–39¼ in (87–100 cm)
- **Weight** 5½–6½ lb (2.5–3 kg)
- **Diet** Mainly fish
- **Location** North Atlantic and Mediterranean

These gannets spend **most of their lives at sea** but nest in dense colonies on steep rocky cliffs and sea stacks. A pair breed for life, using the same nest year after year.

Great frigate bird

Fregata minor

    40 8

- **Length** 33–41 in (85–105 cm)
- **Weight** 2¼–3¼ lb (1–1.5 kg)
- **Diet** Fish and squid
- **Location** Tropical Pacific, Atlantic, and Indian oceans

During courtship, groups of males shake their wings and inflate their magnificent **scarlet throat pouches** like balloons. The female chooses a mate based on his display.

Oriental darter

Anhinga melanogaster

 ? 9

- **Length** 33–38 in (85–97 cm)
- **Weight** 2¼–4½ lb (1–2 kg)
- **Diet** Fish
- **Location** Southern and Southeast Asia

The Oriental darter is often called the snakebird thanks to its **long, snakelike head**. This bird swims with its body submerged, but its head and neck above the water.

Waterbirds

Some of these birds swim and dive, others wade in shallow lakes and swamps or even trot across the water's surface on floating plants. Most waterbirds also fly well. Many swans and ducks migrate huge distances every year between their breeding grounds and the regions where they spend the winter.

FACT FILE

■ **Key features:** Swimming birds such as ducks and swans have webbed feet and waterproof feathers. Some waterbirds feed while they are in the water, either by diving or dabbling for food. Others forage on land.

◀ **HEAD FIRST**
Up-ending, known as dabbling, allows ducks and swans to extend their reach when they search for food in the water.

Mute swan

Cygnus olor

■ **Length** 4–5¼ ft (1.2–1.6 m)
■ **Weight** 16¾–33 lb (7.6–15 kg)
■ **Diet** Aquatic plants, small fish, frogs, and insects
■ **Location** North America, Europe, Africa, Asia, and Australasia

Although they make less noise than other swans, mute swans are **not silent**. They call and sometimes hiss or snort. A mute swan can **fly at over 31 mph** (50 kph). Its wings make a loud creaking sound that can be heard as the swan passes overhead.

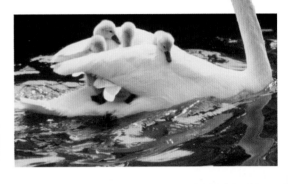

LIFT OFF *To get its heavy body airborne, the mute swan needs a long runway. The bird launches itself with much inelegant pedalling of feet and flapping of wings.*

Black swan

Cygnus atratus

  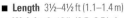

- **Length** 3½–4½ ft (1.1–1.4 m)
- **Weight** 8–19 lb (3.7–8.7 kg)
- **Diet** Plants (mainly aquatic)
- **Location** Australia (including Tasmania); introduced to New Zealand, Europe, and North America

These swans sometimes travel together in colonies numbering many thousands. They usually **nest together**, too, although some breeding pairs may stay apart from the rest. In Europe, black swans are kept as **ornamental** pets.

Goosander

Mergus merganser

- **Length** 23–26 in (58–66 cm)
- **Weight** 3¼–4½ lb (1.5–2 kg)
- **Diet** Fish
- **Location** North America, Europe, and Asia

The goosander is an unusual duck because it has a long, thin bill with **sharp "sawteeth"** along the edges. This means that the bird can get a firm grip on slippery fish. Goosanders hunt by putting their head below the surface of the water and **diving** for their prey.

MALE GOOSANDER

Muscovy duck

Cairina moschata

- **Length** 26–33 in (66–84 cm)
- **Weight** 4½–8¾ lb (2–4 kg)
- **Diet** Leaves, seeds, insects, and small aquatic invertebrates
- **Location** Central America and northern South America

Domesticated muscovy ducks are kept all over the world and appear in many colors. Wild muscovy ducks have **black plumage** with some white feathers in their wings.

Wattled jacana

Jacana jacana

- **Length** 6½–10 in (17–25 cm)
- **Weight** 4⅘–9 oz (136–255 g)
- **Diet** Insects, aquatic invertebrates, and rice seeds
- **Location** Southern Central America and South America

Big, splayed feet spread this bird's weight and allow it to **walk on floating water plants** without sinking. The female wattled jacana usually takes **several mates**. She lays her eggs in floating nests.

Mallard

Anas platyrhynchos

      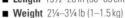

- **Length** 19½–26 in (50–65 cm)
- **Weight** 2¼–3¼ lb (1–1.5 kg)
- **Diet** Aquatic plants, grasses, and small aquatic invertebrates
- **Location** North America, Greenland, Europe, Africa, and Asia; introduced to Australasia

One of the **commonest** of all ducks, mallards are found across the northern hemisphere. Most domestic ducks are descended from the mallard. Both male and female mallards can be recognized by their noticeable **blue wing patch**.

Blue wing patch

Mandarin duck

Aix galericulata

- **Length** 16–19 in (41–49 cm)
- **Weight** 18–22 oz (500–625 g)
- **Diet** Plants, insects, and snails
- **Location** Northwestern Europe and eastern Asia

These ducks are at home both in water and on land. They make their nests high in trees, safe from predators. The **fantastic plumage** of the male mandarin duck (seen here) has made this bird popular in captivity.

Great crested grebe

Podiceps cristatus

- **Length** 18–20 in (46–51 cm)
- **Weight** 1¼–3¼ lb (0.6–1.5 kg)
- **Diet** Fish and aquatic invertebrates
- **Location** Europe, Asia, Africa, Australia, and New Zealand

The black head feathers and **spectacular frill** of the great crested grebe are displayed to full effect during the bird's courtship ceremony. A pair of grebes perform elaborate **dances in the water** and offer one another gifts of weeds.

Dark green head

MALE MALLARD

FEMALE MALLARD

Horned screamer

Anhima cornuta

- **Length** 31–37 in (80–95 cm)
- **Weight** 4½–6½ lb (2–3 kg)
- **Diet** Leaves, grass, and seeds
- **Location** Northern and central South America

Screamers are **heavily built** birds that look rather like large domestic fowl. The horn that juts out from the head of the horned screamer is in fact a long **feather quill**. The bird's calls are hoots and honks rather than screams.

Migration:
Snow geese

Some birds fly thousands of miles each year, following "pathways" in the sky that are only visible to them. These snow geese, for example, follow well-established migration routes in search of richer feeding grounds or to return to their nesting grounds.

WE ARE FAMILY *Snow geese are sturdy birds. They have to be: it can take them more than 10 weeks to reach their nesting grounds, allowing for nighttime rests. They fly in family groups within huge flocks.*

Greater snow goose

Anser caerulescens atlanticus

- **Length** 27–33 in (69–83 cm)
- **Weight** Up to 10 lb (4.5 kg)
- **Speed** Up to 60 mph (95 kph)
- **Location** Canada, Greenland, and northeastern US

This goose is white, apart from the tips of its wings, which are black. Some birds have a **blue-gray plumage**, and were once thought to be a different species, but they are now known to be the same. Pairs stay together for life.

▲ V-FORMATION *Why do migrating birds fly in a V-formation? It means that each bird is flying in the slipstream of the one in front, which is a lot less work and so saves energy. The lead bird changes frequently: it's a tiring place to be!*

▶ GRAZING *Snow geese graze on wetland rich with plant life. They largely feed on aquatic plants, roots, grasses, and grains. They swallow small amounts of sand and grit to help them digest the plants.*

ANNUAL MOVEMENT

Snow geese breed on the Arctic tundra, but fly some 3,000 miles (5,000 km) south away from the Arctic winter in September in enormous, noisy flocks, which may number more than 100,000 birds. They return to the Arctic in the following spring.

Why are we "snow" geese?

Snow geese are named for their white coloring, which, when a large flock descends, looks a little like a blizzard of falling snow. Young birds have more gray feathers, flecked with white, which change to white in their first year.

137

◀ FISH KING *The majestic kingfisher plunges headfirst into the water and grabs its prey in its long, straight bill.*

My feathers really shine.

A kingfisher's feathers shimmer because they are iridescent. The feathers have a semitransparent layer that scatters light like a soap bubble, so you see the vivid colors reflected back at you.

Kingfishers and relatives

Kingfishers are famous for their fishing skills, but they have many relatives that live far from rivers and streams. These include bee-eaters, hoopoes, and hornbills. The birds in this group live in woodland habitats around the world.

FAST FACTS

■ **Number of species:** 218
■ **Key features:** Large heads and bills relative to the size of their compact bodies; legs usually short, with two toes fused near the base of the foot; many have bright plumage; all species nest in holes.
■ **Body size:** The largest of these birds are the hornbills at lengths of up to 4¾ ft (1.5 m); the smallest are the todies at lengths of just 4 in (10 cm).

Size comparison

Common kingfisher

Alcedo atthis

- **Length** 6½–7½ in (16–19 cm)
- **Weight** 1¼ oz (35 g)
- **Diet** Mainly fish
- **Location** Eurasia and North Africa

Stand by a river or stream in Europe, and you might see a flash of brilliant color as one of these **swift, active birds** flies past. The kingfisher returns to a favorite perch after a catch, striking the head of the unfortunate fish before swallowing it whole.

Pied kingfisher

Ceryle rudis

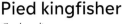

- **Length** 10 in (25 cm)
- **Weight** 3¼ oz (90 g)
- **Diet** Fish
- **Location** Africa, southern Asia, and Southeast Asia

The **breeding behavior of these birds is rather unusual**. The breeding pair raises the young with the help of up to four other kingfishers. Often the helpers are young from a previous brood, but they may be completely unrelated. These birds are equally at home hunting in fresh water or salt water.

European bee-eater

Merops apiaster

- **Length** 11–12 in (27–30 cm)
- **Weight** 2½ oz (70 g)
- **Diet** Stinging insects
- **Location** Europe, Central Asia, and Africa

As its common name suggests, this **brightly colored** bee-eater loves to eat stinging insects such as bees, hornets, and wasps. Before swallowing its meal, the bee-eater rubs the insect's tail against a perch and then squeezes the body in its bill to get rid of the sting. These birds **may eat 250 or more stinging insects** in this way **every day**.

Great Indian hornbill

Buceros bicornis

- **Length** 5 ft (1.5 m)
- **Weight** 6½ lb (3 kg)
- **Diet** Fruit and small animals
- **Location** Southern and Southeast Asia

The **large yellow helmet** on the head of this massive hornbill is **called a casque**. No one knows for sure what purpose the casque serves. It may have developed as a way of attracting a mate, but males have also been known to use it as a battering ram when fighting.

Southern yellow-billed hornbill

Tockus leucomelas

- **Length** 15¾–24 in (40–60 cm)
- **Weight** 9 oz (250 g)
- **Diet** Fruit and insects
- **Location** Southern Africa

This hornbill is a **common sight on the savanna**, where it forages for insects, spiders, scorpions, and fruit such as figs. These birds **team up with dwarf mongooses and act as lookouts**, while the mongooses flush out locusts in return for the favor.

Green wood hoopoe

Phoeniculus purpureus

- **Length** 17¾ in (44 cm)
- **Weight** 2½ oz (75 g)
- **Diet** Insects, earthworms, slugs, snails, and spiders
- **Location** South of the Sahara Desert

Yet another brightly colored bird from this group, the green wood hoopoe is an **agile tree climber** that uses its slender, down-curved bill to probe the bark for insects and other invertebrates. These birds live in close-knit groups of up to 16, headed by a dominant breeding pair.

Blue-crowned motmot

Momotus momota

- **Length** 15¾ in (40 cm)
- **Weight** 3⅗ oz (102 g)
- **Diet** Mainly insects
- **Location** Central America to central South America, and Trinidad and Tobago

The colorful blue-crowned motmot **perches quietly for most of the day**, swinging its racquet-shaped tail feather like a pendulum.

Laughing kookaburra

Dacelo novaeguineae

- **Length** 15¾–18 in (40–45 cm)
- **Weight** 13 oz (350 g)
- **Diet** Insects, snails, and small vertebrates
- **Location** Southern Australia (including Tasmania) and New Zealand

What this bird lacks in color it makes up for with its raucous call. The kookaburra is the **largest of the kingfishers** and maintains its bulk by eating a range of small animals, such as frogs, birds, fish, and snakes.

Lesser flamingo
Phoeniconaias minor

- **Height** Up to 3 ft (1 m)
- **Weight** Up to 4½ lb (2 kg)
- **Plumage** Sexes alike
- **Location** Western, central, southern Africa, India, and Pakistan

This is the **smallest flamingo**, but it is also the most numerous. Like all flamingos, it likes company: some colonies contain more than one million birds! It feeds at dusk and after dark.

AN UNUSUAL BILL

Flamingos wade in shallow water to feed, using their feet to stir up the muddy bottom. They feed with their heads almost upside-down, sweeping their specialized bill from side to side to filter out food particles. Large flamingos feed on crustaceans, mollusks, and worms. Small flamingos feed on microscopic algae.

BRINE SHRIMP

Why so pink? Flamingos get their pink color from pigments in the food they eat. The pigment is made by algae, which are microscopic plantlike organisms. These are either swallowed by the flamingos, or they enter the bird's digestive system after the flamingo eats brine shrimp that have fed on the algae. It's a mini food chain!

Flamingos

Flamingos nest in huge, noisy colonies consisting of many thousands of birds. These colorful birds are found in the tropics and subtropics. Their large nests are spaced so each roosting bird cannot quite reach its neighbor; a tactic that helps to prevent pecking!

I can sleep on one leg.
Flamingos will often stand on one leg. It is thought that this helps to lessen the amount of heat lost through the legs and feet.

FLAMINGOS *make their nests from flattened cones of mud, and a colony will lay eggs within the same few days. After a week or so, the chicks will join large creches.*

Herons and relatives

Lanky legs, snakelike necks, and heavy, stabbing bills are features shared by many of these birds. The group includes storks, egrets, spoonbills, bitterns, and ibises. Most of them live near fresh water and eat fish. The herons are stealth hunters that wait motionless for prey before making a lightning-fast strike.

FACT FILE

- **Number of species:** 121
- **Key features:** Most of these birds have splayed toes that enable them both to wade in shallow water and mud, and to stand in trees. They usually live alone, except in the breeding season. The majority are good flyers.

The numbers show where the featured animals are found.

▼ ON THE RUN *The courtship displays of the gray heron include running and prancing with wings held open. The bird's big, rounded wings measure nearly 5 ft (1.5 m) from tip to tip.*

▶ GOOD CATCH
The rare great white heron, a color form of the great blue heron, lives only in the Florida Keys.

American bittern

Botaurus lentiginosus

- **Height** 23–34 in (58–86 cm)
- **Weight** 13–18 oz (370–500 g)
- **Location** North and Central America

In the reed beds where it lives, the bittern is disguised by its **striped plumage**. When it is startled, the bird **freezes**, with its head pointing straight upward. This pose makes it even more unnoticeable. However, the bird's booming call means that it is easily heard.

Scarlet ibis

Eudocimus ruber

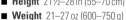

- **Height** 21½–28 in (55–70 cm)
- **Weight** 21–27 oz (600–750 g)
- **Location** South America

The brilliant feathers of the scarlet ibis get some of their color from pigments in the bird's food. Scarlet ibises like wet, muddy areas such as swamps, but for safety they build their nests in trees well above the water. If they can, they **nest on islands**, where their eggs and chicks are less likely to be in danger from predators.

Striated heron
Butorides striata

- **Height** 17–20 in (43–50 cm)
- **Weight** 7–9 oz (200–250 g)
- **Location** Africa, Asia, Australia, and South America

Also known as the green-backed heron, this small, **secretive fish-eater** spends most of its time hidden in dense cover. It sometimes looks for prey at night. The striated heron is a crafty hunter. It drops **bait**, such as an insect, on the water to attract fish to the surface.

Marabou stork
Leptoptilos crumeniferus

- **Height** 3½–5 ft (1.1–1.5 m)
- **Weight** 8¾–20 lb (4–9 kg)
- **Location** Africa

A bald head and neck and **long, dangling throat sac** give the marabou stork a most unusual appearance. When it goes courting, the stork uses the throat sac to make calls and grunts. Marabou storks look magnificent in the air, as they have a wingspan of about 10 ft (3 m). These birds eat almost everything. Fish, insects, eggs, other birds, and dead animals are all on a marabou stork's menu.

Shoebill
Balaeniceps rex

- **Height** 4 ft (1.2 m)
- **Weight** 12–14 lb (5.5–6.5 kg)
- **Location** East central Africa

The colossal bill of this extraordinary-looking stork is in the shape of a wooden clog, hence the bird's name. Sharp-tipped and **saw-edged**, the bill is a fearsome tool for catching prey. A shoebill can **crack the shell of a turtle** or snap off the head of a small crocodile. Shoebills live mostly alone. They pair up to share nest-building and the care of chicks.

Cattle egret
Bubulcus ibis

- **Height** 19–21 in (48–53 cm)
- **Weight** 9½–18 oz (270–512 g)
- **Location** Southern Europe, Africa, Southeast Asia, Australia, and Central and South America

Once the cattle egret was found only in Africa, but it has spread into many other regions. In the breeding season, cattle egrets develop **long plumes** on their heads and backs.

Gray heron
Ardea cinerea

- **Height** 35–39 in (90–98 cm)
- **Weight** 3¼ lb (1.4 kg)
- **Location** Europe, Africa (south of Sahara Desert), and Asia

The long bill has a sharp tip.

While a gray heron waits motionless, on the lookout for fish, it stands with its long neck kinked back. If it spots prey, the heron takes **less than a second to react**, shooting out its neck and bill to grab the victim.

Great blue heron
Ardea herodias

- **Height** 3–4½ ft (0.9–1.4 m)
- **Weight** 4½–5½ lb (2.1–2.5 kg)
- **Location** North America and northern South America

With a wingspan of 6 ft (1.8 m) or more, this bird is **one of the world's biggest herons**. The great blue heron hunts for food on land as well as in water. Its diet includes rodents, lizards, and even snakes. The heron may toss its prey in the air before gulping it down.

African spoonbill
Platalea alba

- **Height** 34⅖ in (90 cm)
- **Weight** 3½ lb (1.6 kg)
- **Location** South of Sahara Desert, and southwestern Sahara region

The African spoonbill goes fishing by **sweeping its bill** from side to side in the water. Its food may include water insects and crustaceans, as well as fish. The bird traps its prey between the flattened tips of its bill.

Parrots

With their vivid colors and loud squawks and calls, parrots, and their relatives, are easily recognized. The group includes parakeets, macaws, lorikeets, cockatoos, cockatiels, and budgerigars. Many are popular as pets.

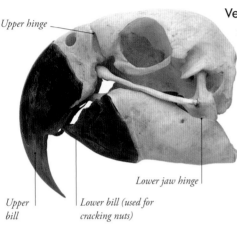

Versatile bill A parrot's bill can move far more than you might think. This is because there is a highly flexible hinge joining the bird's upper bill to its skull. Parrots also use their strong, hooked upper bill like an extra foot, to help them grip the branches as they clamber through the trees.

Upper hinge

Lower jaw hinge

Upper bill

Lower bill (used for cracking nuts)

FACT FILE

■ **Key features:** Hooked bill, large head, and short neck. Strong feet with sharp claws and two toes pointing forward and two pointing backward for a firm grip.
■ **Size:** Smallest are the pygmy parrots (genus: *Micropsitta*), which are about 3 in (8 cm) long. Largest is the hyacinth macaw at 3¼ ft (1 m) long.

Size comparison

Scarlet macaw
Ara macao

FEEDING *Parrots have flexible feet that they use like hands. They often eat by grasping food with one foot and pulling bits off the food with their sharp, agile bill.*

Red-fan parrot
Deroptyus accipitrinus

- **Length** 14 in (36 cm)
- **Weight** 7–11 oz (200–300 g)
- **Diet** Seeds, nuts, fruit, nectar, pollen, and insects
- **Location** Northern South America

Most of the time this parrot attracts little attention. But when it is frightened or excited, it raises its **bright red neck feathers** to form a fan that frames its face. This makes the bird look larger and possibly more scary to a potential predator.

Rose-ringed parakeet
Psittacula krameri

- **Length** 16 in (40 cm)
- **Weight** 4 oz (125 g)
- **Diet** Seeds, nuts, fruit, flowers, and nectar
- **Location** W. to E. Africa, S. and S.E. Asia

This bird can be found in more parts of the world than any other parrot. This is because many **released pet birds are breeding** in the wild in Europe and in North America.

Coconut lorikeet
Trichoglossus haematodus

- **Length** 12 in (30 cm)
- **Weight** 5 oz (150 g)
- **Diet** Pollen, nectar, fruit, seeds, and insects
- **Location** New Guinea, Southeast Asia, and southwest Pacific

This is one of the most colorful of all parrots. Its feathers are usually a stunning mix of vivid colors, although some birds are duller than others. Lorikeets have **bristles on their tongues** to help them gather pollen and nectar from flowers.

Budgerigar
Melopsittacus undulatus

- **Length** 7 in (18 cm)
- **Weight** 1 oz (25 g)
- **Diet** Seeds, grains, and nuts
- **Location** Australia

Most people know these friendly birds as pets, but large flocks of wild budgerigars are a familiar sight over the grasslands of Australia. **Wild birds are always green**, with a yellow face and blue tail. But since budgerigars were first introduced to Europe in 1840, careful breeding has produced birds in many different colors.

MANY COLORS
In captivity, budgerigars are bred so that they come in a wide range of colors: blue, gray, green, yellow, violet, and even white.

Hyacinth macaw
Anodorhynchus hyacinthinus

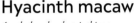

- **Length** 3¼ ft (1 m)
- **Weight** 3¼ lb (1.5 kg)
- **Diet** Palm nuts, seeds, and fruit
- **Location** Central South America

These are the **largest of all parrots**, although half their length is made up of their tail. Often described as gentle giants, these highly intelligent birds love company and are usually seen in a group or with their mates. They stay with the same partner throughout their long lives.

Galah
Eolophus roseicapilla

- **Length** 14 in (35 cm)
- **Weight** 12 oz (325 g)
- **Diet** Seeds, grass, leaves, and fruit
- **Location** Australia (including Tasmania)

The **noisy galah** is the most widespread cockatoo of all. It gathers in huge flocks, and can be a pest to farmers as it will raid fruit and seeds.

Cockatiel
Nymphicus hollandicus

- **Length** 12½ in (32 cm)
- **Weight** 3 oz (90 g)
- **Diet** Seeds, nuts, and fruit
- **Location** Australia

This is **the smallest cockatoo**, but its beautiful coloring and large, bright yellow crest make it a popular pet. The crest is lowered when it rests, and sometimes when it feeds. The underside of the tail is black for a male bird and yellow for a female.

Kakapo
Strigops habroptila

- **Length** 25 in (64 cm)
- **Weight** 4½ lb (2 kg)
- **Diet** Fungus, moss, leaves, seeds, fruit, and pollen
- **Location** New Zealand

Kakapos cannot fly, so they are vulnerable to predators. They almost became extinct, but from 1987 to 1992, the few remaining birds were taken to the safety of three predator-free islands off the coast of New Zealand.

Hummingbirds

These birds beat their wings in a figure-eight pattern, which gives them a lot of flight control. They are the only birds able to fly backward and they can even fly upside down. They also hover, which is necessary when they use their long bills to probe flowers and drink the nectar within.

My wings are a blur!
Small hummingbirds flap their wings about 4,200 times a minute. That's 70 times a second! A tiny bee hummingbird flaps its wings even faster, at about 200 times a second during courtship displays!

Magenta-throated wood star
Calliphlox bryantae

Bee hummingbird

Mellisuga helenae

- **Height** 2–2¼ in (5–6 cm)
- **Weight** ¹⁄₁₆ oz (2 g)
- **Location** Cuba and Isla de la Juventud

Famed as **the smallest bird in the world**, the male bee hummingbird is smaller than the female. Unlike the female, it also has iridescent feathers around its head and neck. The female lays eggs no larger than peas in tiny, walnut-size nests.

▲ IRIDESCENT FEATHERS *are a striking feature of most male hummingbirds. The feathers appear to have a metallic sheen. But why? It is to help the males attract females. When he is looking for a female, the male searches for a perch in the sun, which causes the iridescent feathers to positively gleam.*

▶ NO HUMMINGBIRD *weighs more than around 1 oz (24 g). That is about the weight of a tablespoon of sugar. The largest hummingbird is the giant hummingbird.*

FACT FILE

There are a number of different types of hummingbird, but all of them are found in the Americas. They all have long, pointed bills that probe into flowers so the birds can drink nectar.

Woodpeckers and toucans

These woodland birds all have striking bills— some huge and brightly colored, others long, thin, and finely pointed like a dagger. They can also run up and down the sides of tree trunks with ease, thanks to their super-grip feet.

FACT FILE

- **Number of species:** More than 400 species, divided into six groups or families.
- **Key features:** Large bills and strong, parrotlike feet with two toes pointing forward and two pointing backward, for a firm grip.
- **Nest:** In holes, safely out of sight of predators.

Toes

Size comparison

◄ CACTUS NEST *Gila woodpeckers (*Melanerpes uropygialis*) are unusual: they thrive in deserts, where there are unlikely to be any trees to nest in. Instead, they peck out nest holes in the large cacti that are common in the dry, hot areas of the southwest United States, where this bird lives.*

Strong skull Woodpecker skulls are extra thick. This helps to cushion the brain, which is important for an animal that spends hours every day hammering away at trees with its bill. These birds also have an unusually long tongue, with a barbed or sticky tip for catching insects.

WOODPECKER SKULL

FEEDING *Woodpeckers are born blind and helpless and rely on their parents for many months. This youngster takes a tasty morsel that its father has carried back to the nest.*

Rufous-tailed jacamar

Galbula ruficauda

- **Length** 7½–10 in (19–25 cm)
- **Weight** ⅝–1¹⁄₁₆ oz (18–30 g)
- **Diet** Insects
- **Location** Central America and north and central South America

This beautiful bird, with its shimmering green, red, and gold feathers, likes to keep a low profile. It spends most of the day sitting quietly on a shaded branch, only darting out occasionally to **spear a passing insect** on its daggerlike bill.

Green woodpecker

Picus viridis

- **Length** 12–16 in (30–33 cm)
- **Weight** 6¼–7¾ oz (180–220 g)
- **Diet** Insects, mainly ants
- **Location** Europe and western Asia

The green woodpecker's tongue is nearly twice the length of its bill, with a tip covered in a sticky liquid to help trap **ants, the bird's favorite food**. Although green woodpeckers live in woods, where they peck nest holes in the sides of trees, they also spend a lot of time on the ground, in yards or parks, using their pointed beaks to dig out any insects that are crawling through the grass.

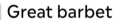

NOISY BIRD *The loud "laughing" cry of the green woodpecker can be heard far and wide over woods and heaths during spring.*

Greater honeyguide

Indicator indicator

- **Length** 8 in (20 cm)
- **Weight** 1¾ oz (50 g)
- **Diet** Bees and beeswax, bee eggs, and ants
- **Location** Central and southern Africa

Honeyguides can **sniff out bees' nests**, their main source of food, using their keen sense of smell. Some African tribes use the bird to guide them to bees' nests, so that they can harvest the honey.

Yellow-bellied sapsucker

Sphyrapicus varius

- **Length** 7½–8½ in (19–20 cm)
- **Weight** 1½–2 oz (43–55 g)
- **Diet** Tree sap and insects
- **Location** North and Central America, and Caribbean

The sapsucker gets its name because it **feeds on the sugary sap** that it sucks out of trees through holes it drills in the trunk. In spring, males drum on trees and other objects to mark their territory.

Great barbet

Psilopogon virens

- **Length** 12½ in (32 cm)
- **Weight** 7–11 oz (200–300 g)
- **Diet** Fruit, nectar, and insects
- **Location** Central and East Asia

Barbets use their large, bristly, pointed bills to dig out nest holes and to peck into tree trunks in search of a meal. This bird's plump body; large head; and stubby, rounded wings make it **a poor, inelegant flyer**. It spends quite a lot of its time bobbing along the ground.

Toco toucan

Ramphastos toco

- **Length** 21–23½ in (53–60 cm)
- **Weight** 17½–30¼ oz (500–860 g)
- **Diet** Fruit, insects, and bird eggs
- **Location** Northeast to central South America

This is one of the largest and **most well known** of all toucans. Its spectacular, brightly colored bill is not solid, but has a honeycomb-like structure, making it much lighter than it appears to be.

Keel-billed toucan

Ramphastos sulfuratus

- **Length** 18–20 in (46–51 cm)
- **Weight** 10–19 oz (275–550 g)
- **Diet** Fruit, insects, and reptile and bird eggs
- **Location** Central and northern South America

Even for a toucan, this bird stands out for its dazzling array of colors. Keel-billed toucans do not fly very well, so spend most of their time hopping along branches in search of food. Having a long bill means they can pick fruit that is often beyond the reach of other birds. Once they have their prize, they toss their heads back sharply, open their surprisingly agile jaws wide, and **swallow the fruit whole**.

Amazing *nests*

Birds' nests come in all shapes and sizes, from the tiny cup-shaped ones of songbirds to the massive platforms of eagles and the complex communal nests of weaver birds. All sorts of materials are used to build nests and some birds spend many weeks constructing them.

WHY DO BIRDS BUILD NESTS?

Most birds build nests, but a nest is rarely a permanent home. Birds usually only start to build a nest when they are ready to breed. This is because they need a safe, warm place to lay their eggs, and for their newly hatched chicks to develop.

NEST INGREDIENTS

Birds use many things for building their nests, including sticks, mud, feathers, stones, twigs, grass, and moss. Long-tailed tits even use sticky cobwebs to hold their moss nests together. They then camouflage the nest with lichen and use feathers to give it a soft lining.

WHITE TERN

No nest The white (or angel) tern does not build a nest. It just sticks its eggs in the fork of a tree branch, using only a glob of mucus to hold them in position.

Just move in Most owls are not keen on nest building. They often lay their eggs in holes in tree trunks. These openings may have been hollowed out by another bird, or they may be natural.

Out of reach Many gulls nest in colonies high up on the cliff face, away from possible predators. They build cup-shaped nests from twigs and plant materials along the rocky ledges.

Family pile Storks build huge nests by piling up sticks, often adding more sticks to the same nest year after year. They like to be up high, in tall trees or on the top of buildings or chimneys.

NEST SHAPES

Some nests are little more than a hole scraped in the ground and lined with pebbles. But many are complex structures, built to last.

▶ *Old World orioles weave sack-like nests that they hang from the branches of trees. They use almost any material, including bits of string.*

◀ *Weaver birds weave nests from shreds of leaves and grass. A long entrance tunnel is woven into the side or base.*

◀ *Many small birds make open, cup-shaped nests.*

Perching birds

More than half of all the bird species in the world belong to a group known as perching birds, or passerines. The feet of perching birds have three toes pointing forward and one backward. This allows them to get a firm grip on even the thinnest and most flexible branches.

My feet don't lose their grip even when I go to sleep.
When a bird lands, the weight of its body presses down on its toes. This makes the toes lock automatically around the branch in a tight grip.

FACT FILE

Perching bird foot

Size comparison

- ■ Number of species: about 5,962.
- ■ Key features: specialized perching feet, with three toes pointing forward and one back. Most perching birds have distinctive songs.
- ■ Size: The crows and ravens are the largest, with lengths of up to 25½ in (65 cm). The short-tailed pygmy tyrant is the smallest perching bird at just 3 in (7 cm) in length.

GOOD SINGERS

Another special thing about perching birds is their ability to sing. They are often referred to as songbirds, and many of them have wonderful voices. Each species has a particular song, which may be made up of a wide range of notes. The best singers include the song thrush and the nightingale.

Great tit

Parus major

- ■ **Length** 5½ in (14 cm)
- ■ **Diet** Insects, fruit, and seeds
- ■ **Location** Europe and Asia

This tit is seen everywhere from woodlands to town gardens. **Bold and bossy,** the great tit does not hesitate to drive smaller tits away from backyard bird tables. Its distinctive two-note *"teacher, teacher"* call is easy to recognize.

Woodpecker finch

Camarhynchus pallidus

- **Length** 6 in (15 cm)
- **Diet** Insect larvae
- **Location** Galápagos Islands

This finch is a **rarity** among animals because it **uses a tool to catch food**. The bird holds a twig or cactus spine in its beak and probes in tree bark with the tool to lever out grubs.

European robin

Erithacus rubecula

- **Length** 5½ in (14 cm)
- **Diet** Insects, worms, and berries
- **Location** Europe, northern Africa, and northwest Asia

The "redbreast" is popular with gardeners in the UK for its **cheerful, bubbling song** and its appetite for harmful insect pests. Elsewhere in its range, the European robin is less inclined to associate with people. For all their charm, robins can be very **fierce** in defense of their territory.

BIRDS

White-throated dipper

Cinclus cinclus

   10

- **Length** 7–8 in (18–21 cm)
- **Diet** Small fish, crustaceans, mollusks, and larvae
- **Location** Europe, northern Africa, northern Asia, and northern and central South Asia

The dipper is found by fast-running streams and rivers. It swims well, and **can walk along riverbeds completely submerged** while it searches for food. When the dipper is not in the water, it perches on rocks by the riverbank, constantly bobbing its body up and down. This dipping action is how the bird got its name.

Song thrush

Turdus philomelos

 17

- **Length** 9 in (23 cm)
- **Diet** Berries, insects, worms, slugs, and snails
- **Location** Europe, North Africa, central and northwestern Asia, introduced to Australia and New Zealand

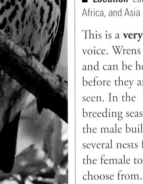

Broken snail shells by a flat stone are a sign that a thrush has been eating there. **Numbers** of thrushes have **fallen dramatically** in Europe due to loss of their farmland habitat.

Wren

Troglodytes troglodytes

   7

- **Length** 3½ in (9 cm)
- **Diet** Insects and spiders
- **Location** Europe, North America, northern Africa, and Asia

This is a **very small bird** with a very loud voice. Wrens usually **live in dense hedges**, and can be heard before they are seen. In the breeding season, the male builds several nests for the female to choose from.

Red-backed fairy-wren

Malurus melanocephalus

- **Length** 4–5 in (10–13 cm)
- **Diet** Insects, fruit, and seeds
- **Location** Northern and eastern Australia

There are several different species of fairy-wren in Australia and Papua New Guinea. The red-backed wren, like all its fairy-wren relatives, has a **long tail** that it carries **cocked upright**. This wren builds its nests in dense undergrowth or among tall grasses. It is sometimes a backyard visitor.

▲ SPLASH OF RED *The vividly colored red-backed wren is the smallest of all the fairy-wrens.*

Red crossbill
Loxia curvirostra

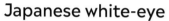

- **Length** 6½ in (17 cm)
- **Diet** Seeds (from pine cones)
- **Location** North America, Europe, and Asia

The crossbill's unusual **crossed-over beak** develops gradually, and is not seen in young birds. This beak is the perfect shape for breaking the seeds off pine cones.

Japanese white-eye
Zosterops japonicus

- **Length** 4 in (10.5 cm)
- **Diet** Invertebrates, fruit, berries, and nectar
- **Location** South, East, and Southeast Asia and Hawaii

White feathers ring this bird's eyes like a pair of glasses. Japanese white-eyes are very common in Asia. They gather in flocks in gardens and woodlands. Their **varied diet** changes from season to season, according to what food is available.

▶ FLOWERS
provide the Japanese white-eye with nectar and pollen

Raggiana bird of paradise
Paradisaea raggiana

- **Length** 14 in (35 cm)
- **Diet** Fruit, insects, and spiders
- **Location** Papua New Guinea

There are many species of bird of paradise. The male birds usually have spectacular **flowing plumes**, which they show off in courtship rituals. Males of the type of bird of paradise shown here gather together to put on a mass display in front of the females.

White wagtail
Motacilla alba

- **Length** 7 in (18 cm)
- **Diet** Insects and seeds
- **Location** Europe, Africa, and Asia

The banks of rivers and streams, and the edges of ponds are good places to see a white wagtail. This bird **loves to be near water**. A wagtail darts about in short, fast runs, flicking its tail, as it hunts for the insects that are the main part of its diet.

Northern house martin
Delichon urbicum

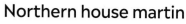

- **Length** 5 in (12.5 cm)
- **Diet** Flying insects
- **Location** Europe, Africa (south of the Sahara Desert), and Southeast Asia

House martins like to be close to people. These birds nearly always use buildings as nesting sites. They stick their **mud nests** under the eaves of houses, in barns, and even under road bridges. About the only time a house martin comes down to the ground is when it is collecting mud for a nest. For most of its life, a martin stays in the air, wheeling and swooping in pursuit of flying insects.

Short-tailed pygmy tyrant
Myiornis ecaudatus

- **Length** 2½ in (6.5 cm)
- **Diet** Insects
- **Location** Northern and central South America

This is one of the smallest birds in the world. Its tail is not much more than a tiny stub. The short-tailed pygmy tyrant belongs to a group of birds called tyrant flycatchers. These birds are **highly skilled at catching their insect prey** in midair. They are called "tyrants" because, despite their generally small size, they are very aggressive.

A breeding pair of ravens can be fierce when they are defending their territory. The couple may attack intruders or chase them over long distances.

Dark-eyed junco

Junco hyemalis

 10

- **Length** 5½–6 in (14–16 cm)
- **Diet** Seeds, berries, and invertebrates
- **Location** North America

Common in woodland, dark-eyed juncos **flock together** during the fall and winter, when the breeding season is over. The male junco sings at most times of the year.

Common raven

Corvus corax

22

- **Length** 25½ in (65 cm)
- **Diet** Fruit, nuts, eggs, carrion, and small animals
- **Location** North and Central America, Europe, Asia, and North Africa

The raven is one of the largest perching birds. It is noted for its aerobatic flight, during which it may twist and turn at high speed. Often, a raven rolls right over in midair and **flies upside down**. The bird makes various calls, including a hoarse croak.

Zitting cisticola

Cisticola juncidis

 ?

- **Length** 4 in (10 cm)
- **Diet** Insects
- **Location** Southern Europe, Africa, Asia, and Australia

This warbler is **hard to see** because its color blends in with the grasslands and scrublands where it lives. In flight, it makes a monotonous **two-note call**.

Red-whiskered bulbul

Pycnonotus jocosus

 11

- **Length** 8 in (20 cm)
- **Diet** Berries, insects, and nectar
- **Location** Asia; introduced into Australia and the US

Bright plumage and an **attractive song** have made the red-whiskered bulbul popular as a cage-bird. These birds are trapped in large numbers. They are still common but may soon need protection.

Bare-faced bulbul

Nok hualon

 11

- **Length** 7⅛ in (20 cm)
- **Diet** Fruit and berries
- **Location** Laos

This bulbul really stands out from other bulbuls because of the **bare patches of skin** around each eye. It lives on the sparsely covered limestone hills of Laos where it can sometimes be seen perching on rocks. It **forages in pairs** when looking for food.

Cliff swallow

Petrochelidon pyrrhonota

10

- **Length** 5–6 in (13–15 cm)
- **Diet** Flying insects
- **Location** Alaska, Mexico, and South America

Buildings as well as cliffs are good nesting sites for cliff swallows. The birds plaster their **cone-shaped mud nests** onto vertical walls. These birds **migrate**, spending spring and summer in the north and going south for the winter.

▶ COLONIES
Hundreds, or even thousands of cliff swallows may nest together at one site.

Australian golden whistler

Pachycephala pectoralis

 15

- **Length** 6–7 in (16–18 cm)
- **Diet** Insects, small arthropods, and berries
- **Location** Indonesia, S. and E. Australia, Tasmania, and Fiji

As its name suggests, the golden whistler is a fine songster. It has a loud, **tuneful voice** and a wide range of notes. Golden whistlers have particularly strong feet for gripping and a stout bill.

◀ COZY NEST
Golden whistlers bind their nests with spiders' webs and line them with soft grass.

Starlings

Starlings are a familiar sight in many countries throughout the world, roosting and flying in huge, noisy flocks. They nest in artificial or natural cavities, perhaps finding a space under roof tiles or a hole in a tree, and have proved immensely successful.

BIRDS

FROM SMALL BEGINNINGS

It is believed that about 60 starlings were deliberately released in New York City in 1890. By the mid-1950s, starling numbers in North America had reached 50 million, and today there are thought to be some 200 million starlings.

Common starling

Sturnus vulgaris

- ■ **Length** 8½ in (21 cm)
- ■ **Weight** 2–3¼ oz (60–96 g)
- ■ **Diet** Insects, earthworms, seeds, and fruit
- ■ **Location** Worldwide except polar regions

Starlings are **stocky birds**, with speckled feathers that shimmer with iridescent purple and green. Their **beaks turn yellow** in the breeding season. They are noisy birds, and often mimic the calls of other birds, and even frogs or cats.

Birds fly in one of two ways: they either flap their wings continually, or they are able to glide on air currents, flapping their wings occasionally. Starlings are flappers, following straight flight lines and beating their wings rapidly to stay aloft.

▲ JUVENILE STARLING *Young birds have a brown plumage, and no iridescent feathers.*

As the bird takes off, its feet are drawn up toward the body.

By flapping its wings up and down, the starling stays in the air.

Murmuration Starlings gather in large flocks, and occasionally more than a million birds will gather. This is known as a murmuration, and it will swoop and soar as one, each bird following its neighbor. Flocks as big as these make strange, dark shapes in the sky.

A *world* of eggs

No two bird eggs are exactly alike; they vary greatly in size, shape, color, and texture. The size of the egg doesn't always relate directly to the size of the bird. An egg laid by an ostrich is the world's largest bird's egg, but it is one of the smallest eggs in relation to the bird's body size.

Common kingfisher
Alcedo atthis

Green broadbill
Calyptomena viridis

Song thrush
Turdus philomelos

Eurasian nightjar
Caprimulgus europaeus

**Common
oystercatcher**
Haematopus ostralegus

Black woodpecker
Dryocopus martius

Ringed plover
Charadrius hiaticula

Madagascar bulbul
Hypsipetes madagascariensis

Gray butcherbird
Cracticus torquatus

Tawny owl
Strix aluco

Emu
Dromaius novaehollandiae

**Rose-ringed
parakeet**
Psittacula krameri

Rock wren
Salpinctes obsoletus

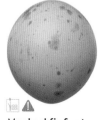

Herring gull
Larus argentatus

**Black-winged
cuckoo-shrike**
Coracina melaschistos

Masked finfoot
Heliopais personatus

Egyptian vulture
Neophron percnopterus

Southern cassowary
Casuarius casuarius

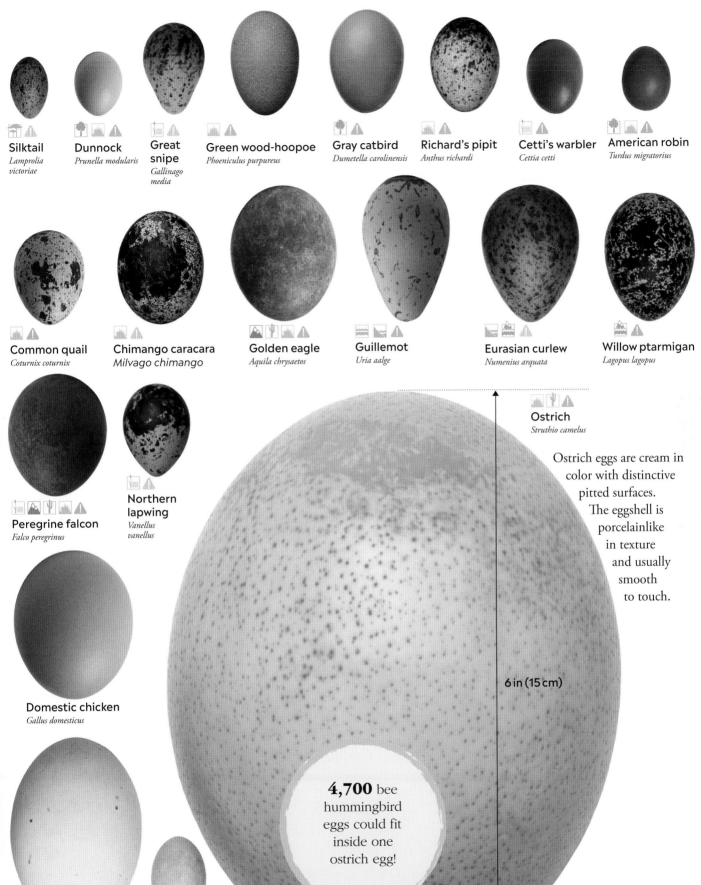

Silktail
Lamprolia victoriae

Dunnock
Prunella modularis

Great snipe
Gallinago media

Green wood-hoopoe
Phoeniculus purpureus

Gray catbird
Dumetella carolinensis

Richard's pipit
Anthus richardi

Cetti's warbler
Cettia cetti

American robin
Turdus migratorius

Common quail
Coturnix coturnix

Chimango caracara
Milvago chimango

Golden eagle
Aquila chrysaetos

Guillemot
Uria aalge

Eurasian curlew
Numenius arquata

Willow ptarmigan
Lagopus lagopus

Peregrine falcon
Falco peregrinus

Northern lapwing
Vanellus vanellus

Ostrich
Struthio camelus

Ostrich eggs are cream in color with distinctive pitted surfaces. The eggshell is porcelainlike in texture and usually smooth to touch.

6 in (15 cm)

Domestic chicken
Gallus domesticus

4,700 bee hummingbird eggs could fit inside one ostrich egg!

Greylag goose
Anser anser

Great crested grebe
Podiceps cristatus

½ in (1 cm)

Bee hummingbird
Mellisuga helenae

159

REPTILES

Definition: A **reptile** is a cold-blooded, usually egg-laying vertebrate. Reptiles are covered with scales or horny plates and they breathe through lungs.

What is a REPTILE?

Reptiles once dominated Earth. Fierce tyrannosaurs and huge *Triceratops* stalked the land, until their sudden extinction 66 million years ago. Although many dinosaurs were wiped out, other reptiles survived, and these creep around nearly every continent today.

WHAT MAKES THEM DIFFERENT?

Like mammals and birds, reptiles are vertebrates (they have a backbone) and breathe air. However, unlike mammals, they are cold-blooded, they have scaly skin, and most species reproduce by laying eggs.

Scaly skin

It's not **furry**.
It's not **slimy**.
It's not **feathery**.
It must be
a **reptile**!

▲ SUPPLE SPINES *All reptiles have backbones, and some have extremely long and bendy ones, such as this emerald tree boa.*

FACT FILE

There are five main groups of reptiles: lizards, snakes, tortoises and turtles, crocodilians, and the tuatara.

■ **Snakes:** Snake senses are sophisticated—they can find their prey with ease, and they make stealthy and cunning predators. They don't chew their food, but always swallow it whole.

■ **Lizards:** This group is highly varied and very common, especially in warm countries. Many lizards can camouflage their skin to match their surroundings.

■ **Tuataras:** This group of reptiles can only be found on two small islands off the coast of New Zealand. They differ from lizards in lots of subtle ways.

■ **Crocodilians:** Crocodiles, caimans, and alligators make up this group. Most are freshwater inhabitants, but a few venture into the sea.

■ **Tortoises and turtles:** These animals had ancestors that lived alongside the dinosaurs. They are the only reptiles with a hard, protective shell.

SCALY SKIN

Reptiles have dry, scaly or scalelike skin. The scales are made of keratin, the same material that makes hair and feathers. All reptiles shed their skin as they grow. Snakes cast theirs off in one piece.

◀ DINO COUSIN
"Dinosaur" means "terrible lizard" in Latin. Today's reptiles are relatives of the dinosaurs.

▲ LIZARD SKIN

▲ SNAKE SKIN

▲ CROCODILE SKIN

STURDY SKELETON

The different groups of reptiles have very different skeletons. This is the skeleton of a chameleon. Reptile skeletons are sturdy, making them suitable for life on land.

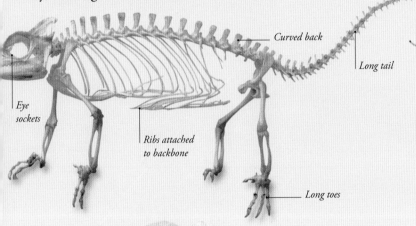

Curved back

Long tail

Eye sockets

Ribs attached to backbone

Long toes

I'M FEELING COLD

Reptiles are often called "cold-blooded." This doesn't mean that their blood is cold. Their temperature depends on their surroundings. If the temperature doesn't suit them, some reptiles can hibernate until the temperatures are right again.

▼ SUNBATHING *If a reptile feels its blood is too cold, it will sunbathe to warm up.*

Chameleon eggs

EGG BEGINNINGS

Most reptiles reproduce by laying eggs. Females lay their eggs in decayed wood, a nest of leaves and mud, or elsewhere on land. Most do not sit on their eggs to incubate them but some snakes do.

◀ BIRTH DAY
A baby tortoise emerges from its egg.

LOOK INTO MY EYES...

An interesting characteristic of reptiles is their eyes. The shape of a reptile's pupil indicates whether the animal is active at night or during the day. Most reptiles active at night have slit-like pupils that can close tightly in bright light. Reptiles active in daytime have round pupils.

ROUND PUPIL

SLIT-LIKE PUPIL

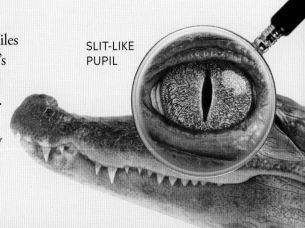

Reptile birthday

These turtles, like most reptiles, have to fend for themselves after they are born. There is safety in numbers so they all hatch at the same time, and usually during the night. Even so, it is estimated that just 1 in 1,000 baby turtles makes it to adulthood.

HEAD FOR WATER *The eggs hatch and hundreds of baby turtles emerge from nests in the sand. Instinctively, they head directly for the water, where they will have the best chance of survival. The babies can swim right away.*

BORN FROM EGGS

Most reptiles, including those that live mainly in water, reproduce by laying eggs on land. Reptile eggs often have a leathery shell that allows water and oxygen to pass through to the developing animal inside. Although many species of reptile lay their eggs, then leave, some reptiles, including the Nile crocodile, make attentive parents.

DAY 1
Mom prepares a nest out of sand, mud, and weeds at the water's edge. She lays 20-60 eggs in the nest. They are protected by a tough, leathery shell.

DAY 5
Even though the mother crocodile stays close by and defends the nest, when she pops out for a cooling dip, the nest is often raided by predators.

I've got to get to the sea. I've got to get to the sea …

The mother turtle is long gone by the time these turtles hatch. They seem to know they have to make for the waves, and fast! Unfortunately, they have to run a gauntlet of predators as they grow, from seagulls to sharks.

DAY 90

The eggs hatch. A baby croc uses its egg tooth to break the shell. Alerted by tiny grunts and chirps, the mother helps her babies out of the nest.

DAY 90

The mother carries the babies to the water where she will continue to watch and protect them for up to two years.

TURTLE CONSERVATION

Sadly, the number of sea turtles has rapidly declined—because of human activity. This includes disturbance of their nest sites due to beach tourism, collection of their eggs, pollution of the seas, and getting caught in fishing nets. To address the problem, beach reserves with assisted breeding programs have been set up and turtle-friendly fishing nets have been introduced. Everyone is keeping their fingers crossed for these amazing creatures.

Tortoises and turtles

Tortoises and turtles are among the longest-living animals on Earth. But they don't need to worry about losing their teeth as they get older, because they don't have any. Instead they have a sharp, horny beak to cut and chew up their food.

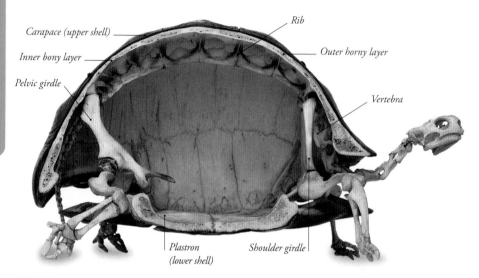

Carapace (upper shell)

Inner bony layer

Pelvic girdle

Rib

Outer horny layer

Vertebra

Plastron (lower shell)

Shoulder girdle

SKELETON

Tortoises and turtles have an unusual skeleton. Their ribs and some of their vertebrae are fused to their upper shell. This means they cannot move their ribs to help pump air in and out of their lungs. Instead, they use muscles at the tops of their legs to do the pumping.

▲ DO NOT DISTURB *Tortoises and turtles living in cooler parts of the world often hibernate in winter, to avoid the cold and shortage of food.*

FACT FILE

- **Number of species:** 356
- **Key features:** Tortoises live on dry land and have round, stumpy legs. Turtles spend most of their time in water and have flipper-like limbs. Freshwater turtles are often called terrapins. They all have a protective shell.

Size comparison

Smallest turtle   Smallest tortoise

Biggest turtle   Biggest tortoise

I AM 150 YEARS OLD!
The Galápagos tortoise (Chelonoidis niger) is the world's biggest at 4 ft (1.2 m) long. They can live to be more than 170 years old.

Desert tortoise
Gopherus agassizii

- **Length** 6–14 in (15–36 cm)
- **Diet** Cacti, grass, and some insects
- **Location** S.W. US and N.W. Mexico

On exceptionally hot days, this tortoise will burrow into the sand, using its **shovel-shaped feet**, to escape the baking desert heat, Males may fight each other for a mate during the breeding season.

Indian star tortoise
Geochelone elegans

- **Length** Up to 11 in (28 cm)
- **Diet** Grass, leaves, and fruit
- **Location** India, Pakistan, and Sri Lanka

Its knobbly, high-domed shell, covered with **star-shaped markings**, make this tortoise one of the easiest to recognize. It is a **thirsty creature** and is usually only very active during the wet monsoon season. When it is dry, it tends to venture out just in the early morning or late afternoon.

Hermann's tortoise
Testudo hermanni

- **Length** 5–11 in (13–28 cm)
- **Diet** Leaves, flowers, and fruit
- **Location** S.E. Europe and Mediterranean islands

This tortoise was once a **popular pet**, but its sale is now restricted by law. It usually **hibernates** during the winter, especially in very cold weather, and spends much of summer resting in the shade.

Green turtle
Chelonia mydas

- **Length** 3¼–4 ft (1–1.2 m)
- **Diet** Seaweed and algae; the young also eat jellyfish, mollusks, snails, worms, and sponges
- **Location** Worldwide

Having been **hunted** for centuries for their meat and eggs, green turtles are now **legally protected**. Special breeding beaches have been set up by conservationists to help save them from extinction.

Leatherback turtle
Dermochelys coriacea

- **Length** 4¼–6 ft (1.3–1.8 m)
- **Diet** Jellyfish
- **Location** Worldwide

Leatherbacks are the **biggest turtles**. Some weigh as much as 1,770 lb (800 kg). They also **swim great distances**. Individuals have been known to cross the Atlantic. Unlike other turtles, they have a leathery outer shell.

Alligator snapping turtle
Macrochelys temminckii

- **Length** 31–39⅖ in (79–100 cm)
- **Diet** Fish, turtles, and other aquatic animals
- **Location** Southeast US

This is the world's **largest freshwater turtle**. Most of its day is spent with its scissor-sharp jaws wide open, as it lures fish toward it by wiggling a small, pink, wormlike tube on the floor of its mouth. Its hooked "beak" delivers a **deadly bite**.

Common snake-necked turtle
Chelodina longicollis

- **Length** 8–10 in (20–25 cm)
- **Diet** Fish, crabs, lobsters, and tadpoles
- **Location** East and south Australia

This turtle uses its **exceptionally long neck** to "snorkel" while it hunts for food in rivers and streams. A long neck is also very handy for lunging at and **grasping prey**. The neck and head together are often longer than the shell.

Loggerhead turtle
Caretta caretta

- **Length** 28–39 in (70–100 cm)
- **Diet** Shellfish, crabs, and lobsters
- **Location** Worldwide

Loggerheads get their name from their exceptionally **big head**. They also have large, powerful jaws, that can easily crunch their way through any passing shellfish, crab, or lobster. These turtles only breed every two years at the most and are **becoming rare**. Many of their breeding areas are now protected.

Snakes

Snakes are highly evolved and deadly predators. They slither along on smooth bellies, hunting by stealth, eating all types of animals, from ants to alligators. The only way they can eat their prey is to swallow it whole, including the horns, hooves, and hair!

Forked tongue

◄ SENSES *Snakes have poor eyesight and hearing. They rely instead on their tongue, which they use to "taste" the air or touch the ground to follow a scent left by their prey. Some have heat-detecting pits on their faces.*

New skin

Cast-off skin

▲ SKIN *Snakes shed their skin between four and eight times a year. Shedding starts around the mouth and nose. Once the skin is loose, the snake rubs against objects to help pull itself out.*

Rib

Skull

Backbone

Anatomy

The skeleton of a snake is very simple. It consists of a skull, and hundreds of ribs set along a long, flexible backbone. The internal organs are mostly long and thin and are arranged to fit along the length of the snake. The jaws are loosely hinged to help swallow food.

FACT FILE

■ **Key features:** Snakes can move in three ways. Undulation is a side-to-side movement where the snake uses rough ground to push itself along. In tunnels a snake will concertina its coils against the walls to thrust itself forward. A snake also uses its belly scales to pull itself along.

Snake movement

Undulation

Concertina

Straight line

Sea snakes have flattened, paddle-shaped tails and spend most of their lives at sea. Because they have lungs rather than gills they visit the surface regularly to breathe. Sea kraits are not sea snakes; they lay their eggs on land.

REPTILES

Olive sea snake
Aipysurus laevis

- **Length** 6 ft (1.8 m)
- **Location** Australasia

The olive sea snake is found on coral reefs in Australia and New Guinea. Although **venomous**, it only attacks if it is provoked. Its body is purplish brown with a light brown underside. These snakes are regarded as true sea snakes because they give birth to **live young in the water**.

Yellow-lipped sea krait
Laticauda colubrina

- **Height** 3¼–5 ft (1–1.5 m)
- **Location** Southeast Asia

Sea kraits live in coastal waters where they hunt fish and eels. They are most **active at night**. Unlike sea snakes, kraits lay eggs on land and leave them to hatch. Sea kraits have **special scales** on their belly that help them crawl on land.

▶ FANGS *Most venomous snakes have two hollow teeth that they use to inject their prey with venom. Venom kills or paralyses the animal, making it easier for the snake to swallow.*

CONSTRICTORS

Constrictors are snakes that kill by wrapping their coils around their prey and squeezing hard so the blood cannot flow around the victim's body. This stops the heart and prevents oxygen reaching the organs. When the animal stops struggling, the snake swallows it head first. Boas and pythons are typical constrictor snakes.

Children's python
Antaresia childreni

- **Length** 30–39 in (75–100 cm)
- **Location** Northern Australia

This small python hides in caves and crevices where it **waits to ambush** lizards, birds, and small mammals. It will even eat bats. If threatened it will strike and bite an attacker, but it is not venomous. Children's pythons are reddish brown in color with **darker blotches**. They lay their eggs in hollow trees or caves.

Anaconda
Eunectes murinus

- **Length** 20–33 ft (6–10 m)
- **Location** South America

The anaconda is the world's **heaviest snake**, and can weigh up to 550 lb (250 kg). Anacondas spend most of their time **submerged** in water, hiding in the plants along the edges of rivers and lakes. They are capable of killing capybaras and small deer and have been known to attack fully grown caimans.

BIG DINNER
This anaconda has killed a caiman. It will not need to eat anything else for several months.

Emerald tree boa

Corallus caninus

20 ⚠

- **Length** 5–6½ ft (1.5–2 m)
- **Location** Northern South America

The emerald tree boa is perfectly adapted for life in the treetops. Its **vivid color** blends in with the rainforest foliage, while its muscular body firmly grips tree trunks and branches. These boas coil themselves around a branch with their heads hanging down, ready to strike a bird or mammal. The prey is seized by the snake's teeth before being **crushed** to death by the snake's body. Each season, a female gives birth to between three and 15 orange-red live young. They turn green after one year.

Carpet python

Morelia spilota

- **Length** 6½–13 ft (2–4 m)
- **Location** Australia

Carpet pythons are found across much of Australia and in many different **habitats**. They vary in color, but all have bold markings on a lighter-colored background. They are **active day and night**. Female carpet pythons lay up to 50 eggs in hollow trees or rotting vegetation and will **incubate** them until they hatch.

Common boa constrictor

Boa constrictor

- **Length** 3¼–13 ft (1–4 m)
- **Location** Central and South America

The common boa is a large snake with a narrow head and a **pointed snout**. Boas are good climbers and able swimmers, but are also happy to hunt on the ground. They detect prey by scent rather than by heat. Boa constrictors have distinctive **dark markings** along their backs against a pink, gray, or gold background. Female boas produce live young.

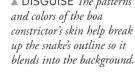

▲ DISGUISE *The patterns and colors of the boa constrictor's skin help break up the snake's outline so it blends into the background.*

Rubber boa

Charina bottae

- **Length** 14–32 in (35–80 cm)
- **Location** S.W. Canada and W. US

This snake gets its common name from the **rubbery** feel of its skin. Both its head and tail are blunt, making them hard to tell apart. When threatened, the snake coils itself up and raises its tail to make attackers think it is its head. Rubber boas live underground, hunting for small animals in burrows and tree holes. These snakes often **hibernate** for long periods in winter.

Reticulated python

Python reticulatus

- **Length** 13–26 ft (4–8 m)
- **Location** Southeast Asia

The reticulated python is one of the world's longest snakes, and it can weigh more than 300 lb (136 kg). These snakes have irregular **diamond-shaped markings** in a variety of colors. They are widely hunted for their skin, which has led to them becoming increasingly **rare in the wild**.

Rosy boa

Lichanura trivirgata

- **Length** 23½–43 in (60–110 cm)
- **Location** S.W. US and N.W. Mexico

The rosy boa is a **burrowing snake** and lives mostly beneath rocks and in crevices, where it forages for food. Rosy boas are actually cream, gray, or buff in color with brown, orange, or black stripes running along the lengths of their bodies. They are very **slow movers** and have to ambush their prey.

African rock python

Python sebae

- **Length** 13–23 ft (4–7 m)
- **Location** Central and Southern Africa

African rock pythons are more **aggressive** than other pythons and will readily **bite** if harassed. They live on grasslands and savannas, often close to water. Farmers like them because they eat cane rats in the fields, but they are less welcome on livestock farms as they will also take larger animals such as gazelles, goats, and even crocodiles.

▼ NOTHING LEFT
Every part of this gazelle will be eaten by a rock python, even though it may take a whole year for it to be digested.

REPTILES

FANG-TASTIC SNAKES!

The majority of snakes do not kill by constriction. Instead, they use their teeth. Most are harmless to humans, but some are armed with grooved or hollow fangs that can inject a deadly venom. One strike from a taipan, for example, contains enough venom to kill 100 people. There are three different fang positions:

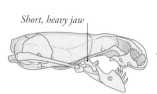

Short, heavy jaw

PRIMITIVE SNAKE
Primitive snakes have a heavy skull and few teeth. Blind snakes, which feed only on small prey such as insects and their larvae, are primitive snakes.

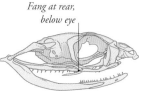

Fang at rear, below eye

REAR-FANGED SNAKE
Rear-fanged snakes' fangs are grooved, not hollow, and their venom is usually weaker than front-fanged snakes. It is more to aid the digestive process than to kill.

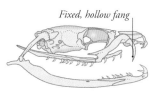

Fixed, hollow fang

FRONT-FANGED SNAKE
The most familiar venomous snakes, such as cobras, are front-fanged. Their venom is potent and their fang position enables venom delivery during a strike or quick bite.

FATAL STRIKE *This rattlesnake hunts by ambushing its victims, striking with venomous fangs before devouring its stunned, or dead, prey.*

Milk snake

Lampropeltis triangulum

- **Length** 1⅓–6½ ft (0.4–2 m)
- **Diet** Insects, frogs, small rodents, and other snakes
- **Location** North America, Central America, and northern South America

These colorful snakes are fairly common within their range, but rarely seen since they are **secretive**. They are usually found near forest edges, but can also live in open woodlands, and grasslands, near streams and rivers, on rocky hillsides, and in suburban areas and farmlands—in other words, just about anywhere.

Grass snake

Natrix natrix

- **Length** 4–6½ ft (1.2–2 m)
- **Diet** Frogs and fish
- **Location** Europe to central Asia and northwest Africa

These non-venomous snakes often take to the water and are **excellent swimmers**, feeding on frogs and fish. When they feel themselves to be in extreme danger, they **"play dead"**—a good surprise tactic.

Western diamondback rattlesnake

Crotalus atrox

- **Length** 6½ ft (2 m)
- **Diet** Small mammals, birds, and lizards
- **Location** Southwest US and northern Mexico

This is North America's most dangerous snake. Its "rattle" is a horny section at the end of its tail, which it vibrates when threatened. It is a **deadly predator** that stalks its prey, strikes, then swallows.

Puff adder

Bitis arietans

- **Length** 6–8 ft (1.8–2.4 m)
- **Diet** Small rodents (mice, rabbits) and birds
- **Location** Africa and southern Arabia

One of the world's most dangerous snakes, the puff adder is big, effectively camouflaged, **highly venomous**, and aggressive. It strikes readily when annoyed or frightened, but usually **puffs up** or hisses loudly in warning. This snake has caused many human deaths.

Indian cobra

Naja naja

- **Length** 4–5½ ft (1.2–1.7 m)
- **Diet** Rodents, frogs, and lizards
- **Location** South Asia

Well known for emerging out of baskets, and seeming to dance to a snake-charmer's music, this snake is **one of the most dangerous in India**, causing 10,000 fatalities each year. Cobras rise up and display their hoods when they feel threatened to make themselves appear as large as possible.

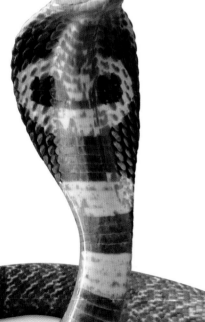

Mangrove snake

Boiga dendrophila

- **Length** 8 ft (2.5 m)
- **Diet** Small mammals, lizards, frogs, snakes, and fish
- **Location** Southeast Asia

Dramatic colors warn predators that this is a venomous snake. The mangrove snake has a slightly flat body with a **ridge down its back**. Before striking, it draws back its head and flares its yellow lip scales.

Kopstein's bronzeback

Dendrelaphis kopsteini

- **Length** 5 ft (1.5 m)
- **Diet** Lizards and frogs
- **Location** Southeast Asia

It's easy to tell when this strikingly colored snake is angry—**it flares its neck** and flashes its orange-red scales. Like many other bronzebacks, it has a venomous bite. It spends most of its time hunting lizards in the treetops.

Black mamba

Dendroaspis polylepis

- **Length** 8¼–11½ ft (2.5–3.5 m)
- **Diet** Small mammals and birds
- **Location** Eastern and southern Africa

This is one of the most venomous snakes, and probably **the fastest moving**. In short bursts it can overtake a running human, making it an extremely dangerous predator.

Corn snake

Pantherophis guttatus

- **Length** 3¼–6 ft (1–1.8 m)
- **Diet** Small rodents and small birds
- **Location** Central and southeast US

This eye-catching snake is not venomous, but it may strike to bite if threatened. It also **vibrates its tail** and excretes a foul-smelling musk to deter intruders. It is largely nocturnal, but may emerge in daytime in cooler weather.

Taipan

Oxyuranus scutellatus

- **Length** 6½–12 ft (2–3.6 m)
- **Diet** Mammals, birds, and lizards
- **Location** S. New Guinea and N. Australia

The **most venomous land snake in the world**, the taipan is the most feared snake in Australia. However, because an effective antivenom has been developed, human fatalities are now relatively rare.

Golden flying snake

Chrysopelea ornata

- **Length** 3–6 ft (1–2 m)
- **Diet** Small vertebrates
- **Location** South and Southeast Asia

Technically a glider rather than a flier, this snake **flattens its body** to twice the normal width so it acts like a wing. It reaches its take-off point by crawling up a tree, gripping the bark with its scales. The flying snake is **considered harmless** because its venom is not dangerous to humans.

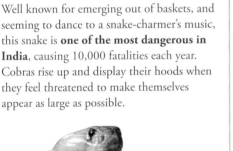

Lizards

Lizards are a large and varied group of reptiles that have successfully adapted to a wide range of habitats. Most lizards have four legs, a long tail, scaly skin, and reproduce by laying eggs.

This lizard has lost the end of its tail.

Dewlap

It can take up to two years to grow a new one.

Five clawed toes

▲ CAMOUFLAGE *Many lizards have patterned skin that helps them blend into their surroundings. This enables them to hide from predators or stalk their prey.*

This pygmy chameleon is no bigger than a fingernail.

▶ SUNBATHERS *Because lizards are cold blooded they need to spend time basking in sunlight before they become fully active.*

Gila monster

Heloderma suspectum

- **Length** 18–24 in (45–60 cm)
- **Location** Southwestern US and northern Mexico

Gila monsters live in desert and semi-arid regions, where they hide under rocks or in burrows. Their **beaded skin** is strongly marked with bands and blotches. Gilas are **venomous** and deliver their poison along grooves in the teeth of the lower jaw. They hunt mainly in the spring, usually for eggs and baby rabbits. After a large meal they store fat in the tail.

Fat-storing tail

Sharp teeth

Beadlike scales

▼ EGG THIEF *Lizards such as the Gila monster often raid nests for eggs and nestlings. They crush the egg with their jaws and let the contents trickle down their throat.*

FACT FILE

- **Key features:** Lizards typically have a tail longer than their body that some species can shed if attacked. Most have external ear openings, movable eyelids, and a tongue that is notched or forked. Lizards also have sharp cusped or serrated teeth running along the edge of the jaw.

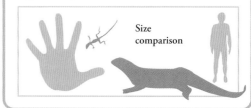

Size comparison

Amphisbaenians are a group of legless lizards that are sometimes mistaken for worms or snakes. They have a cylindrical body and rings of scales that resemble the body segments of worms. Adapted to a life underground, the head is smooth and pointed for burrowing and the small, rudimentary eyes are covered with a transparent scale. The nostrils point backward to prevent them being filled with soil while tunneling. Most amphisbaenians live in tropical regions, which provides them with the constantly warm soil temperatures they need to move underground.

Eye
Mouth

▲ EYES AND MOUTH
Amphisbaenians have only limited vision. The lower jaw is set back to prevent soil entering while digging.

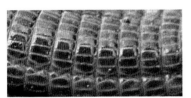

▲ SCALES *Unlike snakes, the scales of amphisbaenians do not overlap and are arranged in rings, making them look like worm segments.*

▼ SKELETON *While they may look like worms from the outside, amphisbaenians have a skeleton similar to that of a snake. However, they also have bones that prove their ancestors had legs. Three Mexican species still have a pair of front legs.*

Speckled worm lizard
Amphisbaena fuliginosa

- **Length** 12–18 in (30–45 cm)
- **Location** Northern South America and Trinidad

Unlike most amphisbaenians, which are pinkish brown in color, this species has a distinctive black and white skin. It spends most of its life underground but may come to the surface at night. Worm lizards move through the soil by pushing their body segments together like a concertina, which provides thrust for forward movement. This species feeds on any small vertebrates and insects it encounters, crushing them in its **powerful jaws**. It will shed its tail if necessary, but cannot grow a new one.

Armadillo lizard
Cordylus cataphractus

20

- **Length** 6½–8¼ in (16–21 cm)
- **Location** South Africa

These tiny lizards live in the deserts of South Africa. They have unusual **square-shaped scales** and a crest of spines along the neck and tail. If attacked they curl round and **bite their tail** to protect their soft belly, just like an armadillo. They also hide in crevices and puff themselves up so they cannot be dislodged. Armadillo lizards are live-bearers and sometimes live in colonies of up to 40 individuals.

Frilled lizard
Chlamydosaurus kingii

20

- **Length** 24–35⅖ in (60–90 cm)
- **Location** N. Australia and New Guinea

Australia's frilled lizard is a spectacular sight when provoked. Rising up on its hind legs, it unfurls a wide **flap of skin around its neck** and hisses loudly. If this tactic doesn't work, it turns tail and runs for the safety of a tree. It comes down to forage for food, eating mainly insects, spiders, and other invertebrates.

▼ BIG FRILL *The neck frill of this lizard is stiffened with cartilage rods to make it stand away from the body.*

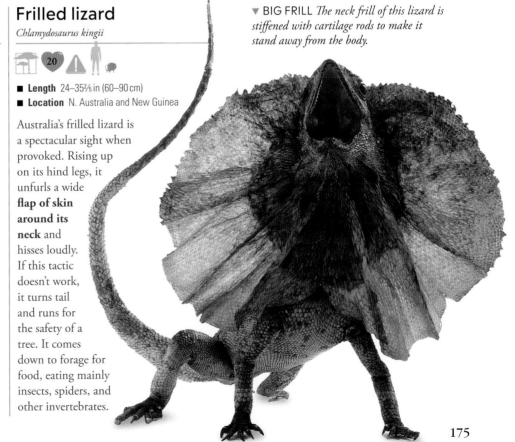

175

Chameleons

With their swivelling eyes and amazing ability to change color, it's no surprise that chameleons often have a special place in folklore. In Madagascar, they are protected by local superstitions and it is considered bad luck to kill one.

I have a twist in my tail.

Chameleons have a long, grasping or "prehensile" tail that can be coiled tightly around branches to act as a secure anchor. When not in use the tail is usually held in a loose spiral.

Panther chameleon

Furcifer pardalis

- **Length** 16–20½ in (40–52 cm)
- **Weight** 9 oz (250 g)
- **Location** Madagascar and Réunion Island, Indian Ocean

A large and **colorful** species, panther chameleons can change color—females do this only when they are pregnant to signal they will not mate, but males flush any combination of red, green, or blue depending on their mood.

The prehensile tail is used to grip branches.

ALL CHANGE!

Special cells called chromatophores in the chameleon's skin contain a variety of pigments that can be displayed at the surface of the cell or hidden. Signals from the chameleon's brain tell each skin cell which colors to show and which to hide, in order to create an overall pattern to suit any occasion.

VEILED CHAMELEON
The bony helmet or casque of some chameleons has several functions, including display and picking up low frequency sounds, like a dish.

COLORFUL FEELINGS
Males use color mainly to communicate. When rivals meet, they adopt aggressive postures and flush a range of colors to intimidate each other.

Each eye moves
independently.

FANCY FOOTWORK
The five toes on each of the chameleon's feet are fused together in groups of two and three to form powerful grippers that provide a secure hold on narrow branches.

Long, sticky tongue

▲ FOOD
Chameleons eat mainly small invertebrates such as insects and spiders, which they catch using a long, sticky tongue that can be shot out at lightning speed and with deadly accuracy.

◄ NEST
Female chameleons lay clutches of up to 50 rubbery eggs, usually in damp soil. The young hatch into miniature versions of their parents and must fend for themselves from day one.

CAMOUFLAGE
A chameleon can display colors that match its background. The disguise is perfected with gentle swaying that mimics the movement of the tree.

Geckos, skinks, and others

Climbing aces of the lizard world, geckos can get a grip on anything with their sticky feet. They are common in the tropics. The slender skinks form the largest group of lizards. Their pointed heads and flattened bodies enable them to slip easily into cracks and crevices.

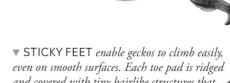

▼ TAKING TO THE AIR *is how Kuhl's flying gecko escapes enemies. It leaps from trees and glides with the help of webbed feet and skin flaps on its sides.*

▼ STICKY FEET *enable geckos to climb easily, even on smooth surfaces. Each toe pad is ridged and covered with tiny hairlike structures that cling firmly to everything they touch.*

Blue tongue

◄ TONGUE POKING *out, the blue-tongued skink defies an enemy. This defensive display, usually accompanied by loud hissing noises, often saves the skink from being attacked.*

Tokay

Gekko gecko

15

- **Length** 7–14 in (18–36 cm)
- **Diet** Insects and small vertebrates
- **Location** Southeast Asia

Sticky toe pad

Big and colorful, the tokay is one of the most striking geckos. It is popular as a pet, despite being aggressive and having a **fierce bite**. When a tokay is annoyed it opens its mouth in a gape to show its **bright red tongue**. Even other geckos have reason to be wary of the tokay. It is a **cannibal** and doesn't hesitate to eat geckos smaller than itself. The tokay gets its name because of its loud "tock-ay" call.

Pupil closes to a slit in daylight.

NIGHT VISION
Because the tokay is active at night, it has big goggle eyes to help it see in the dark. To shut out bright light, the pupils of the eyes close to a slit.

Red tongue

Leopard gecko

Eublepharis macularius

25

- **Length** 8–10 in (20–25 cm)
- **Diet** Spiders, crickets, worms, and young mice
- **Location** South Asia

The tail of the leopard gecko is almost the same width as its body. The gecko uses this **plump tail** as a store for spare food, to be drawn on in times of shortage. Unlike most geckos, this species has **movable eyelids**, so it can blink. The leopard gecko is a popular pet and if kept in the right environment may live for more than 20 years.

Union Island gecko

Gonatodes daudini

?

- **Length** 1½–1¾ in (4–4.5 cm)
- **Diet** Insects
- **Location** Caribbean

Pick up a handful of leaves from the dry forest floor of Union Island and you may find one of these tiny geckos hunting for ants and termites. Although brightly colored, its patterning helps it **blend into the background** in the dappled shade of the forest.

Ibiza wall lizard

Podarcis pityusensis

6

- **Length** 6–8½ in (15–21 cm)
  - **Diet** Insects
  - **Location** Balearic Islands, introduced to Majorca

Slim, **agile**, and shy, Ibiza wall lizards usually run away or climb out of reach extremely quickly when startled. These lizards often gather together in **large groups**. They like sunning themselves on walls and rocks. Ibiza wall lizards are also sometimes seen in yards, where they forage for food on scrap heaps.

REPTILES

Five-lined skink

Plestiodon fasciatus

6

- **Length** 5–8½ in (12.5–21.5 cm)
- **Diet** Insects and spiders
- **Location** E. North America

The fine stripes that give this lizard its name are seen only in females and young skinks. **Males lose their stripes** when they become adult. Young skinks have bright blue tails (right). The lizards tend to live on the ground but can also be found in trees. They **like rotten logs** and tree stumps, which are a good source of insect food.

Web-footed gecko

Pachydactylus rangei

5

- **Length** 4¾–5½ in (12–14 cm)
- **Diet** Crickets and spiders
- **Location** Western southern Africa

The webbing between its toes stops this gecko from sinking into the sand of the deserts where it lives. During the day, the gecko **escapes the heat by staying in a tunnel** that it digs out. At night, it emerges to feed. The gecko's **huge eyes** help it find prey.

Red markings vary in individuals

Broadley's flat lizard

Platysaurus broadleyi

?

- **Length** 6–8 in (15–20 cm)
- **Diet** Flies and berries
- **Location** Southern Africa

Broadley's flat lizard can squeeze itself into the narrowest of cracks, because its body and tail are so flattened. The male (below) is multicolored, but females and young are brown with pale stripes. They **live near waterfalls**, where they feed on swarms of tiny flies.

Black tegu

Tupinambis teguixin

20

- **Length** 3–4½ ft (90–135 cm)
- **Diet** Small vertebrates, snails, eggs, fruit, and plants
- **Location** South America

This large, strong lizard can sometimes be aggressive. It is a **ground-dweller** and digs its own burrows. The black tegu is a good climber but prefers to stay on the ground most of the time. It often **lays its eggs in termite mounds** to protect them from predators.

Madagascar day gecko

Phelsuma madagascariensis

10

- **Length** 9–12 in (22–30 cm)
- **Diet** Insects, spiders, fruit, pollen, and nectar
- **Location** North Madagascar

There are several different types of day gecko and all of them are active during the daytime. The day gecko is one of the largest species. Unlike its relatives, this gecko is **fiercely territorial**. The males drive away any other male that comes near their home ground.

Iguanas, monitors, and relatives

Lizards come in all shapes and sizes. The largest lizard in the world is the Komodo dragon, which hunts animals such as deer and wild pigs. Others are tiny, and light enough to glide through the air.

◀ FEEDING
Komodo dragons can eat 80 percent of their body weight in one feeding. Dragons sometimes swallow smaller animals whole, regurgitating the horns, hooves, and hair later as pellets.

▲ DEADLY SALIVA
Being bitten by a Komodo dragon can be fatal. Its saliva contains bacteria that can kill an animal within 24 hours—if it doesn't die from blood loss first!

Komodo dragon

Varanus komodoensis

- **Length** 6½–10 ft (2–3 m)
- **Location** Indonesia

Komodo dragons are the **top predator** on the islands where they live. Although they feed mainly on carrion, they will also ambush live prey. They can run quickly for short sprints and young dragons can climb trees. Dragons are usually **solitary** creatures.

I am the biggest lizard of all.
Komodo dragons are not the sort of lizard most humans would want to bump into. They have thickly folded, scaly skin; a huge, muscular tail; and powerful jaws that can tear off large chunks of flesh.

Green basilisk

Basiliscus plumifrons

- **Length** 23½–30 in (60–75 cm)
- **Location** Central America

This bright green lizard lives in trees overhanging streams and ponds. Also known as the plumed basilisk, it has **three crests** along its head, neck, and tail that it uses when swimming. This lizard has the unique ability to escape a predator by running very quickly across the surface of a pond on its hind feet.

Thorny devil

Moloch horridus

- **Length** 6–7 in (15–18 cm)
- **Location** Australia

Thorny devils are small, spiky lizards that live in the Australian desert. Their **spines** protect them against predators and also act as channels to **collect water** for drinking. Devils eat only one type of black ant. They will sit by an ant nest for hours, eating up to 3,000 ants one by one.

SCARY DEVIL
The spines of thorny devils are not their only defense. They can also take in air to inflate their size.

Spiny scale

Rainbow lizard

Agama agama

- **Length** 5–11⅞ in (13–30 cm)
- **Location** Africa

Rainbow lizards are usually brownish gray, but the males develop a blue body and tail and an **orange-red head after basking** in sunlight. Rainbow lizards live in open habitats and are often found near buildings. The rainbow's tail is twice as long as its body.

Flying lizard

Draco spilonotus

- **Length** 6–8 in (15–20 cm)
- **Location** Southeast Asia

Flying lizards have flaps of skin along their ribs that they can stretch out to form a **"wing"** on either side of their body. They use these wings like a parachute to escape predators and glide to safety. Another flap under the chin is used to **attract mates** and threaten rivals.

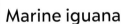 

Green iguana

Iguana iguana

- **Length** 5¾–6½ ft (1.75–2 m)
- **Location** Central and South America

Green iguanas are found across most of northern South America, particularly the Amazon rainforest. Iguanas have a **fleshy dewlap** under the chin and a crest of spiky scales running down their back. Although they are agile climbers, iguanas can also **swim, using their tail** to propel them through the water.

Nile monitor

Varanus niloticus

- **Length** 5–6 ft (1.5–1.8 m)
- **Location** Central Africa

The Nile monitor lives near water, where it feeds on crabs, mollusks, and fish as well as small birds and eggs. In cooler climates Nile monitors hibernate together in **communal dens**. If threatened by crocodiles or pythons, they will use their teeth, claws, and tail to defend themselves. Females lay their eggs in **termite mounds**.

Marine iguana

Amblyrhynchus cristatus

- **Length** 20–39 in (50–100 cm)
- **Location** Galápagos Islands

Marine iguanas live on the rocky shores of the Galápagos Islands off the coast of Ecuador. They are the only iguanas to **swim in salt water**, diving for the algae on which they feed. They can only spend a short time in the cold sea and have to bask in sunlight to warm up again. During this time they are vulnerable to predators.

Crocodiles and alligators

Large, scaly reptiles including crocodiles and alligators are collectively known as crocodilians. They live on land and in water and are excellent swimmers, using their tails to propel themselves along. Their jaws are strong enough to crush bones when they close, but the muscles that open the jaws are very weak.

Nostrils close when underwater.

Skin is covered in armor-like plates, called scutes.

Dwarf crocodile
Osteolaemus tetraspis

75

- **Length** 5½ ft (1.7 m)
- **Weight** 68 lb (31 kg)
- **Diet** Fish, frogs, and toads; young eat worms and insects
- **Location** Western and central Africa

Among the **smallest** of crocodiles, this is one of the most aggressive. During the day, it burrows among tree trunks at the water's edge and **at night it hunts**. The female usually lays about 10 eggs. When they hatch, she carries each baby to the water in her mouth.

▲ *Crocodilians are cold-blooded, so they depend on the temperature of their environment to warm up or cool down.*

Spectacled caiman
Caiman crocodilus

40 !

- **Length** 6½–8 ft (2–2.5 m)
- **Weight** 99 lb (45 kg)
- **Diet** Reptiles, fish, and waterbirds
- **Location** Central America and northern South America

This crocodile has a **bony ridge** around its eyes that looks like glasses. It spends almost all its time in fresh water, floating on the surface during the day and hunting at night. It is a good swimmer and hunts fish such as piranhas and catfish. It also **snatches mammals**, including wild pigs, that come to the water to drink.

▼ *Crocodilians have see-through eyelids that they close when they are underwater.*

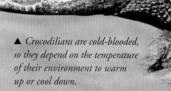

Gharial
Gavialis gangeticus

60

- **Length** 13–23 ft (4–7 m)
- **Weight** 353 lb (160 kg)
- **Diet** Fish, frogs, and insects
- **Location** Northern India

A crocodile with a long, **narrow snout**, the gharial rarely leaves the water. It is one of the largest crocodilians and cannot walk on land, so it **belly slides** across the ground.

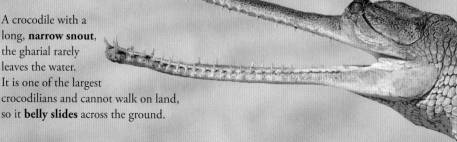

The first crocodilians

Crocodiles appeared with the first dinosaurs, about 200 million years ago. They have remained virtually unchanged ever since.

▶ KILLING TIME
As it waits for prey, a crocodilian floats almost completely submerged. Only its nostrils and eyes are fully above the water.

Slender snouted crocodile

Mecistops cataphractus

   50

- **Length** 10–14 ft (3–4.2 m)
- **Diet** Crabs, frogs, fish, birds, and small mammals
- **Location** Central and western Africa

Gray-green to almost black, this crocodile lives in rivers, lakes, and coastal waters. Although it prefers fresh water, it can tolerate salt water and may **swim over to islands** near the African mainland. Females lay between 13 and 27 eggs in riverbank nests.

▲ *A crocodilian can open its mouth wide underwater—a flap of skin on its throat stops water going into its lungs.*

American alligator

Alligator mississippiensis

    50

- **Length** 9¼–16 ft (2.8–5 m)
- **Weight** 330 lb (150 kg)
- **Diet** Fish, small mammals, and birds
- **Location** Southeast US

A large, **heavy predator,** the American alligator lives mostly in the rivers, lakes, and **swamps** of Florida and Louisiana. Females lay 25–60 eggs. The young have yellow and black stripes. They stay with their mother for up to three years.

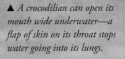

Nile crocodile

Crocodylus niloticus

      40

- **Length** 11–20 ft (3.5–6 m)
- **Weight** 1,100 lb (500 kg)
- **Diet** Fish and large mammals including antelopes, zebras, and buffaloes
- **Location** Africa and western Madagascar

This crocodile feeds on fish, as well as larger animals including antelopes and zebras. It **pulls big prey into the water**, then spins round and round to tear off chunks that it can swallow.

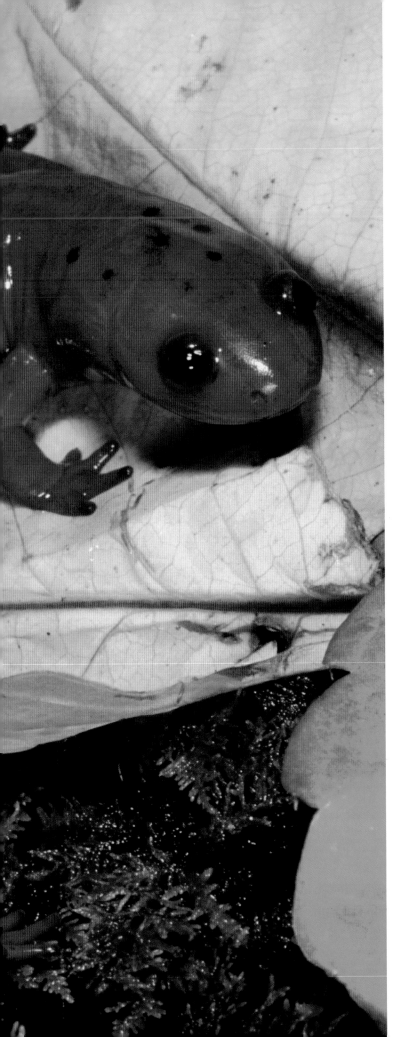

AMPHIBIANS

Definition: **Amphibians** comprise three groups: newts and salamanders, frogs and toads, and caecilians. They are cold-blooded and live both in water and on land.

What is an amphibian?

Amphibians have three life stages: eggs, larvae, and adults. Many amphibians start life in water, and breathe through gills, then change into adults that can live on land, and breathe through lungs. This happens in a process called "metamorphosis."

IT'S A FROG'S LIFE

… and a toad's, and a newt's, and a salamander's, and a caecilian's. All these creatures are amphibians. The least well known of these is the caecilian. It is a wormlike animal, rarely seen by humans because it lives either in soil burrows or underwater. It has a good sense of smell to sniff out earthworms that it catches with sharp, curved teeth.

◄ CAECILIAN LIFE CYCLE
Caecilians, such as the Mhadei caecilian, have varied life cycles: some lay eggs, while some keep the eggs in their bodies until they are ready to hatch into larvae.

I might go ashore now to wander around.
Most amphibians are equally at home on land or in water, but many live entirely in water.

FACT FILE

There are three groups of amphibians: frogs and toads, newts and salamanders, and caecilians. Altogether, there are 8,614 species.

■ **Frogs and toads**
Frog and toad larvae are called "tadpoles." They eat algae until they become adults when they become carnivorous.

■ **Newts and salamanders**
These animals have tails and short legs. They are carnivorous in both their larval and adult stages.

■ **Caecilians**
These form a small group. They have long, thin bodies and no legs. They only live in tropical, humid places.

A LONG WALK HOME

Most amphibians live on land as adults but return to water to breed. Some species migrate long distances to get back to the same pond where they started out themselves. In some cases this can mean a mass of frogs moving across rough terrain during the breeding season to get "home."

▶ EGG-CELLENT
When frogs find a pond, they mate and lay their eggs.

SPECIAL SKIN

The skin of an amphibian is naked and smooth, and highly specialized. It is very thin and absorbent—thin enough to breathe through. Mucus glands keep it damp, which helps gases pass through.

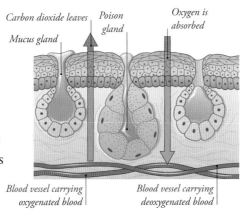

Carbon dioxide leaves

Poison gland

Oxygen is absorbed

Mucus gland

Blood vessel carrying oxygenated blood

Blood vessel carrying deoxygenated blood

▲ SPOT THE FROG *Many amphibians have amazing camouflage. It's as though their skin has been painted to make them disappear.*

STURDY SKELETON

Amphibians have a fairly simple body structure, well adapted to life in water and on land. They have large eye sockets to make room for their big eyes, and wide mouths to fit in large prey.

Wide mouth

Long toes

◄ LEAP FROG
Take a quick glance at a frog skeleton and it is obvious how it moves. It looks poised to leap. It has a short, squat body; wide mouth; and large eye sockets—all the better to see its prey.

Four fingers

Ribs

Spine

Five toes

Long back legs

▲ SALAMANDER STRUT
This creature walks along one foot after the other. It has a long tail to help propel it through water. Its long backbone is flexible and bends.

MORPHING

Most amphibians start life in water, as one egg among a cluster of eggs (in the case of frogs, this is called "frog spawn"). After a few weeks the eggs hatch into larvae. These are like little fish with tails; they swim and breathe through gills. Gradually, they start to change and develop lungs until metamorphosis is complete and they can leave the water.

Newt's egg

2 weeks later— newt larva hatches

3–4 months later—adult newt

▲ NEWT LIFE CYCLE
Like frogs, newts have an egg, larva, and adult stage. They keep their tails.

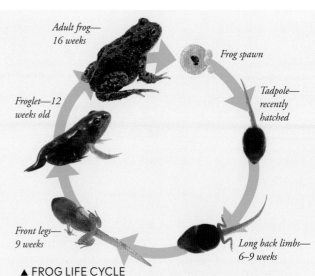

Adult frog— 16 weeks

Frog spawn

Froglet—12 weeks old

Tadpole— recently hatched

Front legs— 9 weeks

Long back limbs— 6–9 weeks

▲ FROG LIFE CYCLE
Frogs start out as frog spawn, which hatches into tadpoles. Legs gradually grow, tail shrinks, and, finally, they become frogs.

Salamanders and newts

There is no real difference between newts and salamanders. Newts are a subgroup of salamanders which means all newts are salamanders, but not all salamanders are newts! Newts generally spend more of their adult life in water than salamanders. Both groups are amphibians.

It's hair-raising being a newt!

This great crested newt is still a baby. It spends all its time underwater, breathing through its long, feathery gills. At about four months old, its gills shrink and disappear. It begins to breathe air through lungs and is ready to leave the water.

Chinese giant salamander

Andrias davidianus

- **Length** 6 ft (1.8 m)
- **Diet** Fish, crustaceans, and insects
- **Location** China

This is the **largest amphibian** in the world. It lives in mountain streams, preferring fast-running water, and hunts mainly at night for shrimp, fish, and insects. Certain males make masterful fathers. In the mating season, one male controls the movements of all breeding pairs in his territory and later **guards all the eggs** until they hatch.

Fire salamander

Salamandra salamandra

- **Length** 7–11 in (18–28 cm)
- **Diet** Worms, slugs, and insects
- **Location** N.W. Africa, Europe, and W. Asia

The **yellow markings** on this sturdy creature warn predators that it is poisonous, and would make a disgusting meal. It often **lives on mountain slopes** in woodland. During the cold winter months, it curls up underground, in a cozy hole. It emerges when it's warmer, especially after rain, to eat slugs and worms.

Jordan's salamander

Plethodon jordani

- **Length** 3¼–7½ in (8.5–18.5 cm)
- **Diet** Millipedes, beetles, and insect larvae
- **Location** Eastern US

This salamander is also distasteful to predators, thanks to a **slime that oozes from its tail**. Its breeding habits show the varied behavior of salamanders: males breed every year, females breed every two years.

Great crested newt

Triturus cristatus

- **Length** 4–5½ in (10–14 cm)
- **Diet** Insects, worms, woodlice, slugs, and snails
- **Location** Europe and Central Asia

This is a male great crested newt; you can tell by the **crest on his back** that develops during the breeding season. He does a complex dance underwater to attract a female. After mating, the female **lays one egg at a time**, and wraps each one in a leaf. It's a big job as she lays more than 200 eggs.

Pacific giant salamander

Dicamptodon tenebrosus

- **Length** 6½–13½ in (17–34 cm)
- **Diet** Invertebrates, other amphibians, snakes, and mice
- **Location** S.W. Canada and N.W. US

This large salamander lives in or around streams, and **comes out at night**. Some never leave the water, and never lose their gills, and some do leave the water and do lose their gills! Their numbers have dipped because of logging and the resulting silting up of streams.

Emperor newt

Tylototriton shanjing

- **Length** 5½–7 in (14–18 cm)
- **Diet** Worms and fish
- **Location** Southern and Southeast Asia

During the winter or dry weather, this **warty newt** stays underground. It comes out for the monsoon, when it rains a lot. It then makes a journey to a breeding pond and sticks its eggs onto water plants. Emperor newts are highly toxic and, when grabbed by predators, their warts ooze poison.

Olm

Proteus anguinus

- **Length** 8–12 in (20–30 cm)
- **Diet** Invertebrates
- **Location** Southern Europe

This is one of the few amphibians that **makes its home in a cave**, sometimes deep below ground. It lives in total darkness, and is **almost blind**. It eats small animals that live in underground streams, and never leaves the water.

Frogs and toads

These cold-blooded creatures form the largest and best-known group of amphibians. They come in a variety of shapes, sizes, and colors. The goliath frog is as big as a cat, but some frogs are so small they can fit on your fingernail.

WELCOME TO MY PAD *The male of each species has a different call. The gray tree frog* (Hyla versicolor) *has a vocal sac that fills with air to produce a really loud call. On hearing it, females know where they can find a mate.*

LEAP FROG *Frogs can crawl, climb, and hop along, and are able to leap 10 times their body length. They launch themselves out of danger, like this tiger-striped leaf frog.*

FACT FILE

- **Number of species:** About 7,600
- **Key features:** Short body, long hind legs, moist skin, no tail.
- There is no scientific distinction between frogs and toads.
- Frogs usually have smooth, moist skin, are slimy, and jump. They spend most of their lives in or near water. Toads tend to be dry, warty-looking, and walk rather than jump. They spend more time living on land.
- A group of frogs is called an "army." A group of toads is called a "knot."

Australian green tree frog

Litoria caerulea

 15

- **Length** 2–4 in (5–10 cm)
- **Habitat** Terrestrial
- **Location** S. New Guinea, N. and E. Australia

This frog is well known for its **tame** behavior, and its habit of living in or near buildings. A night hunter, it eats mosquitoes, bugs, and even mice, so is a **much appreciated guest**. The frog is well adapted to seasonally wet or dry regions as its skin can control evaporation.

Red-eyed tree frog

Agalychnis callidryas

 5

- **Length** 1½–2¾ in (4–7 cm)
- **Habitat** Terrestrial
- **Location** Central America and northern South America

Many scientists believe the red-eyed tree frog developed its **vivid scarlet eyes** to shock predators into questioning their meal choice. Any small hesitation gives the frog the split second it needs to leap to safety. Red-eyed tree frogs are **nocturnal**, and feed on moths and crickets, which they catch with their long, sticky tongues.

American bullfrog

Lithobates catesbeianus

 16

- **Length** 3½–8 in (9–20 cm)
- **Habitat** Mostly aquatic
- **Location** S.E. Canada, W., C., and E. US

These big frogs have a **big appetite!** They will eat almost anything that moves and that they can swallow, including invertebrates and small mammals, birds, reptiles, fish, and even turtles and other frogs. They usually live among vegetation along the edge of large, slow-moving rivers and streams.

Mexican burrowing toad

Rhinophrynus dorsalis

 10

- **Length** 2¼–3¼ in (6–8 cm)
- **Habitat** Terrestrial/burrowing
- **Location** Southern US to Central America

This toad spends most of its life underground, burrowing into soft soil, slurping up ants and termites. It comes out to breed after heavy rain, the males **inflating their bodies** to make a low "whoo-oa" call. As rain may fall at any time, this call can be heard **all year round**.

Cope's gray tree frog

Hyla chrysoscelis

 5

- **Length** 1¼–2⅓ in (3–6 cm)
- **Habitat** Mostly terrestrial
- **Location** South Canada and central and east US

This small frog is well camouflaged to match the lichen-covered tree branches it lives on, concealing it from predators. It is never far from water. In the north of its range, it lives in regions with very cold winters, and during hibernation, its body produces a natural antifreeze that ensures it does not freeze solid.

Goliath bullfrog

Conraua goliath

 15

- **Length** 4–15¾ in (10–40 cm)
- **Habitat** Mostly aquatic
- **Location** Cameroon and Equatorial Guinea

The goliath is the **biggest frog in the world**, and can leap the length of a car. It is shy, sharp-eyed, and quick to **dive out of sight**. The eggs and tadpoles of its early stages give no hint of its future size, since they are not much larger than those of any other frogs. Only after metamorphosis does it begin to grow and grow.

Javan horned frog

Megophrys montana

 6

- **Length** 2¾–5½ in (7–14 cm)
- **Habitat** Mostly terrestrial
- **Location** Southeast Asia

This forest floor frog does an amazing impression of a dead leaf. Its pointed snout, **hooded eyes**, and sharp folds in its skin add to the effect. The frog **stays still** and waits for its prey—insects and spiders— to pass by.

Carbine frog

Mixophyes carbinensis

 ?

- **Length** 2⅓–3 in (6–7.5 cm)
- **Habitat** Mostly terrestrial
- **Location** N.E. Australia

Carbine frogs live on the rainforest floor of northeast Australia, where they hunt small invertebrates and make burrows among the wet leaves. During the breeding season they make a deep "wonk" call to attract mates. The **tadpoles are twice the size of the adults** and take two years to change into frogs.

I think
I'm in love!
Frogs and toads gather in breeding ponds. Here they mate, the female lays eggs, and then they take off again. The survival rate is low. Out of 2,000 eggs, fewer than five frogs or toads will make it back to the same pond to breed there.

EUROPEAN COMMON TOADS *pair up in breeding ponds in spring. The female is much bigger than the male, especially at this time of year, when she is laden with eggs.*

Brown tree toad

Rentapia hosii

- ■ **Length** 2–4 in (5–10 cm)
- ■ **Habitat** Mostly on land
- ■ **Location** S.E. Asia

Unusually for a toad, this one is a **good climber**. It likes to "hang out" in the branches of trees over rivers. The female lays long strings of toad spawn in rivers and the **tadpoles have sucker-like mouths** to cling on to rocks.

Oriental fire-bellied toad

Bombina orientalis

- ■ **Length** 1¼–2 in (3–5 cm)
- ■ **Habitat** Mostly in water
- ■ **Location** East and Southeast Asia

This toad has a **bright orange belly** for a reason—when threatened it arches its back, flattens its body, and lifts its legs over its head to display the vivid colors—and hopefully scare off any predator. It **lives in mountain streams** near the coast, and hides under rocks and logs during winter.

Surinam toad

Pipa pipa

- ■ **Length** 2–8 in (5–20 cm)
- ■ **Habitat** Always in water
- ■ **Location** Northern South America

Pipa pipa has powerful hind legs to swim fast, and **feelers on its fingers** to help it find prey in muddy water. When the female lays her eggs, they are absorbed into the skin on her back, where they **develop in capsules** and emerge as mini toads.

Midwife toad

Alytes obstetricans

- ■ **Length** 1¼–2 in (3–5 cm)
- ■ **Habitat** Mostly on land
- ■ **Location** W. and C. Europe

This toad has a very **unusual way of breeding**. The female lays large, yolk-filled eggs in strings, which are transferred to the male during mating. The male then wraps these strings around his legs, and carries them around until they are ready to hatch. At which point, he pops them into a pool.

European common toad

Bufo bufo

- ■ **Length** 3¼–8 in (8–20 cm)
- ■ **Habitat** Mostly on land
- ■ **Location** Northwestern Africa and Europe to Central Asia

Bufo bufo is Europe's most widespread amphibian. Apart from during the breeding season, the toad spends its time on land, **hunting slugs and insects**. If threatened it stands on tiptoe, with rigid legs, and **takes gulps of air** to puff up its body. It is mainly nocturnal.

African clawed toad

Xenopus laevis

- ■ **Length** 2⅓–5 in (6–13 cm)
- ■ **Habitat** Mostly in water
- ■ **Location** Southern Africa

With **eyes on the top of its head** to spy food above, and long fingers to shovel small fish and insect larvae into its mouth, this toad is a **voracious underwater feeder**. Its skin colors make effective camouflage—good protection from hungry herons.

Marine toad

Also known as the cane toad, the world's largest toad has a hidden weapon. Its skin is highly toxic, and could be lethal to any animal that attacks it. If it is squeezed—or even threatened—a creamy white poison will ooze from glands on its shoulders and body. An animal that eats this toxin may die rather quickly.

▼ STAY BACK! *As well as using poison, the marine toad will raise itself up if threatened, to look far larger than it is. Most predators have learned to take extreme care with a marine toad.*

Be careful ...
I eat small snakes!

Marine toads do eat snakes,
but some snakes, such as the
toad-eater snake shown here, can eat
marine toads without being affected
by the toad's toxins. However, this toad
may be too big a mouthful for this
particular snake. Marine toads
are stocky, and find it easier
to walk on flat rather than
bumpy ground.

Marine toad
Rhinella marina

- **Length** 2–9 in (5–23 cm)
- **Weight** Up to 4½ lb (2 kg)
- **Habitat** Mostly terrestrial
- **Location** Central America, South America, introduced to Australia and elsewhere.

You can see white toxins seeping out of large **glands on the shoulder** of this marine toad. These toads tend to be active at night, choosing to hide during the day under leaves or stones, or burrowing down into loose soil.

CONSERVATION

The introduction of the marine, or cane, toad to Australia in 1935 is an example of the danger of bringing non-native species into an ecosystem. It is now a serious pest, and has successfully competed against native frogs and toads for space and food, and caused their numbers to decline.

NEW GENERATIONS

Marine toads lay a lot of eggs—it's estimated about 30,000 at a time. Though perhaps just a few of these make it to adulthood, it's partly why marine toads are so successful. The eggs hatch in three days, and the young grow rapidly.

▲ DIET *Marine toads will eat anything they can catch. Their diet consists largely of insects, but may include a variety of rodents, smaller frogs and toads, and snakes. If hungry, they will even eat their own young. They are common near houses, where they will eat dog food if it is left out.*

195

Poison dart frogs

These jewel-like frogs of the jungle are colorful for a reason—bright colors warn predators that they are highly toxic. In fact, the family name comes from the use by local tribes of the frogs' powerful poison to tip their blowgun darts when hunting.

FACT FILE

- There are 339 species of poison dart frog.
- Nearly all species are brightly colored.
- Most are small.
- They live in tropical rainforests of Central and South America.
- Males buzz and chirp to attract females.
- They have tiny suction cups on their toes that cling to slippery leaves and branches.
- They eat termites, ants, flies, crickets, and other insects, which they catch with quick flicks of their sticky tongues.

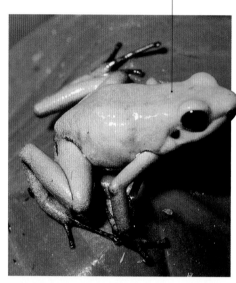

Glands in a poison dart frog's skin ooze poison.

▲ BREEDING AMONG THE TREES
The male takes care of the eggs in most poison dart frog species. He guards them and keeps them moist by collecting water. When the tadpoles are ready to hatch, he lets them wriggle onto his back and carries them to a suitable pool of water.

◄ THE MOST POISONOUS FROG
on Earth is the golden poison dart frog—with enough poison in its skin to kill 10 humans. This frog is thought to be the only animal that can kill a human by touch alone. It is one of the biggest poison dart frogs, at 2 in (5 cm) long.

BEAUTY WITH BITE
The spots, stripes, and brilliant colors may look pretty, but to predators, they mean only one thing: DON'T EAT THEM.

Dyeing poison dart frog
Dendrobates tinctorius

- **Length** 2 in (5 cm)
- **Habitat** Forest floor
- **Location** Northern South America

Only discovered in 1968, dyeing poison dart frogs are active during the day and can be found hiding among boulders and debris near streams. They **lack toe webbing** and are poor swimmers, so they are **never found in the water**.

Red-banded poison dart frog
Oophaga lehmanni

- **Length** 1¼ in (3 cm)
- **Habitat** Forest floor, low bushes
- **Location** Colombia

This frog is also known as Lehmann's poison frog. It is listed as **critically endangered** because it lives in just one area of rainforest that is less than 4 sq miles (10 sq km). Groups of frogs are spread around within this area with no contact between each group. This puts this little frog at even greater risk. Unfortunately, the quality and extent of their habitat are also in decline.

Harlequin poison dart frog
Oophaga histrionica

- **Length** 1–1½ in (2.5–4 cm)
- **Habitat** Forest floor
- **Location** Western Ecuador and Colombia

It is one of the **most poisonous** of these frogs, as well as one of the smallest. The poison that oozes from every bit of its body is collected from the **toxic bugs** it eats and then deposited in its skin.

Doris Swanson's poison dart frog
Andinobates dorisswansonae

- **Length** ⅔–⁷⁄₁₀ in (1.7–1.8 cm)
- **Habitat** Forest floor
- **Location** Colombia

This tiny frog lives in an area of forest that covers less than 0.2 sq miles (0.5 sq km), which means that it is extremely vulnerable to extinction. It **hides in bromeliad plants** and is thought to lay its eggs in the water that collects there. Two of its toes are fused together on each hind foot, giving it the appearance of having **only four toes**.

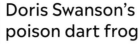

Strawberry poison dart frog
Oophaga pumilio

- **Length** ¾–1 in (2–2.5 cm)
- **Habitat** Forest floor
- **Location** Southern central America

This little frog is also small, but less poisonous than the harlequin poison dart frog. However, it would still give a predator a **nasty stomach ache**. Its **color can vary** from bright red, to brown, blue, or green, depending on where it lives. It is most commonly found in the humid rainforests of Panama.

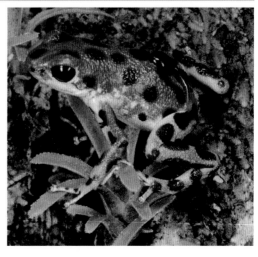

Green and black poison dart frog
Dendrobates auratus

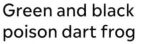

- **Length** 1–2⅓ in (2.5–6 cm)
- **Habitat** Forest floor
- **Location** Central and South America and Hawaii

These little frogs have one habit that is unusual among amphibians— it is the **female that takes the lead** in mating. She entices the male to mate by patting him on the back with her hind feet. People have introduced these frogs to Hawaii, where they have flourished. In highly populated areas, they sometimes **leave their eggs in broken bottles** or discarded cans.

Yellow-headed poison dart frog
Dendrobates leucomelas

- **Length** 1¼–2 in (3–5 cm)
- **Habitat** Forest floor, sometimes in trees
- **Location** Northern South America

The male of this species is **very territorial**. If another male of its kind happens into its territory, it will grasp it belly to belly, and make **a loud buzzing call** in its ear. That's why another name for this frog is the bumble bee frog.

Frogs and *toads*

Frogs and toads form the largest group of amphibians. There's actually no clear difference between them. They range in size from the tiny Brazilian flea frog to the enormous Goliath bullfrog, both shown here at their maximum life sizes.

Australian green tree frog
Litoria caerulea

Tomato frog
Dyscophus antongilii

American bullfrog
Lithobates catesbeianus

The goliath bullfrog can reach just over 15¾ in (40 cm) in length. The Brazilian flea frog is just under ⅜ in (1 cm).

BIGGEST FROG
Goliath bullfrog
Conraua goliath

Solomon Islands horned frog
Ceratobatrachus guentheri

Green mantella
Mantella viridis

SMALLEST FROG
Brazilian flea frog
Brachycephalus didactylus

Monte Iberia Eleuth frog
Eleutherodactylus iberia

Yellow-headed poison dart frog
Dendrobates leucomelas

Emerald glass frog
Espadarana prosoblepon

European tree frog
Hyla arborea

Golden poison dart frog
Phyllobates terribilis

Malabar flying frog
Rhacophorus malabaricus

Red-eyed tree frog
Agalychnis callidryas

Natterjack
Epidalea calamita

Mexican burrowing toad
Rhinophrynus dorsalis

Turtle frog
Myobatrachus gouldii

Javan horned frog
Megophrys montana

Surinam horned frog
Ceratophrys cornuta

Parsley frog
Pelodytes punctatus

Green toad
Pseudepidalea viridis

Surinam toad
Pipa pipa

Woodhouse's toad
Anaxyrus woodhousii

Red-spotted toad
Anaxyrus punctatus

Couch's spadefoot toad
Scaphiopus couchii

Marine toad
Rhinella marina

FISH

Definition: **Fish** are cold-blooded animals that live in water. Most fish have gills that absorb oxygen from the water, and the majority have fins and scales.

What is a FISH?

More than half of all vertebrates are fish. They first evolved on Earth at least 500 million years ago. All fish breathe using gills and are cold-blooded; most have a body covered with scales and move using fins. They live in fresh water or in the sea—and some live in both.

FACT FILE

There are more than 33,000 species of fish. They are broadly divided into three groups: jawless, cartilaginous, and bony fish.

- **Jawless fish** (hagfish and lampreys) are eel-like fish that lack scales and jaws.

- **Cartilaginous fish** (sharks, skates, and rays) have skeletons made of cartilage, not bone. They are covered with a skin with hard scales.

- **Bony fish** are the largest group. They have hard, bony skeletons.

- **Size:** Fish range from one tiny minnow that reaches just ¼ in (7 mm) in length to the whale shark, at up to 62 ft (19 m).

FINS

Fish use their fins, combined with body movements, to propel themselves through the water and steer in the right direction. Some fins come in pairs. These are the pectoral (behind the head) and pelvic (on the underside). Other fins are unpaired: the dorsal (top), caudal (tail), and anal (nearest the tail).

CAUDAL (OR TAIL) FIN *In most bony fish this provides the power that propels the fish forward.*

ANAL FIN *This fin acts as a stabilizer.*

PELVIC FINS *Paired pelvic fins add stability and may be used to slow the fish down.*

NEW LIFE

Most fish begin life as eggs. Some hatch as larvae and change by stages into the adult form, while others look like tiny adults when they hatch. Other species are born as live young.

A baby trout hatches from a fertilized egg.

Fish egg

EGG SAC *The eggs of the dogfish develop inside a leathery sac, or "purse." Long threads anchor the egg sac to rocks or seaweed.*

On the inside

The skeleton of a bony fish is made up of three main parts: the skull, the backbone and ribs, and the fins.

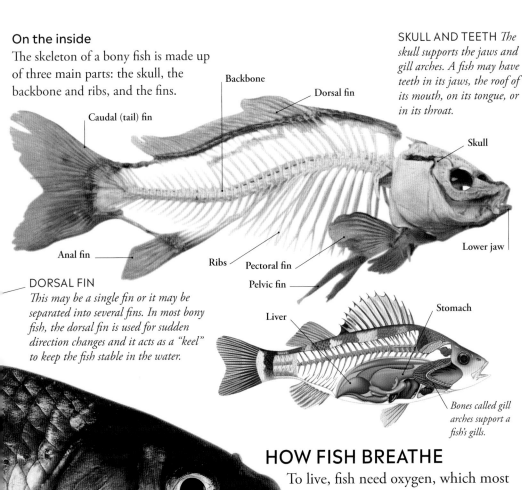

Caudal (tail) fin

Backbone

Dorsal fin

SKULL AND TEETH *The skull supports the jaws and gill arches. A fish may have teeth in its jaws, the roof of its mouth, on its tongue, or in its throat.*

Skull

Lower jaw

Anal fin

Ribs

Pectoral fin

Pelvic fin

Liver

Stomach

Bones called gill arches support a fish's gills.

DORSAL FIN
This may be a single fin or it may be separated into several fins. In most bony fish, the dorsal fin is used for sudden direction changes and it acts as a "keel" to keep the fish stable in the water.

HOW FISH BREATHE

To live, fish need oxygen, which most obtain from the water. A fish takes in water through its mouth and sends it out over its gills (feathery structures found along the sides of the head). As the water flows out of the fish's body, the surfaces of the gills extract the oxygen, which then passes into the bloodstream.

OPERCULUM *This bony flap covers the gills.*

PECTORAL FINS *A fish uses these fins on each side of its head to change direction. The pectoral fins can also be used for tasting, touching, support, and to give the swimming fish a power boost.*

Odd fish

Among the more unusual fish, there are those that appear to fly, others that have no jaws, and some that can "walk" out of water on their fins.

▼ **LAMPREYS** *have sucker pads instead of mouths. They latch onto prey with their teeth and either rasp off the flesh or suck blood.*

Lampreys are jawless fish.

▼ **MUDSKIPPERS** *can live out of water for long periods. They move over mudflats by using their pectoral fins to pull themselves along.*

▼ **FLYING FISH** *cannot fly, but their large, winglike pectoral fins allow them to glide briefly above the water's surface.*

Parental care

Some fish take an active part in caring for their young. Both parents may take care of the eggs and tend the new hatchlings when they emerge. Parental duties can include feeding the young, fanning water over them to supply oxygen, and chasing away predators.

▲ **YELLOWHEAD JAWFISH** *The males carry fertilized eggs in their mouths until they are ready to hatch.*

▶ **FATHERS**
Male seahorses are unusual in that they carry their young. Female seahorses put their eggs in a pouch on the male's abdomen where they are fertilized and begin to develop.

203

A *world* of sharks

There are more than 440 species of shark. They range from small pygmy sharks that are just a little bit longer than the width of this page to the whale shark, which can grow to the length of a truck! Most have a pointed nose and a triangular dorsal fin.

Shortfin mako shark
Isurus oxyrinchus

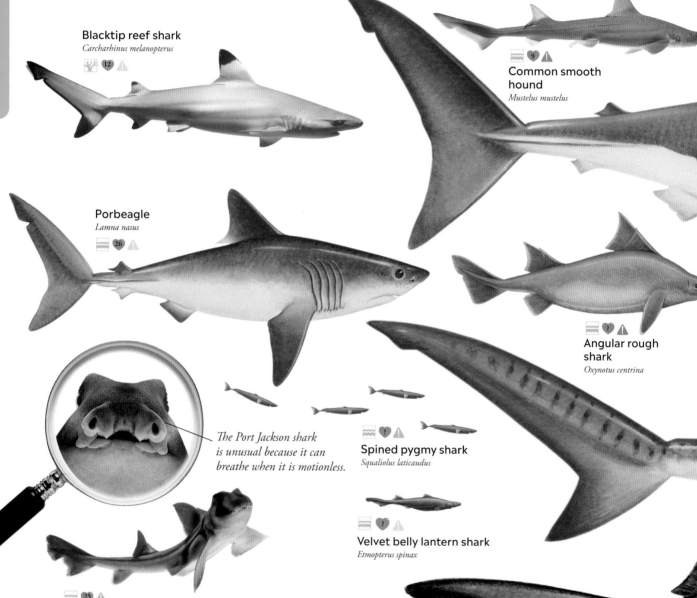

Blacktip reef shark
Carcharhinus melanopterus

Common smooth hound
Mustelus mustelus

Porbeagle
Lamna nasus

Angular rough shark
Oxynotus centrina

The Port Jackson shark is unusual because it can breathe when it is motionless.

Spined pygmy shark
Squaliolus laticaudus

Velvet belly lantern shark
Etmopterus spinax

Port Jackson shark
Heterodontus portusjacksoni

Nurse shark
Ginglymostoma cirratum

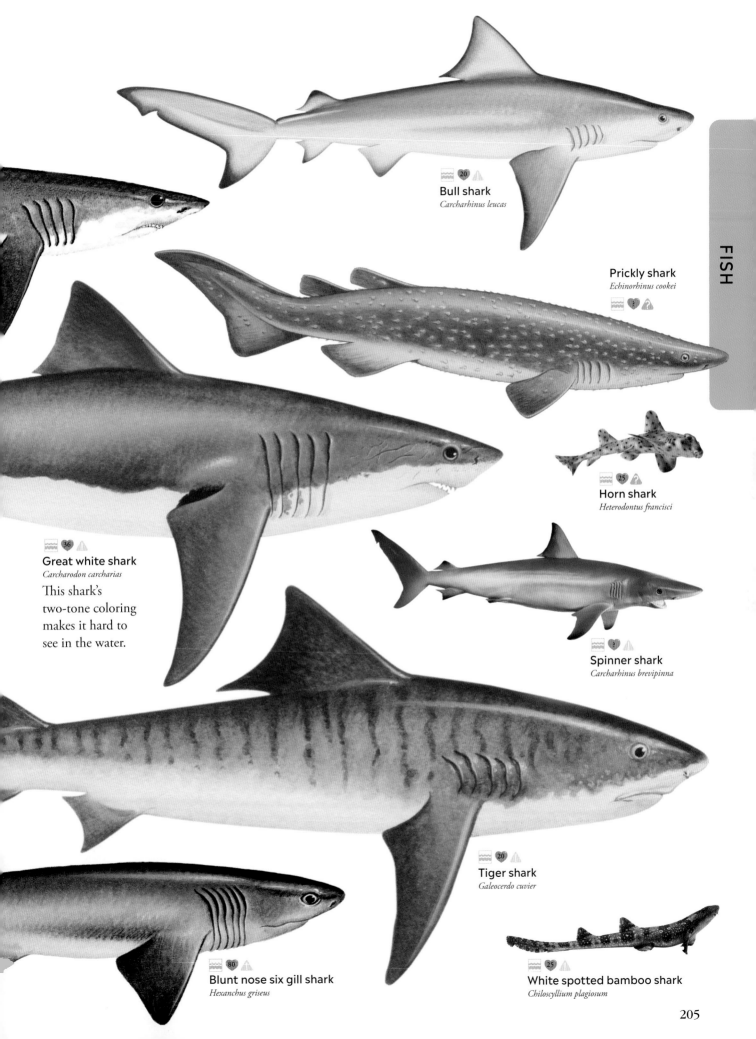

20 **Bull shark**
Carcharhinus leucas

Prickly shark
Echinorhinus cookei

25 **Horn shark**
Heterodontus francisci

36 **Great white shark**
Carcharodon carcharias
This shark's two-tone coloring makes it hard to see in the water.

Spinner shark
Carcharhinus brevipinna

20 **Tiger shark**
Galeocerdo cuvier

80 **Blunt nose six gill shark**
Hexanchus griseus

25 **White spotted bamboo shark**
Chiloscyllium plagiosum

Great hammerhead shark

Sphyrna mokarran

- **Length** 11½–19½ ft (350–600 cm)
- **Weight** 507–992 lb (230–450 kg)
- **Diet** Small sharks, rays, bony fishes, and squid
- **Location** Worldwide (warm temperate and tropical waters)

This is the **largest of nine species** of hammerhead. They live in warm coastal waters. Females produce 20–40 pups that are 28 in (70 cm) in length.

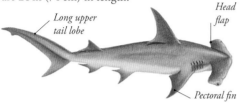

Long upper tail lobe

Head flap

Pectoral fin

KEY FEATURES

Great hammerhead sharks have a wide head with an eye at both ends. The head moves in a constant sweeping motion so the shark can see in every direction. Other characteristics are a first dorsal fin that is large and pointed, and teeth that are triangular with serrated edges.

▼ PREY *Hammerhead sharks are sometimes cannibalistic, but generally they live on a diet of fish, including rays. They eat other sharks, octopuses, squid, and crustaceans. Their favorite meal is stingray, which they pin down using their hammer-shaped head. They look fierce, but there have been few attacks on people.*

Hammerhead sharks use their sensory organs to detect the electrical fields of their prey.

Electrical field

Stingray hiding under the sand

The *big-headed* hammerhead

Hammerhead sharks stick together, and there can be up to 100 in a school. They are formidable hunters and have more sensory organs in their head than typical sharks. These organs pick up electrical signals in the water from potential prey, allowing the hammerhead to hunt effectively.

Killer sharks?

Most people think of sharks as sleek, fast-moving killers equipped with banks of viciously pointed teeth. Some sharks do live up to this description. But there are many other types, from sluggish, toothless giants to glow-in-the-dark fish not much bigger than a person's hand.

Leopard shark

Triakis semifasciata

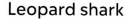

- **Length** 6½ ft (2 m)
- **Weight** 22–39 lb (10–18 kg)
- **Diet** Crustaceans, worms, and fish
- **Location** Eastern North Pacific coast

Sensory organs in the leopard shark's nose allow it to find and pull out prey buried in deep mud. The shark's **striking body pattern** makes it popular with anglers.

Spined pygmy shark

Squaliolus laticaudus

- **Length** 10 in (25 cm)
- **Weight** Not recorded
- **Diet** Squid, shrimp, and small fish
- **Location** Atlantic, western Indian Ocean, and the western Pacific

This deep-water species is **one of the smallest sharks** in the world. Unusually for a shark, it has a dorsal spine. Light-emitting organs in its belly glow in the dark. This may conceal its silhouette from predators swimming below.

Whitetip reef shark

Triaenodon obesus

- **Length** 5–7 ft (1.6–2 m)
- **Weight** 40 lb (18 kg) and more
- **Diet** Fish, octopuses, and crustaceans
- **Location** Tropical Pacific and Indian oceans

Whitetip reef sharks **feed around coral heads**, where divers often meet them. These sharks are not usually aggressive toward people, although they have been known to grab fish from a diver's spear.

◀ SEA FLOOR
These sharks rest on the sea floor or in underwater caves.

Whale shark

Rhincodon typus

- **Length** 39–62¼ ft (12–19 m)
- **Weight** 26,500 lb (12,000 kg) and more
- **Diet** Plankton and fish eggs
- **Location** Warm seas worldwide

This is the **biggest fish in the world**. Despite its name, the whale shark is not related to whales. With a mouth that may be up to 4½ ft (1.4 m) wide, this shark looks dangerous but, in fact, it is quite harmless. Slow-moving and mostly solitary, whale sharks are usually seen cruising near the surface of the ocean. They feed largely by sucking water into their mouths to trap plankton—floating mats of tiny crustaceans and plants. Whale sharks give birth to live young, and pregnant females have been found carrying hundreds of developing young.

▼ DEEP DIVER *Whale sharks are capable of diving more than 3,300 ft (1,000 m). They plunge to such depths in search of eggs released by spawning fish.*

Great white shark

Carcharodon carcharias

- **Length** 20–26 ft (6–8 m)
- **Weight** 4,410 lb (2,000 kg) and more
- **Diet** Seals, dolphins, and large fish
- **Location** Warm seas worldwide

The great white shark is one of the most feared creatures of the sea. There are many stories of its attacks on humans, although the shark's reputation as a human killer has been exaggerated. However, the great white's muscular, streamlined body makes it a swift and deadly predator. With rows of sharp, pointed teeth designed for **ripping and tearing**, the shark can take the head off prey such as a seal with one bite. Great white sharks live and hunt alone, but they sometimes gather together to share a kill. When feeding in groups, the sharks usually show no aggression toward each other.

Atlantic angel shark

Squatina dumeril

- **Length** 5 ft (1.5 m)
- **Weight** 60 lb (27 kg) and more
- **Diet** Small fish and mollusks
- **Location** North Atlantic

Also known as the sand devil or monkfish, this fish is one of several species of angel sharks. It **lives mostly on the sea floor**, keeping its flat body partly concealed in the sand. When the shark spots its prey, it bursts out of its hiding place to make a sudden grab that takes the victim by surprise. A potential meal rarely escapes!

▲ TASTY SHARK
The Atlantic angel shark is fished for its succulent flesh.

Thresher shark

Alopias vulpinus

- **Length** 18 ft (5.5 m)
- **Weight** 992 lb (450 kg) and more
- **Diet** Shoaling fish, such as herring and mackerel, and squid
- **Location** Warm seas worldwide

Using its immensely long tail like a whip, the thresher shark rounds up its fish prey into tight schools. The shark then often **stuns or kills its victims** with blows from its tail. Thresher sharks are strong swimmers and are occasionally seen leaping right out of the water.

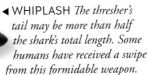

Basking shark

Cetorhinus maximus

- **Length** 33–49 ft (10–15 m)
- **Weight** 13,228 lb (6,000 kg)
- **Diet** Plankton
- **Location** Cool to warm seas worldwide

This giant shark is second in size to the whale shark. It feeds simply by swimming along with its **vast mouth gaping wide**. As the water rushes in, and then out again through the fish's gills, sieve-like projections filter out minute food particles. The basking shark takes its name from its habit of lolling in the sun's light at the surface of the water.

◀ WHIPLASH *The thresher's tail may be more than half the shark's total length. Some humans have received a swipe from this formidable weapon.*

Skates and rays

These fish appear to fly through the water, the larger ones using their fins almost as wings. They have a flattened shape, and some live on the seabed while others swim in open water. Some are able to stun unsuspecting fish with an electrical charge!

Marbled electric ray

Torpedo marmorata

- **Length** 39 in (1 m)
- **Weight** 6⅗ lb (3 kg)
- **Depth** 33–328 ft (10–100 m)
- **Location** Eastern Atlantic and Mediterranean

This ray creates **electric shocks** powerful enough to stun or kill other fish and contact with it can be dangerous for humans, but there are no reports of people actually dying after suffering a shock from it. There are stories that suggest the ancient Greeks may have used them to stun patients before surgery. It is nocturnal, and buries itself in the seabed during daylight hours.

Long-nosed skate

Dipturus oxyrinchus

- **Length** 5 ft (1.5 m)
- **Weight** 37 lb (17 kg)
- **Depth** 50–2,950 ft (15–900 m)
- **Location** Eastern Atlantic, Mediterranean, and Canary and Madeira islands

The long-nosed skate is distinguished by its narrow, sharp nose, while its tail is armed with **three rows of spines**. It tends to rest on the seabed, almost buried but with its eyes just visible. Long-nosed skates are under threat, partly because they develop slowly: they take eleven years to mature to an age at which they can breed.

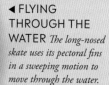

◄ FLYING THROUGH THE WATER *The long-nosed skate uses its pectoral fins in a sweeping motion to move through the water.*

Common stingray

Dasyatis pastinaca

- **Length** 4½ ft (1.4 m)
- **Weight** 66 lb (30 kg)
- **Depth** 16–656 ft (5–200 m)
- **Location** Northeast Atlantic and Mediterranean seas

Common stingrays have **barbed spines full of venom** that can be up to 14 in (35 cm) long. The spines may break off when the common stingray attacks; however, these can grow back. These fish are caught and eaten, while oil is sometimes extracted from their wings.

▼ *Common stingrays are not aggressive—they prefer to flee rather than stay and confront their attacker.*

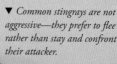 

The flying filter feeders

Manta rays use the **large lobes** on either side of their heads to *funnel* prey into their mouths. Water and prey goes into the mouth, but the water is *filtered* out through the gills while the prey is digested. Mantas prey on small fish as well as sifting plankton from sea water.

Manta ray

Manta birostris

- **Width** 29½ ft (9 m)
- **Weight** 5,070 lb (2,300 kg)
- **Depth** 0–394 ft (0–120 m)
- **Location** Surface tropical waters worldwide, and sometimes warm temperate areas.

This ray is **the biggest in the world**. It is also known as the devil ray, but because of its appearance not because it is aggressive: it ignores divers. Despite its size, this ray can leap out of the water, occasionally giving birth to its young while doing so.

Undulate ray

Raja undulata

- **Length** 4 ft (1.2 m)
- **Weight** 15 lb (7 kg)
- **Depth** 148–656 ft (45–200 m)
- **Location** Eastern Atlantic and Mediterranean

▶ LAYING EGGS *Females are known to lay up to 15 eggs in muddy or sandy flats.*

The undulate ray is also known as **the painted ray** because of its detailed markings. In fact, it is a popular fish for large aquariums because of its markings. The undulate ray feeds on crabs, flatfish, and other seabed invertebrates.

◀ *Seen from below, an undulate ray looks completely different.*

Blonde ray

Raja brachyura

- **Length** 49 in (1.25 m)
- **Weight** 31½ lb (14.3 kg)
- **Depth** 33–1,247 ft (10–380 m)
- **Location** Eastern Atlantic

If you felt the back of this fish and it was smooth, you'd know that it was a young blonde ray, because the **adults develop prickles**. The young hatch from rectangular, horned egg cases in the summer months. Blonde rays have large eyes and a short snout. The outer angles of their wings are almost right angles.

◀ WHERE ARE YOU?
The underside of a blonde ray is white, but the top is covered in small brown spots and larger creamy spots. This camouflages it well against stones on the sea floor.

Thornback ray

Raja clavata

- **Length** 41–47 in (105–120 cm)
- **Weight** 39½ lb (18 kg)
- **Depth** 66–1,890 ft (20–577 m)
- **Location** N.E. Atlantic, North Sea, Mediterranean, and the Black Sea

The thornback ray feeds on crustaceans such as shrimp and crabs. It also eats small fish such as herring, sand eels, and flatfish. The thornback (as its name suggests) has **thorns on its back and tail.** Females are longer than males.

▼ EGGS IN WAITING
Females lay their eggs in the summer, which then hatch during the winter.

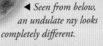

Bony fish

Bony fish are the largest and most varied group of fish; 9 out of 10 species of fish are bony fish. Some live in salty oceans and seas, some live in fresh water, while a few can survive in both habitats. However, they all share one thing in common: they have a light but strong internal bony skeleton.

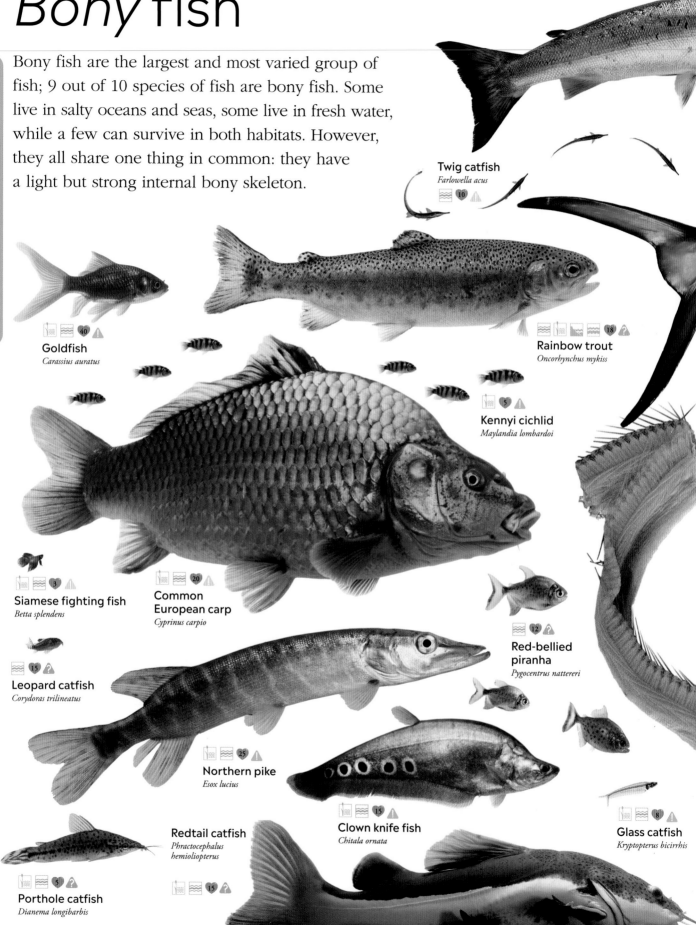

Twig catfish
Farlowella acus

Goldfish
Carassius auratus

Rainbow trout
Oncorhynchus mykiss

Kennyi cichlid
Maylandia lombardoi

Siamese fighting fish
Betta splendens

Common European carp
Cyprinus carpio

Red-bellied piranha
Pygocentrus nattereri

Leopard catfish
Corydoras trilineatus

Northern pike
Esox lucius

Clown knife fish
Chitala ornata

Glass catfish
Kryptopterus bicirrhis

Redtail catfish
Phractocephalus hemioliopterus

Porthole catfish
Dianema longibarbis

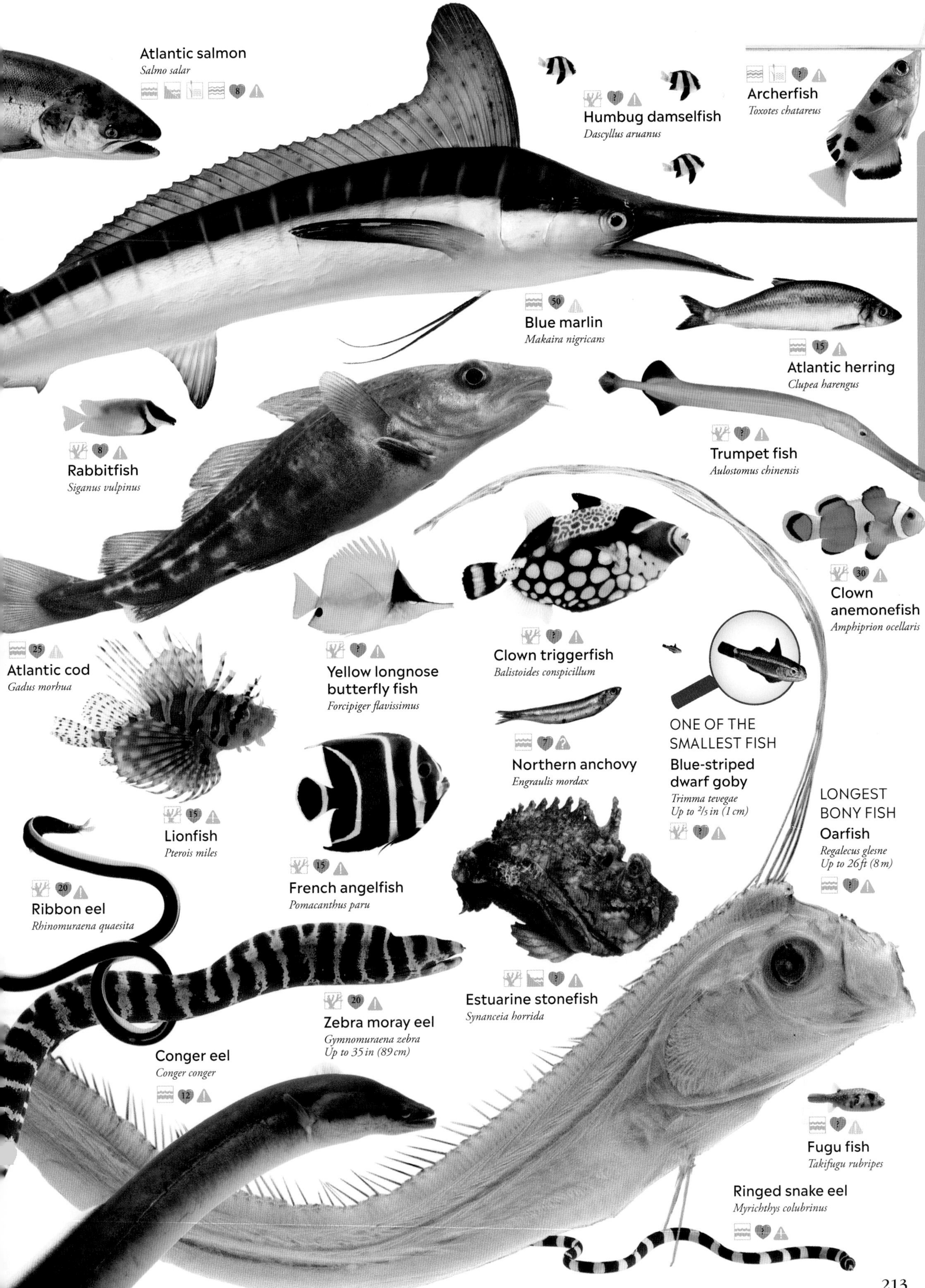

Atlantic salmon
Salmo salar

Humbug damselfish
Dascyllus aruanus

Archerfish
Toxotes chatareus

Blue marlin
Makaira nigricans

Atlantic herring
Clupea harengus

Rabbitfish
Siganus vulpinus

Trumpet fish
Aulostomus chinensis

Clown anemonefish
Amphiprion ocellaris

Atlantic cod
Gadus morhua

Yellow longnose butterfly fish
Forcipiger flavissimus

Clown triggerfish
Balistoides conspicillum

ONE OF THE SMALLEST FISH
Blue-striped dwarf goby
Trimma tevegae
Up to ²/₅ in (1 cm)

Northern anchovy
Engraulis mordax

LONGEST BONY FISH
Oarfish
Regalecus glesne
Up to 26 ft (8 m)

Lionfish
Pterois miles

French angelfish
Pomacanthus paru

Ribbon eel
Rhinomuraena quaesita

Estuarine stonefish
Synanceia horrida

Zebra moray eel
Gymnomuraena zebra
Up to 35 in (89 cm)

Conger eel
Conger conger

Fugu fish
Takifugu rubripes

Ringed snake eel
Myrichthys colubrinus

213

Schools

There is safety in numbers for fish who swim in schools. They are able to confuse attackers, as the size of the school can be bigger than the attacker itself. It is harder for a predator to isolate and catch a single fish among a fast-moving group. Fish in a school have an advantage over the fish who are after them because they have more pairs of eyes on the lookout!

BAIT BALL

Copper sharks, or bronze whalers, swallow mouthfuls of sardines as they push their way through a bait ball, showering blood and fish scales around them. Bait balls are collections of fish that by instinct swim tightly together when faced with a larger predator.

SCHOOL OR SHOAL?

Schooling fish swim close together in a synchronized fashion whereas a shoal is a looser collection of fish that swim in a group. Shoals can be made up of mixed groups of fish. Fish benefit from living in a shoal because they can search for food together, defend themselves from attacks, and have more chance of finding a mate.

▶ DIVING FOR DINNER *Cape gannets dive into a bait ball of sardines. They are plunge divers and will slam into shoals of fish from heights of up to 99 ft (30 m).*

▲ PROTECTION FOR PREDATORS
Fish who are predators also need to have protection from their attackers. Young barracudas live in shoals during the day to help each other keep safe and to look for food. However, most adult barracudas hunt alone.

HOW DO THEY WORK?

■ Fish use vision and sensory systems to help them respond to slight movements around them. This ability allows them to swim in schools and shoals.

■ The "oddity effect" is a theory that if a fish stands out in a shoal it is more likely to be noticed by predators. So fish join shoals of fish that are similar to themselves.

■ Shoaling fish use various tactics when being attacked. They disperse into all directions, they flee away and then come back and swim past both sides of the attacker, or they split into smaller groups.

Fishing for food

Some fish are accomplished at fishing for food. Heavy disguise helps them hide from predators, and also hide from prey. Equipped with a whiplike rod on their head that often has a lure at the end that looks deceptively like a small marine organism, they sit and wait for their prey to fall for the bait.

Angler

Lophius piscatorius

- **Length** 6½ ft (2 m)
- **Weight** 128 lb (58 kg)
- **Location** Eastern North Atlantic, Mediterranean, and the Black Sea

The angler is called by a few other names: sea devil, fishing-frog, or frogfish. It is also known as the monkfish when it is sold as a fish to eat. The angler is able to camouflage itself on the seabed, helped by its broad, flattened body. It sits and waits for a small fish to swim by and then opens its mouth and **sucks in its prey**. It has a large head and a wide jaw containing sharp teeth that slant inward so it can stop prey from trying to escape from its mouth.

▲ HIDDEN AWAY *It is difficult to see the angler on the seabed because its marbled skin and flaps blend in so well with the sediment.*

◀ SUPERB SHUFFLER *The angler has strong pectoral and pelvic fins that it uses to shuffle itself over the seabed. It looks as if it is walking!*

Smooth anglerfish

Phyllophryne scortea

- **Length** 4 in (10 cm)
- **Weight** Not recorded
- **Location** South Australia and Southern Ocean

Like the angler, the smooth anglerfish also goes by the name of the frogfish. It is part of the large anglerfish family. The smooth anglerfish is a **small fish with a large head**. It differs from other anglerfishes in that it has three extended dorsal fin spines on its head. It uses the first dorsal spine like a fishing rod to attract other smaller fish, which it then sucks into its mouth.

Psychedelic anglerfish

Histiophryne psychedelica

- **Length** 2½–3½ in (6.5–9 cm)
- **Weight** Not recorded
- **Location** Southeast Asia

This anglerfish gets its name from the **swirling pattern of white stripes** on its body. These stripes are different on every fish and can be used to identify individuals. Unlike other anglerfishes it has a broad, flat, frilly face with forward-facing eyes. Its body skin is thick and loose and hangs in folds over its pectoral fins. As well as walking along the sea floor, it swims by pushing water out of its gills to jet itself forward.

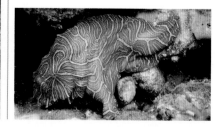

Warty frogfish
Antennarius maculatus

- **Length** 6 in (15 cm)
- **Weight** Not recorded
- **Location** Western Pacific and Indian oceans

The warty frogfish is another member of the anglerfish family. Many anglerfish live in the deep sea, but the warty frogfish lives in shallow waters—mainly in coral reefs. This fish is adorned with various patches and spots on its body. It eats other small fish and **occasionally it eats other warty frogfish**. A flap of colored skin at the end of the long spine on its dorsal fin acts like bait on a fishing rod—it wiggles it to attract prey.

Sargassum fish
Histrio histrio

- **Length** 8 in (20 cm)
- **Weight** 14 oz (400 g)
- **Location** Tropical and subtropical seas worldwide

This fish's Latin name means "the actor" because it blends in so well with the sargassum weeds in which it lives. The sargassum fish feeds by lying in wait for its prey, and it is a hungry fish. It has been known to **swallow a fish as large as itself**, while adults are cannibalistic, which means they will eat each other. Sargassum fish are unusual in their courtship behavior. Males pursue females by chasing them and nipping at them.

It uses its dorsal fin spine as a fishing rod and lure.

▲ DINNER
The sargassum fish lives on a diet of other fish, small squid, and crustaceans.

Estuarine stonefish
Synanceia horrida

- **Length** 24 in (60 cm)
- **Weight** Not recorded
- **Location** Indo-Pacific

As its name suggests, the estuarine stonefish is able to hide on the gravelly seabed without being seen by its prey. It is the **most venomous fish** in the world.

HIDE AND WAIT

The estuarine stonefish does not have any scales on its body. Its color and shape provide brilliant camouflage. It uses its pectoral fins to make a shallow hole on the sea floor. It then piles up sand and mud around itself that adds to the illusion. Its head and eyes remain outside of the sand so it can see its prey. The estuarine stonefish is a slow swimmer so it relies on catching fish that swim near its hideout.

◄ VENOMOUS SPINES *The estuarine stonefish has 13 dorsal spines that have sharp tips and glands full of venom. Stepping on one of the sharp spines can be fatal for a human.*

SHARP SPINES

Can you see me?

Giant grouper

One of the largest of all the grouper fish, the giant grouper swims close to the bottom of the ocean in warm, shallow waters. It usually swims by itself and likes to stay in the same area, around coral reefs. It also swims in caves and near shipwrecks.

Don't come too close!
As its name suggests, the giant grouper is known for its size. It is the largest bony fish to live in coral reefs. The young are preyed upon by other fish, but adults are only at risk from humans.

Giant grouper

Epinephelus lanceolatus

- **Length** 9 ft (2.7 m)
- **Weight** 882 lb (400 kg)
- **Location** Indian Ocean and W. and C. Pacific

The giant grouper is a fish of many names. It is known as the brown spotted cod, brindle bass, bumblebee grouper, and, in Australia, as the Queensland grouper. Its **color changes** as it gets older. Young fish have irregular black and yellow markings. Adults are darker.

Tail fin   *Heavy body*

FISHY FOOD

The giant grouper eats a range of food, including small sharks, fish, rays, and small sea turtles. Its main diet consists of crustaceans, such as spiny lobsters, and it occasionally eats crabs. As giant groupers are so big, they require plenty of food in order to survive.

▲ DIVERS *can usually approach the giant grouper without harm, but there are reports of fatalities.*

CONSERVATION

Giant groupers are being wiped out because cyanide and explosives are used to fish on reefs. Their size and sluggish behavior also makes them easy to hunt by spearfishing. Moves have been made to protect them in some areas, but some giant grouper species are struggling to survive.

Deep-sea fish

Down in the depths of the oceans it is extremely cold, and food and oxygen are scarce. It is also dark. Yet fish manage to survive here, having evolved to live in the harsh conditions. There is still a lot to learn about these deep-sea fish, because equipment to reach the deep sea is expensive. There's another problem, too: deep-sea fish often die when taken out of their natural environment to be studied.

Hey! What are you looking at!
Some deep-sea fish have large eyes that make the most of what little light there is. Other fish have small eyes, but they can also detect vibrations and have an excellent sense of smell.

▼ POPULAR FOOD *Lantern fish are an important source of food for many animals including tuna, sharks, whales, dolphins, grenadiers, sea birds, penguins, and large squid.*

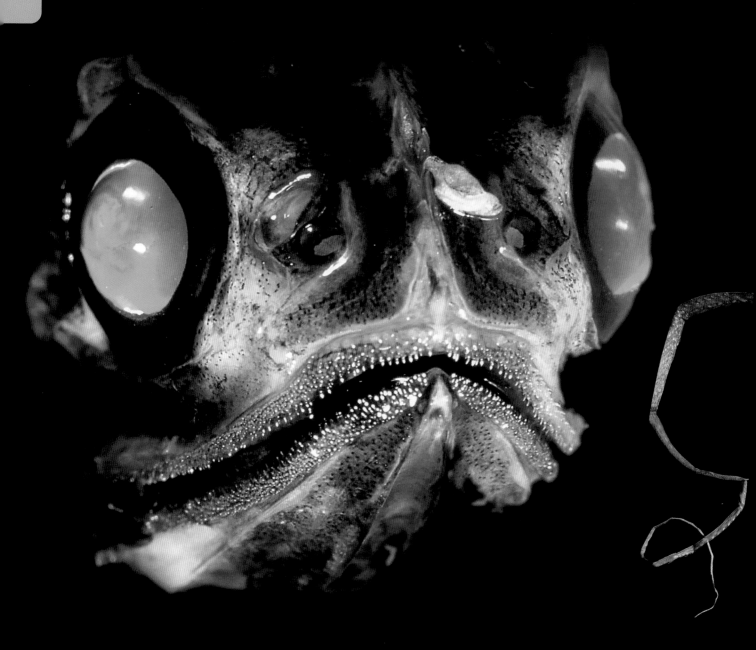

Metallic lantern fish

Myctophum affine

- **Length** 3 in (8 cm)
- **Weight** Not recorded
- **Depth** 0–1,970 ft (600 m)
- **Location** E. and W. Atlantic

Metallic lantern fish have **thin, silvery scales**. They have good vision because of their large eyes; these help them detect changes in light. Metallic lantern fish have photophores that look like small, bright studs on their flanks, undersides, and heads. These bright studs let out light in shades of green, yellow, or blue. Photophores help groups of fish see each other in darkly lit waters, enabling them to recognize each other and stay together.

Atlantic football fish

Himantolophus groenlandicus

- **Length of a female** 2 ft (60 cm)
- **Length of a male** 1½ in (4 cm)
- **Depth** 3,280 ft (1,000 m)
- **Location** Atlantic, Indian, and Pacific oceans

Female football fish are much bigger than males and have larger mouths. They are **poor swimmers** that lie in wait for their prey.

▶ LUMINOUS TAIL *The tail of a pelican eel is luminous to attract prey. It moves its tail like a whip to propel itself forward in the water.*

Sloane's viperfish

Chauliodus sloani

- **Length** 8–14 in (20–35 cm)
- **Weight** 1 oz (30 g)
- **Depth** 1,550–9,190 ft (473–2,800 m)
- **Location** Tropical, subtropical, and temperate waters worldwide

Sloane's viperfish is one of nine species of viperfish living in Earth's oceans. They swim up to depths of less than 1,970 ft (600 m) during the night because prey is more plentiful in shallower waters. This fish has fearsome **fangs that are transparent!** The largest fangs won't fit in the mouth, so they protrude when the jaws close.

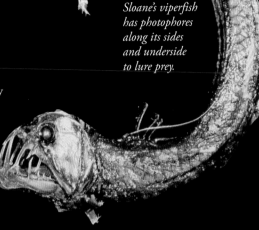

◀ LURING LIGHTS
Sloane's viperfish has photophores along its sides and underside to lure prey.

Lowcrest hatchetfish

Argyropelecus sladeni

- **Length** 3 in (7 cm)
- **Weight** Up to ½ oz (13.2 g)
- **Depth** 0–9,600 ft (2,926 m)
- **Location** Atlantic, Indian, and Pacific oceans

The lowcrest hatchetfish gets its name because its body is shaped like the blade of an ax. It can be found at great depths during the day, but at night it swims to shallower waters to feed. Hatchetfish use light as a form of **protective camouflage**—the photophores on their belly shine downward to mimic light coming from above.

Pelican eel

Eurypharynx pelecanoides

- **Length** 24–39 in (61–100 cm)
- **Weight** 2 lb (1 kg)
- **Depth** 1,640–25,000 ft (500–7,625 m)
- **Location** Tropical and subtropical waters worldwide

The pelican eel is also called the umbrella mouth gulper eel and is rarely seen by humans. Its **enormous mouth** is much wider than its body. Its stomach can expand so it can feed on fish much larger than itself.

Frilled shark

Chlamydoselachus anguineus

- **Length** 7 ft (2 m)
- **Weight** Not recorded
- **Depth** 164–4,921 ft (50–1,500 m)
- **Location** Worldwide

The frilled shark has an **eel-like body** and looks quite different from typical sharks. This species reproduces infrequently. It can take up to two years after fertilization for the female frilled shark to give birth.

Yellow goosefish

Lophius litulon

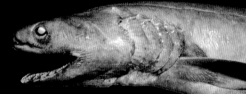

- **Length** 59 in (150 cm)
- **Weight** Up to 7⅗ lb (3.5 kg)
- **Depth** 82–1,837 ft (25–560 m)
- **Location** Northwest Pacific: Japan, Korea, and the Yellow and East China seas

The yellow goosefish is fished for food; its liver is considered a delicacy in Japan while elsewhere it is sold as "monkfish." It is also used in Chinese medicine. **Females are larger than males.**

Spawning salmon

The life cycle of the sockeye salmon shown here is anadromous. This means that it is born in fresh water, then migrates to the ocean, before returning to fresh water to breed (which is also called spawning). On spawning, the sockeye salmon turns a dramatic bright red.

ON A MISSION

From birth to the point at which they return to spawn, some four years later, these sockeye salmon may have traveled up to 930 miles (1,500 km). At the end of its amazing journey, each female will lay more than 4,000 eggs.

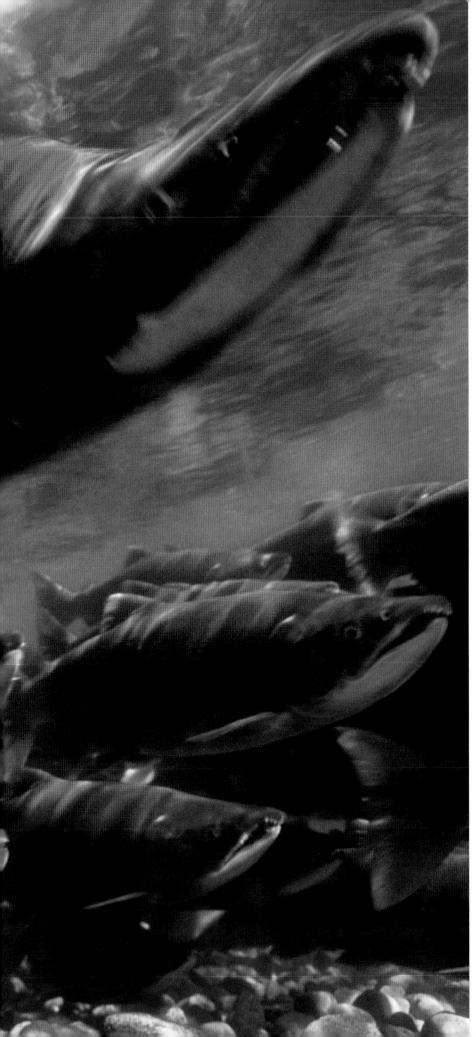

Atlantic salmon

Salmo salar

- **Length** 5 ft (1.5 m)
- **Weight** 103 lb (46.8 kg)
- **Status** Locally common
- **Location** Northeast North America, west and north Europe, and North Atlantic

Atlantic salmon are farmed as a source of food. They are **strong swimmers with powerful tails** that give them the ability to leap up waterfalls and weirs on their way back up the fresh water streams where they spawn. Most salmon die after spawning, but the Atlantic salmon sometimes survive and head back to the ocean.

AN OBSTACLE COURSE

Salmon have well-developed swimming muscles that are useful on their long journey from river to ocean and back. However, even their swimming skills can't save them from fishing nets. Salmon is a popular choice of food for people.

▶ BEAR ATTACK
Humans are not alone in enjoying a meal of salmon. Bears catch salmon when they return to fresh water rivers in the spawning season.

INVERTEBRATES

Definition: **Invertebrates** are animals without a backbone. They include insects, mollusks (such as snails and shellfish), sponges, jellyfish, and worms.

What is an INVERTEBRATE?

Invertebrates are animals that have neither a backbone nor a bony internal skeleton. This group makes up more than 95 percent of the animal kingdom. It is incredibly varied. Some invertebrates are little known, such as the microscopic rotifers. Others are more familiar. Snails and spiders, fleas and flatworms, centipedes and corals: these are all invertebrates. There are simple invertebrates, such as sponges, that have no brain or internal organs. And there are complex ones, such as the highly intelligent octopus.

◄ ARTHROPODA—INSECTS, ARACHNIDS, CRUSTACEANS (1,000,000 NAMED SPECIES) *Arthropods, as these animals are known, have a hard outer covering called an exoskeleton, which is divided into sections. Examples of an exoskeleton are the shell of a crab and the casing of a beetle. Arthropods also have jointed limbs, which are arranged in pairs.*

◄ MOLLUSCA—SQUID, SNAILS, BIVALVES (85,000 SPECIES). *Most mollusks live inside a hardened shell of some sort. This may be a single shell, like that of a snail, or in two halves joined by a hinge, like that of a clam or a mussel. However, mollusks also include animals, such as the octopus and the cuttlefish, which have either no shell or an internal one.*

◄ CNIDARIA—JELLYFISH, CORALS, HYDRAS (11,000 SPECIES). *This group contains various aquatic animals, including jellyfish, sea anemones, and corals. Cnidarians, as they are called, all possess tentacles that bear stinging cells. Some cnidarians can swim, others are attached to the seabed.*

◄ ANNELIDA—EARTHWORMS, LEECHES, POLYCHAETES (22,000 SPECIES). *These are called annelid worms and they all have bodies that are divided into segments. The common earthworm belongs to this group. Some polychaetes are also known as bristle worms. There are aquatic and land-dwelling annelids.*

◄ PORIFERA—SPONGES (9,000 SPECIES). *Sponges may seem like plants but they are not. They are the simplest of all living animals. Their bodies are basically a tube of fibers. Sponges live attached to rocks on the seabed. Water currents carry food into their bodies.*

► ECHINODERMATA—STARFISH, SEA URCHINS, SEA CUCUMBERS (7,000 SPECIES). *The common name of this group of marine animals is echinoderms. A key feature of many of them is an extremely prickly body. Nearly all echinoderms live on the seabed and most of them can move around to feed.*

FACT FILE

An estimated five million species of invertebrates exist today. This could double as we learn more about the habitats of invertebrates.

- **Nematodes**, or roundworms, are possibly the most numerous creatures on Earth. Some are so tiny that as many as 90,000 can be counted on one rotting apple.

- **Invertebrates** sometimes gather together in huge numbers. One of the biggest locust swarms on record contained 72,000,000,000 insects and covered 463 sq miles (1,200 sq km).

- **Octopuses** have shown that they are brainy. A female octopus in a German zoo watched keepers unscrewing the lids of jars of shrimp—and learned how to do it herself.

▲ IT TAKES TWO *butterflies to produce fertilized eggs. Nearly all insects start off as eggs, then pass through various stages, such as caterpillar and pupa, before becoming adult.*

Invertebrates from the past

One of the first animal groups to appear on Earth were the sponges, some 600 million years ago. Fossils of soft-bodied invertebrates, such as jellyfish, are rare. However, fossils of trilobites, crustacean-like arthropods, are abundant. Trilobites (above) survived for 300 million years, becoming extinct about 250 million years ago. Other fossil finds include giant griffinflies with 30 in (75 cm) wingspans, water scorpions 6½ ft (2 m) long, and giant marine mollusks with shells 30 ft (9 m) long.

Living on others

Among the invertebrates are most of the world's parasites. These are animals that live on the outside or the inside of other animals, including humans. Many, though not all, are harmful. Common parasites include worms of various kinds that live in their host's intestines. Pests such as warble flies (above) lay eggs in the hair of mammals such as horses and cattle. When the grubs hatch, they burrow into the skin, causing sores. Some insects lay their eggs on other insects, and the emerging grubs eat their host.

CREATING NEW LIFE

Invertebrates reproduce in various ways. Not all of them need to find a mate. Sponges and starfish can create new individuals from bits of their own bodies. The red tree sponge, for instance, breaks away a part of its body that then floats away and settles to grow elsewhere. Many insects lay unfertilized eggs that hatch and develop into replicas of their parent. Stick insects, water fleas, and aphids all reproduce like this.

▼ SINGLE PARENTS *such as aphids can produce young from unfertilized eggs. This is a quick way of building up numbers.*

Sponges

Sponges live at the bottom of virtually all seas. Although they grow rooted to the spot like plants, sponges are in fact simple animals. They were once among the most abundant forms of life in the oceans, and their skeletons formed vast reefs. These days they must jostle for space on the seabed with corals and other marine organisms.

SHAPES AND SIZES

The 9,000 different types of sponge come in a range of shapes and sizes. The smallest are simple tube-shaped animals a few millimeters long. The largest can reach three feet or more across and have bulbous, branching shapes. Most species have a skeleton made of a soft, springy material.

▼ TOXIC SPONGES *Many sponges, including this elephant ear sponge, grow on reefs. Some contain toxic substances, which act as a defense against predators. These toxins are used in the manufacture of drugs and medicines.*

Elephant
ear sponge
Ianthella basta

Elephant ear sponge

Ianthella basta

■ **Location** Indian and Pacific oceans and adjoining seas

These large, fan-shaped sponges intercept and feed off the water currents passing over the reefs. Their **springy skeleton** enables them to flex slightly so they are not damaged by stormy seas. There are several species of *Ianthella*, and they come in a variety of shapes, sizes, and colors.

FACT FILE

■ **Anatomy** The sponge's body cells work together, but do not form organs, tissues, or obvious body parts. Sponges reproduce in two ways—by budding off tiny clones and by releasing sperm to fertilize egg cells.

■ **Feeding** Sponges obtain energy by taking in food. They collect this from seawater, which is taken in through tiny pores and passes through a system of channels in the body. The channels are lined with cells bearing tiny hairs that trap the food. The filtered water passes out again through an opening called the osculum.

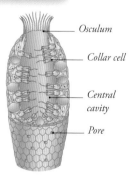

Osculum
Collar cell
Central cavity
Pore

▲ FILTER SYSTEM
Sponges are known as "filter feeders."

Red sponge

Negombata magnifica

■ **Location** Red Sea

A dramatic-looking, shallow-water sponge that can grow into the branching structure seen below, or as a spreading crust on rocks. It **produces a toxic protein** called latrunculin to deter predators. This doesn't scare everyone and the sponge is still eaten by a species of sea slug. The sea slug stores the toxin in its own body and benefits from the toxin's protection without being poisoned itself.

Bread crumb sponge

Halichondria panicea

■ **Location** Atlantic Ocean, Baltic, and Mediterranean Sea

This sponge often grows on rocky overhangs in strong currents. It can reach up to 24 in (60 cm) across. The name refers to the **crumbly looking surface**, which is covered with craterlike openings.

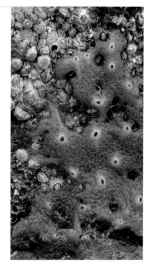

Azure vase sponge

Callyspongia plicifera

■ **Location** Caribbean Sea

This colorful sponge is a member of the class Demospongia, which includes all the soft, squashy, bath-type sponges. It **lives in sunlit shallow waters** and grows up to 18 in (45 cm) tall. A large specimen can filter hundreds of gallons of water per hour, extracting algae, plankton, and other tiny particles of food.

Calcareous sponge

Sycon ciliatum

■ **Location** All oceans

Sycon sponges are common members of the calcareous sponge class. They are small, with a **delicate skeleton** made of chalky calcium carbonate. They often grow attached to seaweeds or reef organisms, in order to position themselves in a good feeding current. A **crown of fine spicules** deters predators and helps prevent debris blockages.

Glass sponge

Euplectella aspergillum

■ **Location** Western Pacific Ocean

This tube-shaped sponge is supported by an extraordinary lacy lattice of brittle spicules, which gives it the alternative name "Venus' flower basket." The tube is often **home to pairs of small sponge shrimps**, which enter as juveniles and live their whole lives inside the sponge, eventually growing too big to leave.

Sea anemones

These "sea flowers" are usually found in shallow waters or tidal pools but as many as 50 percent live in the depths of the oceans. Sea anemones look delicate but they are efficient predators that shoot their prey with poisoned barbs. Most sea anemones do not move around much or swim. They stay anchored by a fleshy foot to rocks or dig their soft bodies into sand on the sea floor.

STINGERS

The tentacles of sea anemones are lined with stinging cells (nematocysts). Each cell contains venom, a barbed needle, and a "trigger" hair. When prey touches the hair, the needle shoots out, injecting the victim with venom. The needle stays attached to the anemone by a thread.

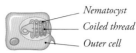

Nematocyst
Coiled thread
Outer cell

Before discharge

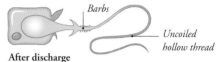

Barbs

Uncoiled hollow thread

After discharge

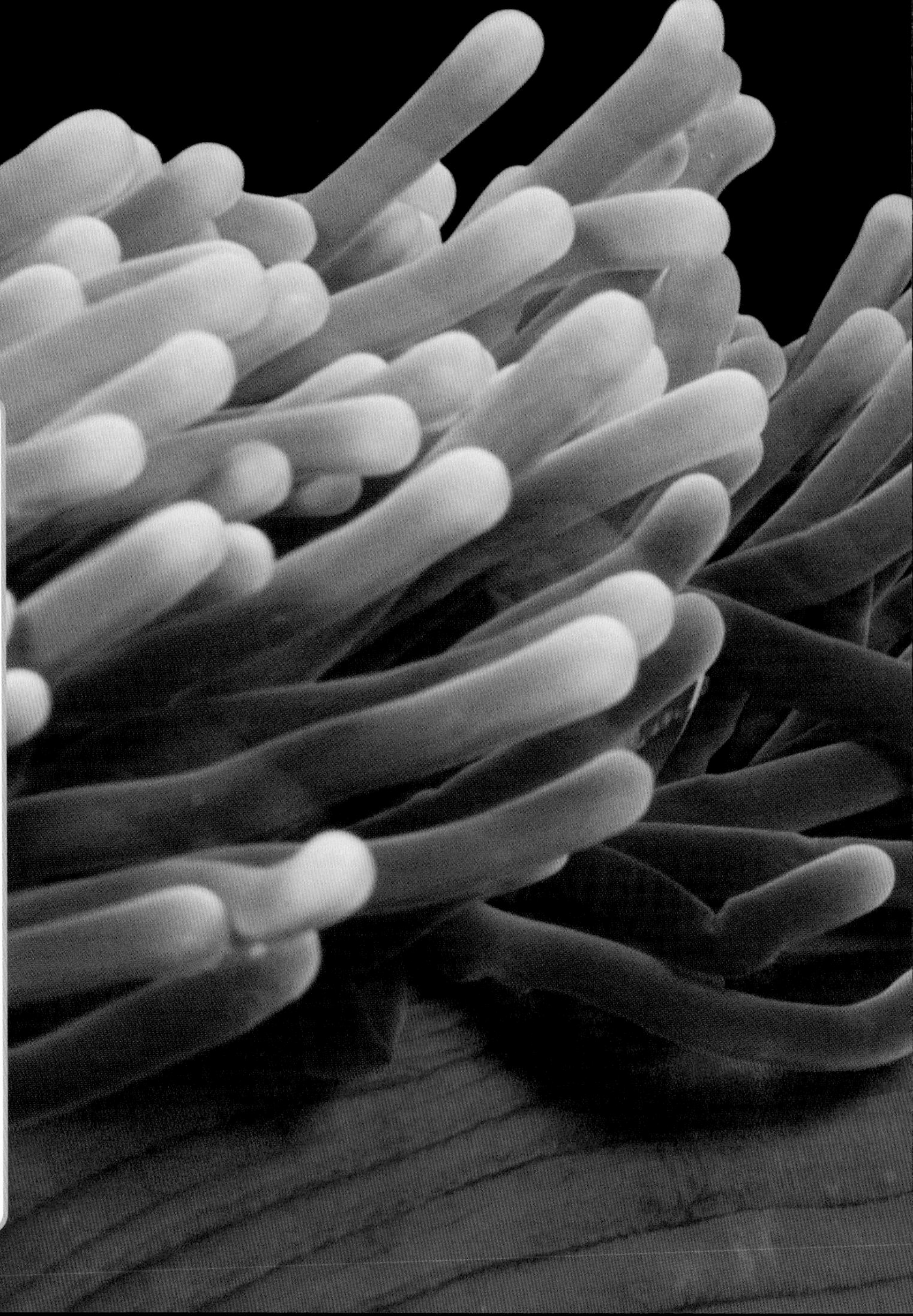

FACT FILE

■ **Sea anemones range in size** from less than ½ in (15 mm) to nearly 3 ft (1 m) in diameter. They can have from 12 tentacles to as many as several hundred.

■ **A sea anemone** is made of a soft body sac, which is attached to the seabed by a sticky foot. The body is cylinder-shaped with a flattened top called an oral disk. A mouth opens in the middle of this disk. The stinging tentacles that surround the mouth can be retracted (pulled in).

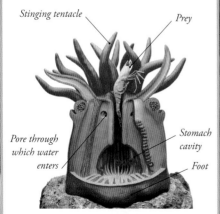

Stinging tentacle

Prey

Pore through which water enters

Stomach cavity

Foot

Cross section of a pink beadlet anemone

Aggregating anemone

Anthopleura elegantissima

- **Diameter** ¾–2 in (2–5 cm)
- **Diet** Small marine animals
- **Location** Western Pacific

Anemones of this species **live in colonies**. They are often found in tidal pools. When the tide goes out, they pull in their tentacles and **cover themselves with sand** and fragments of shell to prevent themselves from drying out.

Swimming sea anemone

Stomphia coccinea

- **Diameter** 2–2¾ in (5–7 cm)
- **Diet** Small marine animals
- **Location** North Atlantic and North Pacific

The swimming anemone behaves differently from its relatives. If scared, it bounces off the rock to which it is attached and **swims away** by swaying its body back and forth. When safe, it sinks back to the seabed again.

Long-tentacled sea anemone

Macrodactyla doreensis

- **Diameter** 4–6 in (10–15 cm)
- **Diet** Shrimp and small fish
- **Location** Indian Ocean

The tentacles of this anemone are up to 6½ in (17 cm) long. They are often twisted, giving the species its other popular name of **corkscrew anemone**. This anemone likes to embed its foot into soft mud on the sea bottom. It has several **color variations**, most commonly shades of gray or purple. The tentacles are striped with white.

I'm a friend, not prey.
Clown fish like this one often take refuge within the tentacles of sea anemones. Mucus on their skin protects them from being stung.

Jellyfish

Jellyfish are simple, free-swimming animals, with stinging tentacles to stun and draw in their prey. The wobbly, jellylike body is what gives this group of mostly marine invertebrates its name. There are around 300 species.

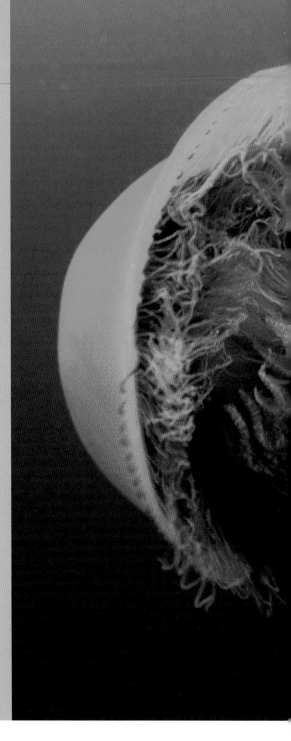

The main body of a jellyfish is called the "bell." It surrounds a central cavity, which acts as a gut.

The opening into the gut brings food in and takes away waste. It is fringed with stinging tentacles, used for drawing in the food.

◀ SOGGY BODY *Jellyfish are almost completely made of water. This is fine for life in the ocean, but their lack of a supporting skeleton makes them collapse in a heap if they are washed up on a beach.*

HOW A JELLYFISH MOVES

READY ... *Jellyfish either float with the current or move by a form of jet propulsion if they want to go in a particular direction.*

STEADY ... *The bell of the jellyfish extends upward and water collects underneath it. The jellyfish prepares to push forward.*

GO ... *The muscle cells slowly contract, forcing water out of the bell. As water leaves its body, the jellyfish starts to move.*

... AND AWAY *The force produced by pushing water away from its bell gently propels the jellyfish in the opposite direction.*

I make a tasty snack!
So many Nomura's jellyfish get caught up in fishing nets that people in China and Japan began to eat them instead of the fish.

GIANT JELLY *A diver swims alongside a Nomura's jellyfish off the coast of Japan. These massive sea creatures can grow 6½ ft (2 m) wide and weigh 480 lb (220 kg).*

▼ STAR JELLYFISH
This new species of jellyfish gets its name from the small pigmented dots inside its body that look like tiny stars.

▲ OUCH! *The tentacles of the Pacific sea nettle are covered in thousands of stinging cells that hold on to prey so it can be drawn into the jellyfish's mouth.*

Nomura's jellyfish

Nemopilema nomurai

- **Width** 6½ ft (2 m)
- **Weight** 480 lb (220 kg)
- **Location** Waters surrounding China, Korea, and Japan
- **Diet** Plankton and some crustaceans

Nomura's jellyfish usually drifts in **shallow waters** but sinks to greater depths to avoid schools of swordfish, tuna, and other **predators**. The population of this giant jellyfish has exploded in recent years, and many are **caught up in fishing nets**. The sheer weight of jellyfish can then crush the catch and even **destroy the nets**.

Corals

There are two types of corals: hard and soft. Hard corals have an internal skeleton made of limestone. These types build the huge coral reefs found in tropical seas. Most soft corals, which often look like plants, have a flexible internal skeleton. All corals grow from one tiny animal called a polyp. This animal produces new polyps, and a colony slowly develops, forming the coral.

FACT FILE

■ **Number of tentacles:** The polyps of hard corals have tentacles in multiples of six; the polyps of soft corals have eight.

■ **First appearance:** The first corals appeared on Earth some 540 million years ago.

■ **Reproduction:** Coral colonies in a reef usually reproduce by "broadcast spawning," which means they all release eggs and sperm into the water at the same time, often at full moon.

Pillar coral

Dendrogyra cylindrus

- **Height** 6½ ft (2 m)
- **Depth** 3–60 ft (1–20 m)
- **Location** Western Atlantic Ocean, Caribbean, and Gulf of Mexico

This is a reef-building hard coral. Pillar coral grows straight upward in **thick spires**. If it is in an area where it is safe from damage, the coral may become very large. Its furry appearance is caused by the **extended tentacles** of its polyps reaching out to feed.

Staghorn coral

Acropora cervicornis

- **Height** Not recorded
- **Location** Upper to mid-reef slopes and lagoons in clear water in the Caribbean

There are 120 species of staghorn coral. Most form branching shapes, like **antlers**. These corals grow quickly but are **easily damaged** by rough waves if the seas are stormy.

Mushroom soft coral

Anthomastus ritteri

- **Diameter** 6 in (15 cm)
- **Depth** 655–5,000 ft (200–1,500 m)
- **Location** Eastern Pacific Ocean

When this deep-water coral extends its fragile tentacles to trap food, it resembles a **strange**, **underwater flower**. With the tentacles pulled in, the coral lives up to its name and looks more like a mushroom.

Orange cup coral

Tubastraea coccinea

- **Diameter** ½–¾ in (1–2 cm)
- **Depth** 3–436 ft (1–130 m)
- **Location** Indian and Pacific oceans

Often found in tidal pools, orange cup coral **likes to attach itself to shady rocks**. The tiny cups have two ways of feeding. Sometimes, they put out tentacles to trap food. Alternatively, the coral keeps its tentacles withdrawn and catches food simply by holding open a mouth in the cup.

Great star coral

Montastraea cavernosa

- **Height** Not recorded
- **Depth** 40–100 ft (12–30 m)
- **Location** Atlantic Ocean

Colonies of great star coral often form **huge mounds**. In deeper waters the coral tends to spread out in flat plates. The polyps extend their tentacles to feed at night.

Grooved brain coral

Diploria labyrinthiformis

- **Height** Not recorded
- **Diameter** 6 ft (1.8 m)
- **Location** Western Atlantic Ocean

The polyps that form this rounded coral arrange themselves in wandering lines. This gives the coral colony a **heavily wrinkled appearance**, very like that of a brain. If sand becomes trapped between the grooves, the individual polyps push it out again to keep the coral clean.

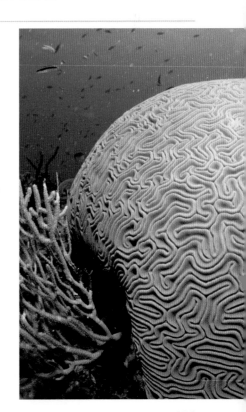

Worms

Most people think of worms as the squishy, slimy creatures wriggling around in soil. But there are thought to be more than a million different types that are found in a wide range of different places. Some do live in burrows in the ground, but others live in rivers or the sea, and some are parasites that are responsible for causing deadly diseases in humans and other animals.

Life around deep-sea vents
Deep below the ocean surface lie volcanic ridges that are dotted with submarine vents. These gush out plumes of water rich in minerals, which are used as nutrients by bacteria. These feed a variety of animals that can grow to be much bigger than similar creatures living in shallower waters.

Giant tubeworm

Riftia pachyptila

- **Length** 6–8 ft (2–2½ m)
- **Diet** Chemicals transformed to food by bacteria in tubeworm's body
- **Location** Pacific Ocean

Peeping out from the top of its hard, **protective white tube**, this bright red worm resembles a giant lipstick. It is found around **deep-sea, hydrothermal vents** on the floor of the Pacific. Here it **absorbs chemicals** from the water erupting from the vents. These chemicals are converted into usable food by **special bacteria** living inside the worm, which it digests. It has few enemies, but some fish and crabs will nibble at any worm that is protruding from its tube.

Earthworm

Lumbricus terrestris

- **Length** 3½–12 in (9–30 cm)
- **Diet** Decaying plant matter
- **Location** Worldwide

Earthworms burrow just below the soil's surface, feeding as they go. Any undigested matter passes out of their body to form the muddy "worm casts" that are often most noticeable on grass. Segmented worms like this **move in a series of muscular waves** as the segments expand and narrow. Stiff bristles on the segments grip the soil.

Flap-like "legs" covered with bristles, or chaetae

King ragworm

Nereis virens

- **Length** 12–31½ in (30–80 cm)
- **Diet** Small marine animals, rotting algae, and plants
- **Location** Atlantic Ocean

These giant worms have strong **pincer jaws** that they use for seizing prey and which can easily deliver a painful bite to a human. King ragworms belong to the **bristle worm** group. These marine animals crawl around on the surface of the sea floor and make burrows in the soft mud or gravel, feeding on anything that comes within reach of their jaws. They are also **good swimmers**.

Sea mouse

Aphrodita aculeata

- **Length** 3–8 in (7–20 cm)
- **Diet** Mainly other worms and small bivalves
- **Location** Atlantic and Mediterranean

This marine worm is covered in what looks like dense fur but is, in fact, **bristles**. It also has **long hairs** that shimmer from red to green according to the way light falls on them. Sea mice live in mud or sand on the seabed, often in deep oceans.

Medicinal leech

Hirudo medicinalis

- **Length** Up to 8 in (20 cm) and more
- **Diet** Blood
- **Location** Europe and Asia

The leech has a flattened body with **suckers** at both ends. At the head end there is a mouth with jaws. When a leech bites it **injects substances** that numb pain and stop blood from clotting. Leeches may need to feed only every few months.

Peacock worm

Sabella penicillus

    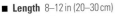

- **Length** 8–12 in (20–30 cm)
- **Diet** Small marine animals and tiny plankton
- **Location** Europe, North America, and the Caribbean

This long, thin-segmented worm spends its entire life encased in a **flexible tube** that it builds around itself, using a mixture of sand and mud that it binds together with mucus. The tube is anchored to a rock in coastal waters. Surrounding the worm's mouth is a **crown of feathery tentacles**, banded in red, brown and purple. This protrudes from the protective tube when the worm is feeding. Particles of food suspended in the water drop onto the crown, where tiny hairlike cilia on the tentacles move the particles down to the mouth.

Flexible tube in which the worm lives.

The feeding tentacles fan out to catch food.

Mollusks

Mollusks are a large and incredibly diverse group of invertebrates. They have a huge range of body shapes and sizes, ranging from around 1/50 inch (1/2 mm) snails (*Ammonicera rota*) to the colossal squid (*Mesonychoteuthis hamiltoni*), which is more than 46 ft (14 m) in length and one of the largest animals on Earth.

Emperor nautilus
Nautilus pompilius

The nautilus and its now extinct relatives, the ammonites, were once one of the most successful groups of animals found in the world's oceans. However, all except the nautilus became extinct at the same time as the non-flying dinosaurs, 66 million years ago.

We have been on Earth for 500 million years!

TYPES OF MOLLUSK

Most mollusks have a shell or at least the remnants of one. The shell is made out of calcium carbonate and is produced by the mantle, part of a mollusk's fleshy body.

■ **Gastropods**, also called univalves, usually have a single shell. Sometimes they have no shell at all. Snails, slugs, and sea slugs are all gastropods. Gastropods usually have a muscular foot that they use for crawling.

■ **Bivalves have shells made up of two pieces.** When a bivalve needs to close its shell, powerful muscles pull the two halves together, sealing it safely inside. Clams and oysters are bivalves.

■ **Cephalopods** include large invertebrates such as squid. The shells of squid have become internal and support the animal's soft body from the inside. Octopuses have lost the ability to make shells altogether.

Size comparison
Ammonicera rota

Mesonychoteuthis hamiltoni

Shell made of calcium carbonate

Eye

Tentacle

Muscular foot

Giant Pacific octopus
Enteroctopus dofleini

- **Size** 9¾–16 ft (3–5 m) arm span
- **Weight** 110 lb (50 kg)
- **Diet** Crabs, lobsters, fish, and other octopuses
- **Location** North Pacific Ocean

This is the **largest** octopus in the world. It can change the color and texture of its skin almost instantly, either to hide from large predators or to warn them away. Along with other octopuses it is the **most intelligent** of the invertebrates.

Butterfly bubble shell
Hydatina physis

- **Length** Shell 1¾ in (45 mm)
- **Diet** Small worms
- **Location** Indo-West Pacific and Atlantic Ocean

This is a **brightly colored** sea snail with a thin shell. It can withdraw into its shell, although it rarely does as the shell gives little protection. It usually crawls along the sandy seabed, but unlike most shelled gastropods, **it can also swim**.

Pyjama sea slug
Chromodoris quadricolor

- **Length** Up to 1¾ in (4.5 cm)
- **Diet** Sea sponges
- **Location** Mediterranean and western Indian Ocean

Some mollusks have lost all trace of their shells, and sea slugs, of which there are 3,000 species, are one such group. To protect themselves, some, such as the colorful pyjama sea slug, use **bright patterns** to warn potential predators that they are full of foul-tasting chemicals and are **not pleasant to eat**. If attacked, a sea slug secretes these chemicals from glands just under the skin.

Blue sea slug
Glaucus atlanticus

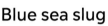

- **Length** 1⅛ ft (3 cm)
- **Diet** Portuguese man-of-war
- **Location** Worldwide

The blue sea slug is a **predator** and feeds on the poisonous Portuguese man-of-war (commonly thought of as a jellyfish, but actually a colony of hydrozoans). The blue sea slug is immune to the man-of-war's venomous stings. In fact it **stores the stings** in feather-like "fingers" that stick out from its body, firing these out if it is attacked.

Flat oyster
Ostrea edulis

- **Length** 1½–4 in (4–11 cm)
- **Diet** Plant and animal matter
- **Location** European Atlantic coast

A bivalve, this oyster spends its life permanently attached to a rock. **It starts as a male**, then becomes female when it is about three years old. Like other oysters, if a tiny piece of food or sand becomes trapped in its shell, the **oyster covers it with a secretion** of minerals and proteins to eventually make a pearl.

Queen scallop
Equichlamys bifrons

- **Length** 4 in (110 mm)
- **Diet** Plankton
- **Location** Australia, Tasmania

The shells of this bivalve are usually light purple on the inside. Like all scallops, the queen scallop **moves rapidly** through the water by opening and closing its shell, producing a jet of water that pushes it along. Humans like to eat queen scallops.

Giant clam
Tridacna gigas

- **Length** 4 ft (1.2 m)
- **Weight** 440 lb (200 kg)
- **Location** South Pacific and Indian oceans

At 3¼ ft (1 m) wide, the giant clam is the **largest bivalve** on Earth. It usually lies in shallow waters. Billions of algae live on its **fleshy lips**. They produce sugars and proteins that the clam feeds on. In return, the clam gives the algae a safe home as well as access to sunlight so the algae can make their own food.

Snails and slugs

Slugs are the slimy, jellylike creatures that live in gardens and eat plants, and snails are like slugs with spiral-shaped shells. They both belong to a class called Gastropoda. All gastropods have a large head and tentacles, plus a soft body they drag around on a single, sucker-like foot.

▲ FLOATING RAFT
Also known as a bubble raft snail, the violet sea snail floats upside down on the surface of warm seas, anchored there by bubbles of its own mucus. These snails are blind, with a paper-thin shell.

▶ ROCK CLINGERS
Limpets cling to rocky shores by sucking on tight with their soft, muscular foot. When the tide is high, they move slowly, feeding on algae. When the tide is low, they lock themselves into position on the rocks.

LAND AND SEA

Some gastropods live on land, while others live in water: all of them lay eggs. The eggs of water-dwelling gastropods develop into larvae and grow in stages to become adults. Land-dwellers hatch as tiny versions of adults. Gastropods have a row of tiny teeth and feed on a widely varied diet.

WARNING SHADES
Because they don't have shells to protect them, sea slugs carry a sting; their bright coloring warns enemies to stay clear.

Lettuce sea slug

Elysia crispata

- **Length** 3 in (8 cm)
- **Diet** Algae
- **Location** Tropical Atlantic waters

Named for its **ruffled body**, which looks like leafy lettuce, this sea slug is solar powered! It gets some of its food from algae that it takes into its tissues and which **turn sunlight into energy**. The ruffles maximize the sea slug's surface area, so it can absorb as much sunlight as possible.

Dog whelk

Nucella lapillus

- **Shell length** 1–2 in (2–4 cm)
- **Diet** Other gastropods
- **Location** North Atlantic coasts

Also called the Atlantic dog winkle, this creature **feeds by boring through the shells of prey**, then sucking out the tissue.

▲ ROCKY NEST
In spring, dog whelks lay clusters of eggs and attach them inside rock crevices.

Garden snail

Cornu aspersum

  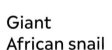

- **Shell length** 1–1½ in (2.5–4 cm)
- **Diet** Plants
- **Location** Worldwide

Disliked by gardeners, this snail has **a thin shell** with four or five spirals. When it's resting or threatened, it **retracts inside**. The head has **four tentacles**, with eyes in the top two. The garden snail is a close relative of the edible snail, *Helix pomatia*.

Garden slug

Arion distinctus

- **Length** About 1¼ in (3 cm)
- **Diet** Plants
- **Location** North America and Europe

Hated by gardeners around the world, the common slug feeds on cultivated plants, tubers, and bulbs using a rasping tongue known as a *radula*. Mostly **active at night**, it spends the day in moist, hidden places. This yellow-gray slug breeds throughout most of the year.

Giant African snail

Lissachatina fulica

    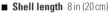

- **Shell length** 8 in (20 cm)
- **Diet** Plants
- **Location** East Africa

The **world's biggest land-dwelling snail**, this creature can cause serious damage to crops in the areas where it thrives. Native to the tropics, it's a hardy species that can survive cold or even snowy conditions by hibernating inside its shell. Typically, adults live for five to six years.

▼ TROPICAL MONSTER
Giant African snail shells are light brown, banded with dark brown and cream.

Octopuses and squid

Believe it or not, these sea-dwelling creatures are mollusks and related to slugs and snails. They are called cephalopods. Equipped with long arms and a poisonous bite, they have little trouble catching prey. They propel themselves through the sea by taking in water and squirting it out.

OCTOPUS *arms are flexible. The octopus can use them to investigate tight spaces as well as to open shells and hold prey. They "taste" things with their suckers before deciding to eat them.*

Maori octopus

Macroctopus maorum

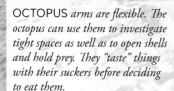

- **Length** Up to 6½ ft (2 m)
- **Arm span** Up to 10 ft (3 m)
- **Location** Australia and New Zealand

Octopuses eat crabs, lobsters, and mollusks. They have very **good eyesight** and stalk their prey, hiding then pouncing on their victim. They often swim above their prey then fall on to it, using their body **like a net**.

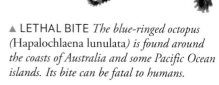

▲ LETHAL BITE *The blue-ringed octopus (Hapalochlaena lunulata) is found around the coasts of Australia and some Pacific Ocean islands. Its bite can be fatal to humans.*

You can't fool me ...
Octopuses are highly intelligent. They have the largest and most advanced brain of any invertebrate. In tests, octopuses have learned to find their way through a maze and take the lid off a container.

CHAMPION HUNTERS

Squid and cuttlefish have an internal shell. As well as having eight arms, these animals have two long tentacles, each with a sucker on the end. They use these to grab prey such as fish and other mollusks.

Size comparison

◄ COMMON SQUID (Loligo vulgaris) *Squid live in deep, open water and hardly ever come near the shore. They have a torpedo-shaped body, which helps them move through the water. Two fins at the end are used for steering. Squid often swim in groups for protection.*

◄ COMMON CUTTLEFISH
(Sepia officinalis) This animal's flat body is ideal for its life on the seabed. Its internal shell is the familiar cuttlebone that is often found on beaches. Like other cephalopods, cuttlefish change color and squirt ink to confuse predators.

A *world* of shells

Mollusks with shells include gastropods, which usually have coiled, single shells, and bivalves, which have two-piece shells. Not all mollusks have shells: octopuses and squid are mollusks, but they have no external shell.

INVERTEBRATES

West Indian worm shell
Vermicularia spirata

Clear sundial shell
Architectonica perspectiva

Ocellate cowrie
Cypraea ocellata

European prickly cockle
Acanthocardia echinata

Matchless cone shell
Conus cedonulli

⚠ **Hebrew cone shell**
Conus ebraeus

Precious wentletrap
Epitonium scalare

Pacific thorny oyster
Spondylus princeps

Rayed pearl oyster
Pinctada radiata

⚠ **Imperial harp shell**
Harpa costata

Giant razor shell
Ensis siliqua

Australian trumpet shell
Syrinx aruanus

Tiger maurea shell
Maurea tigris

Listers keyhole limpet
Diodora listeri

Great scallop
Pecten maximus

Japanese wonder shell
Thatcheria mirabilis

Common blue mussel
Mytilus edulis

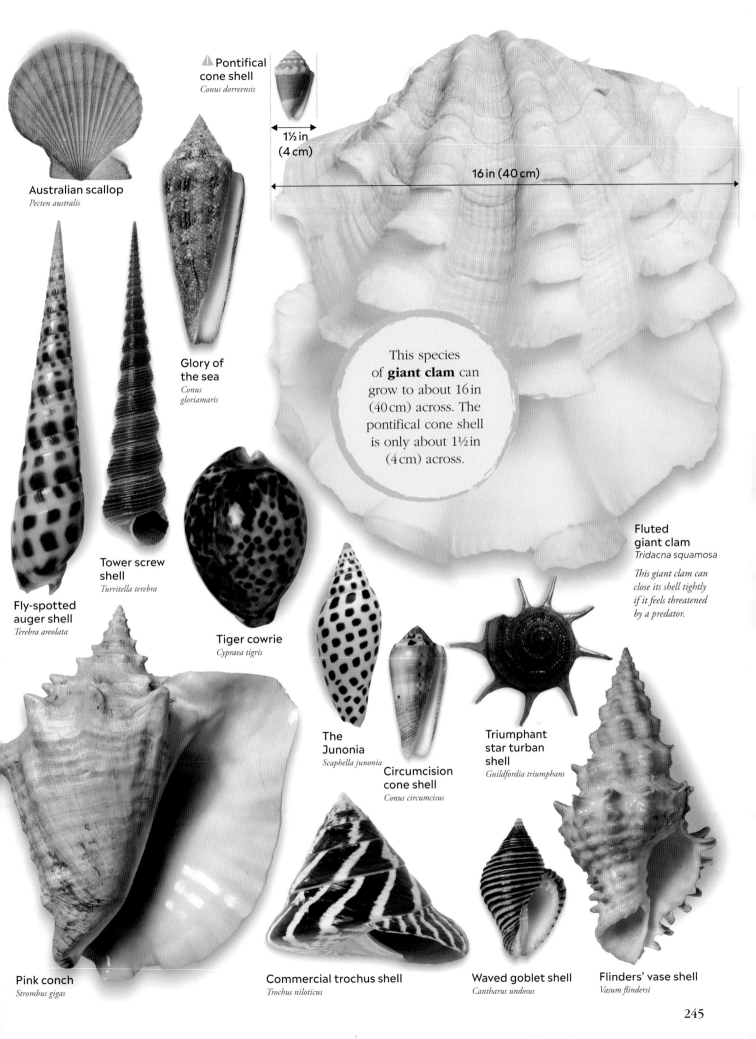

Australian scallop
Pecten australis

⚠ **Pontifical cone shell**
Conus dorreensis

1½ in (4 cm)

16 in (40 cm)

This species of **giant clam** can grow to about 16 in (40 cm) across. The pontifical cone shell is only about 1½ in (4 cm) across.

Glory of the sea
Conus gloriamaris

Fluted giant clam
Tridacna squamosa

This giant clam can close its shell tightly if it feels threatened by a predator.

Fly-spotted auger shell
Terebra areolata

Tower screw shell
Turritella terebra

Tiger cowrie
Cypraea tigris

The Junonia
Scaphella junonia

Circumcision cone shell
Conus circumcisus

Triumphant star turban shell
Guildfordia triumphans

Pink conch
Strombus gigas

Commercial trochus shell
Trochus niloticus

Waved goblet shell
Cantharus undosus

Flinders' vase shell
Vasum flindersi

Arthropods

More than 80 percent of all the animal species we know about on Earth are arthropods. They are a diverse group of animals ranging in size from microscopic gall mites to Japanese spider crabs that measure up to 13ft (4m) across—the same length as a car. Arthropods are found in almost every habitat imaginable, from seals' noses and pools of gasoline to crushing depths and frozen glaciers.

DEER TICKS (*IXODES RICINUS*)

- **Ticks cannot jump like fleas**. Instead, they wait for their host to walk by, and then grab ahold.
- Although they mainly target deer, these **parasites** will nestle on any large mammal, including humans.
- Ticks carry several **diseases** and can pass these on to their host.
- Ticks use their **legs** to **grip tightly** onto the chosen host.

The tick stabs its harpoon-like mouthparts into the flesh until it hits a blood vessel.

It will now expand to almost 200 times its original size as it gorges on blood.

SHEDDING ITS SKIN
The reef lobster, like most arthropods, has a hard exoskeleton, which it sheds as it grows. The new exoskeleton takes time to harden, leaving the lobster vulnerable to predators.

INSECTS	CENTIPEDES AND MILLIPEDES	CRABS, LOBSTERS, AND SHRIMP	SPIDERS, SCORPIONS, TICKS, AND MITES	SEA SPIDERS	HORSESHOE CRABS

Butterfly

Wasp

Grasshopper

Centipede

Millipede

Crab

Squat lobster

Prawn

Raft spider

Gold scorpion

Red-legged earth mite

Sea spider

Horseshoe crab

INVERTEBRATES

Insects are one of the most adaptable and diverse groups of animals on Earth, with over a million species.

These many-legged arthropods have long, segmented bodies. Centipedes have a pair of poisonous claws.

Crustaceans are mainly aquatic. They have a hard exoskeleton, two pairs of antennae, and a pair of compound eyes.

This group is known as arachnids. They have four pairs of legs, but don't have wings or antennae.

Despite the name, these marine arthropods aren't spiders. Species range in size from 1/32–30 in (1 mm to 75 cm).

These aren't true crabs; they are closer to arachnids. They have the rare ability to regrow lost limbs.

Imperial scorpion
Pandinus imperator

- **Length** 4¾–9 in (12–23 cm)
- **Location** Africa

Relying on its size and **powerful, serrated pincers,** the imperial scorpion has no need for deadly venom, unlike other scorpions. Instead, it sneaks up and grabs, crushing its prey's external skeleton or **cutting through its flesh**. Small, pincerlike mouthparts then pull it to pieces. A female scorpion gives birth to live young. She protects, feeds, and carries them on her back until they are able to fend for themselves.

Once gripped by the pincers, prey can be stabbed repeatedly with the stinger.

A scorpion will crush its prey with powerful pincers.

Horseshoe crab
Limulus polyphemus

25

- **Length** 11–24 in (28–60 cm) (including tail)
- **Weight** 10 lb (4.5 kg)
- **Location** East coast of North America

These creatures haven't changed much in nearly 300 million years. They are considered **living fossils** and are close living relatives to the now extinct trilobites. Despite their common name, **they are not crabs**, but are related to arachnids. A female horseshoe crab will lay between 15,000 and 60,000 eggs. Horseshoe crabs grow slowly and it can take 12 years for the young crabs to become adults.

Sea spider
Colossendeis australis

5

- **Leg span** 20 in (50 cm)
- **Location** Worldwide oceans

Sea spiders are found all over the world, from coastal tropical waters to the poles. *Colossendeis australis* are **giant deep-sea inhabitants**, with leg spans reaching more than 20 in (50 cm). They **suck the juices** from soft-bodied invertebrates, or graze on small aquatic animals. Other sea spider species are smaller and can be found in coastal waters and on reefs.

FACT FILE

- **Number of species:** 5,000
- **Key features:** All dragonflies and damselflies have a long, thin body that is perfect for flying. They have two pairs of large, transparent wings that are held either out to the side (dragonflies) or folded along the back (damselflies) when resting. Their huge compound eyes can see really well. They are ferocious hunters. The larva, known as a nymph, lives entirely underwater.

Dragonflies
and damselflies

If you had been alive around 300 million years ago, you would have seen insects flying around that were almost identical to today's dragonflies and damselflies. The adults, with their striking colors and amazing flying skills, are a familiar sight. But these elegant, eye-catching insects spend most of their lives as water-dwelling larvae, or nymphs, well hidden in the murky depths of rivers and lakes.

Southern hawker
Aeshna cyanea

- **Length** 2½–2¾ in (6.5–7 cm)
- **Wingspan** 2¾–4 in (7–10 cm)
- **Location** Europe

The nymphs take up to three years to gain their wings, but an adult has just a few weeks in which to mate before it dies. The males zoom off at speeds of up to **19 mph (30 kph)** to establish their breeding territories, fiercely driving off intruders and any rival males.

Emperor dragonfly

Anax imperator

- **Length** 2¾–3 in (7–8 cm)
- **Wingspan** 4–4¼ in (10–11 cm)
- **Location** Europe, C. Asia, and N. Africa

This is one of the biggest and most powerful dragonflies. It also **holds the record for being the fastest** and can swoop and dive through the air at speeds of up to 24 mph (38 kph). Adults seize and eat their prey, which include butterflies and other flying insects, on the wing. The larvae, or nymphs, take up to a year to become winged adults, but then live for only around 10 days. Males often fight to the death over territory.

Common darter

Sympetrum striolatum

- **Length** 1½ in (38 mm)
- **Wingspan** 2⁹⁄₁₀ in (58 mm)
- **Location** Europe, Asia, and North Africa

Common darters are given their name because they **fly in an unpredictable way**. They are often colorful and have strong bodies. They prefer to live in wet areas. In order to lay their eggs females hover above water and then release them into the water.

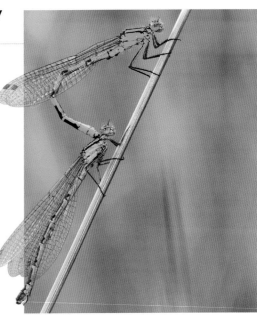

Four-spotted chaser dragonfly

Libellula quadrimaculata

- **Length** 1⅔–1¾ in (4–4.5 cm)
- **Wingspan** 2¾–3 in (7–7.5 cm)
- **Location** Europe, North Asia, and North America

Like most insects, chaser dragonflies can **see color** and their eyes are also very sensitive to movement. These aggressive creatures can spot prey from several yards away. They then swoop up from under their target, gathering it using the **sharp spines** on their legs.

Common blue damselfly

Enallagma cyathigerum

- **Length** 1¼–1½ in (3–3.5 cm)
- **Wingspan** 1½–1⅓ in (3.5–4 cm)
- **Location** Europe

The moment a female lands in his territory, a male blue damselfly will fly over to her and hover just in front of her. He is hoping to impress her with his **brightly colored body**, and prove that he is a suitable mate. He may also hover over and make several landings on the water that runs through his territory. He does this to convince the female that it is a good place for her to lay her eggs, so that the nymphs that hatch out have the best chance of survival.

MAYFLIES

The ancestors of mayflies were probably among the first insects to take to the air about 354 million years ago and, like their dragonfly cousins, have changed little since then.

- **Adult mayflies never eat.** Only the larvae, known as nymphs, feed. It can take as long as three years for a nymph to develop fully into an adult. But once it is an adult, it may live for just a few hours.

- **Number of species:** 2,500

- **Key features:** Adult mayflies have two pairs of transparent wings, which are held upright above the body. Two or three long tails project from the tip of the abdomen. Like dragonflies, their antennae are short, but their eyes are slightly smaller.

Common mayfly

Ephemera danica

- **Length** ⅜–1½ in (1–3.5 cm) excluding tail filaments
- **Location** Europe

The artificial flies used for trout fishing are modeled on these mayflies, which are also **known as green drakes**. They lay eggs in rivers and lakes. Nymphs chew their way into the silt on the bottom and feed on tiny plants and animals that live there.

Three tails

Stick and leaf insects

These remarkable insects bear an uncanny resemblance to the twigs and leaves on which they live. The stick insects, or walking sticks, are found around the world but, like leaf insects, most species live in dense vegetation in tropical regions. Thanks to their odd appearance, many people like to keep these unusual insects as pets.

LEAFLIKE INSECTS *Found in the humid rainforests of Southeast Asia, the leaf insect Phyllium celebicum has a pattern of lines on its body that look exactly like the veins of a leaf.*

I can change color.
Some young leaf insects change color after they hatch. They take on their distinctive green color after the first molt, which is around a week or more after hatching.

Leaf insects
Family Phylliidae

- **Length** 1¼–4¼ in (3–11 cm)
- **Species** More than 50
- **Diet** Plants
- **Location** Australasia, Southeast Asia, Mauritius, and the Seychelles

Leaf insects **mimic leaves** with their flat, round bodies and dull green and brown coloration. Some leaf insects have spots and blotches that add to the effect, while others simply look like dead, wrinkled leaves.

MASTERS OF DISGUISE
True to their name, stick insects have slender, twiglike bodies to blend in with their surroundings and avoid being eaten. Some sway in the breeze to add to the disguise.

RECORD BREAKERS
Stick insects come in different shades of green and brown, with bumps on their bodies to make them look more like twigs. They are the longest insects in the world. The longest species lives in Borneo and grows up to 12 in (30 cm) in length.

Grasshoppers and crickets

With more than 20,000 species, there is a huge variety of these insects, both in behavior and appearance. Most communicate with a chirping noise called their "song" and, during the breeding season, this sound fills the air in many warm parts of the world.

Roesel's bush cricket
Metrioptera roeselii

INVERTEBRATES

GROWING UP

All grasshoppers and crickets undergo incomplete metamorphosis. This means that young insects change gradually as they mature, molting several times. Those species that develop wings have tough forewings that protect delicate hindwings. Crickets grow much longer antennae than grasshoppers, often longer than their bodies.

▲ EARDRUM *Bush crickets hear using drumlike membranes on their forelegs. Grasshoppers have membranes on their sides for hearing. The membranes pick up the songs of potential mates. Grasshoppers sing by rubbing their legs against their wings, while crickets rub their wings together.*

One, two, three, jump.

Grasshoppers and crickets have long, powerful hind legs. Even those species that have wings often jump away from danger instead of flying. It makes it more difficult for a predator to catch them.

FACT FILE

■ Many grasshoppers have colorful wings to startle predators. Others use camouflage as a defense.

■ Locusts are grasshoppers that form swarms. They can cause great damage to crops.

■ Crickets eat a variety of food, from plants to kitchen scraps. Many are hunters or scavengers.

■ Weta crickets have enormous, spiny back legs, which they show to predators to warn them to keep away.

Milkweed grasshopper

Phymateus morbillosus

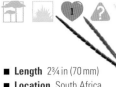

- **Length** 2¾ in (70 mm)
- **Location** South Africa

Males of this species of grasshopper can fly a short distance, but females do not fly even though they have wings. This is probably because females are too heavy to get off the ground. This insect's **bright colors act as a warning** to predators to leave it alone. If it is attacked, it will give off **foul-tasting foam**.

▲ DIET *This species feeds on a variety of plants.*

Stripe-winged grasshopper

Stenobothrus lineatus

- **Length** ¾ in (18 mm)
- **Location** Central and southern Europe to western Asia

This species of grasshopper has a narrow white stripe along the edge of its forewings. This grasshopper is usually green but it can come in a **variety of colors**, from green to yellow, brown, and red. The insect has one of the **quietest songs** among grasshoppers.

European mole cricket

Gryllotalpa gryllotalpa

- **Length** 1¾ in (45 mm)
- **Location** Europe

Mole crickets have short, broad, toothed front legs for digging. Females dig chambers to lay their eggs. Males dig trumpet-shaped burrows that make their songs sound louder. There are about 60 species of mole cricket. They are covered with **short, velvety hairs**, like the burrowing mammal from which they get their name.

Desert locust

Schistocerca gregaria

- **Length** 2⅘ in (72 mm)
- **Location** Africa and western Asia

The desert locust is known for forming **huge swarms** that can stretch for hundreds of square miles and contain 40 to 80 million locusts. The locusts **change color** from green to brown when they are overcrowded. They can be solitary, but lack of food makes them swarm. The swarms fly up to 80 miles (130 km) a day.

Speckled bush cricket

Leptophyes punctatissima

- **Length** ¾ in (18 mm)
- **Location** Europe

As its name suggests, this cricket's body is covered with tiny black speckles. It **cannot fly but can jump a long way** on its long, slender legs. The male's song is difficult for humans to hear because it is so high-pitched. But female crickets can hear it, and they answer with their own song.

African cave cricket

Pholeogryllus geertsi

- **Length** 1½ in (38 mm)
- **Location** Northern Africa and southern Europe

Cave crickets can be recognized by their **humped backs**, and they are sometimes known as camel crickets. They have **extra-long hind legs** for jumping, and even longer, sensitive antennae. They use their antennae to help them detect predators. There are about 250 species of cave cricket around the world.

With a triangular-shaped head and the curious ability to turn it around to see behind, mantids are strange-looking creatures. The common name "praying mantis" refers to the way the insect holds its forelegs.

Who's behind me?
The praying mantis has the ability to turn its head through 300 degrees—this means it can see what is lurking behind it.

Devil's flower mantis
Idolomantis diabolicum

- **Length** 5½ in (14 cm)
- **Location** South of the Sahara Desert

The African devil's flower mantis is **one of the biggest mantises in the world**. It lives in the dry, bushy scrublands of eastern Africa. Here it lurks around pretending to be a nectar-bearing flower—a very attractive sight to many insects.

▲ **PRAYING IN WAIT**
Mantids are ambush predators. Hunting during the day with their specially adapted vision, they patiently lie in wait for their prey to get close.

▲ **LASH AND GRAB**
Mantids use their powerful spiked forelegs to lash out at fantastic speed and grab their prey. The mantid's body remains amazingly still and steady.

▲ **A NASTY BITE?**
Mantids do pinch and bite, but they don't possess a venom. They rely on their size and camouflage to defend themselves.

INVERTEBRATES

255

Cockroaches

These robust, leathery insects have flat, oval bodies so they can squeeze into tight spaces to escape predators or find food. Most cockroaches live in dark, damp places and come out at night to feed. In their natural habitat, they eat fallen fruits, leaves, and other plant material, but some will also eat the remains of dead animals. A few cockroaches are pests that infest houses and spread disease.

▲ EGG-LAYING MACHINES *An adult American cockroach lives for a year or more, but in this short time the female will produce an average of 150 young. The young roaches, or nymphs, hatch from egg cases called oothecae. The nymphs mature into adults within a year.*

LIVE BEARERS *Cockroaches such as the giant hissing cockroach give birth to live young. The female lays eggs in an egg case but then draws it back inside her abdomen so the young develop inside her body.*

FACT FILE

■ **Number of species:** There are some 4,600 species of cockroach, grouped into nine families.

■ **Key features:** Flat, oval, leathery bodies with long, whiplike antennae.

■ **Size:** Cockroaches grow quite big—the giant cave cockroach can reach 4 in (10 cm) in length.

Size comparison

Giant hissing cockroach

Gromphadorhina portentosa

- **Length** 2–3 in (5–7.5 cm)
- **Weight** ⅘ oz (23 g)
- **Location** Madagascar

This large cockroach lives on the forest floor among the leaf litter and rotting logs. It **comes out at night** to feed on fruit and plant material. When fighting or mating it makes a hissing noise by forcing air through its breathing holes. Hissing is also used as an **alarm call** to the rest of the colony. Males hiss more often than females.

Giant burrowing cockroach

Macropanesthia rhinoceros

- **Length** 3¼ in (8 cm)
- **Weight** 1 oz (35 g)
- **Location** Australia

A true giant, this is the **heaviest species** of cockroach in the world. Giant burrowing cockroaches construct and **live in burrows** up to 39 in (1 m) under the ground. They come out at night to collect leaf litter and other dead plant material, which they take back to their burrow to eat.

Leathery, segmented abdomen

Austral ellipsidion

Ellipsidion australe

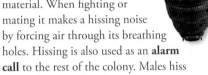

- **Length** 1 in (2.5 cm)
- **Location** Australia

These bush cockroaches are active during the day, where they can be found wandering over plants in Australia. The younger nymphs are equally **striking**, with bands of bright yellow dots running across the abdomen. Like all

cockroaches, the nymphs grow into adults by **shedding their outer skin** in stages. This species feeds on pollen, honeydew, and mold fungus.

German cockroach

Blattella germanica

- **Length** ½–⅝ in (12–15 mm)
- **Location** Worldwide, except for cold climates

German cockroaches are found wherever there is human habitation, but they do not like the cold. In the wild, they live in warm, dark, damp crevices. Although they have wings, they **rarely fly**. They are most active at night, when they scavenge for food. **Unfussy eaters**, they will eat soap, glue, toothpaste, or even each other when food is scarce.

Death's head cockroach

Blaberus craniifer

- **Length** 1½–2½ in (4–6 cm)
- **Location** Central America; introduced to southern US

This cockroach takes its common name from the **"skull"** or "vampire" markings on the pronotum—part of the thorax just behind the insect's head. The nymphs lack wings, while adults have wings but do not fly. These roaches cannot climb up glass so they **make good pets** for open aquariums. They feed mostly on plant material, but will eat other foods that may be available.

Green banana cockroach

Panchlora nivea

- **Length** 1 in (2.5 cm)
- **Location** Caribbean and US Gulf Coast

These **small, green cockroaches** are also known as Cuban cockroaches, reflecting their origins. They have since spread to the US on shipments of Caribbean fruit. As nymphs, these cockroaches burrow under logs and other debris, but the adults are usually found crawling on shrubs and trees. They **emerge at night** and are drawn to bright lights.

American cockroach

Periplaneta americana

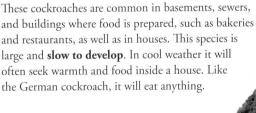

- **Length** 1–1½ in (2.5–4 cm)
- **Location** Worldwide

This **pest thrives** in warm, moist conditions indoors as well as outdoors. These cockroaches are common in basements, sewers, and buildings where food is prepared, such as bakeries and restaurants, as well as in houses. This species is large and **slow to develop**. In cool weather it will often seek warmth and food inside a house. Like the German cockroach, it will eat anything.

Bugs

To a biologist, the word "bug" means a very particular group of insects, also known as hemipterans. Bugs come in an enormous variety of shapes and have very varied lifestyles, but they share a special way of feeding and have a distinctive wing structure.

STAB AND SUCK A close look at a bug reveals it has no mouth, only a stout "beak" shaped like a reinforced drinking straw. This is used to stab prey or tap into plants and suck up body fluids or sap. Bugs cannot bite or eat solid food.

CLASSIC BUG *This forest shield bug shows typical bug characteristics: toughened front wings covering small, delicate hindwings, and stout drinking-straw mouthparts.*

FACT FILE

■ **Number of species:** Entomologists have so far described more than 80,000 species of bug, and there may be at least as many still to be discovered.

TWO TRIBES *Bugs can be grouped into two main types. The heteropterans have front wings with hardened bases and membranous tips and they feed on animals and plants, while the homopterans have uniform front wings and usually suck fluids from plants.*

Thorax

Split wings

Thorax

Uniform wings

Shield bug
Typical heteropteran

Leafhopper
Typical homopteran

Cottony cushion scale

Icerya purchasi

- **Length** About ¼ in (5 mm), not including egg sac
- **Status** Pest
- **Location** Originally from Australia, now worldwide

These small sap-sucking insects are a **major pest of citrus crops** such as orange and lemon groves. Males are found occasionally, but most scales are hermaphrodites and are able to reproduce without mating.

Periodical cicada

Magicicada septendecim

- **Length** 1½ in (4 cm)
- **Status** Occasional pest
- **Location** Eastern United States

The largest of the periodical cicada species, with an **amazing 17-year life cycle**. Larvae spend 17 years developing into adults in the soil before emerging simultaneously in huge numbers. Swarms of cicadas can damage young trees and **have been known to stop traffic and cause accidents**! Newly emerged adults mate, produce eggs, and die within a few weeks and all is quiet for another 17 years.

Assassin bug

Eulyes illustris

- **Length** ¾ in (2 cm)
- **Status** Neutral
- **Location** Southeast Asia

The black-spotted red assassin bug shown here is just one of thousands of species of assassin bug. As the name suggests, these insects are **predators**. Some live by sucking blood. Assassin bugs are found worldwide, especially in tropical and subtropical regions. They make their homes in plants, on the ground, and in leaf litter. Some can **transmit diseases to humans** through their bite.

Water strider

Gerris lacustris

- **Length** ⅖–⅗ in (10–15 mm)
- **Status** Neutral
- **Location** Mainly Europe

Water striders are **predatory bugs** that stalk the surface film of still pools and ponds. Their long, thin legs allow them to spread their weight over a wide area and water-repellent hairs on the feet prevent them from sinking. They use the water surface as a spider uses a web, using vibrations to track down potential prey. Water striders leave the water to **hibernate in winter**.

Cabbage aphid

Brevicoryne brassicae

- **Length** ⅖–1 in (2–2.5 mm)
- **Status** Pest
- **Location** Originally from Europe, but spreading

Like other aphids, this species **feeds on plant sap** and can occur in such vast numbers that the plant host is destroyed. Cabbage aphids also **transmit a number of plant diseases**. They are one of about 250 aphid species listed as plant pests.

Forest shield bug

Pentatoma rufipes

- **Length** ½ in (14 mm)
- **Status** Occasional pest
- **Location** Mainly Europe

This **common species** occurs in natural forests and plantations. It is associated with oak trees, but can become a nuisance in commercial fruit orchards. It eats plant fluids and insects. Females lay eggs in crevices on tree bark during the winter. The larvae hatch the following spring.

Lantern bug

Fulgora laternaria

- **Length** 1¼ in (3 cm)
- **Status** Neutral
- **Location** Central and South America

One of a large group of strange-looking insects with a **greatly enlarged head** section. The species is also known as the peanut-headed lantern fly. The hindwings bear large eyespots to deter predators, and further protection is given by plant poisons extracted from tree sap and stored in the lantern bug's body.

Water scorpion

Nepa cinerea

- **Length** ¾ in (2 cm)
- **Status** Neutral
- **Location** Europe

This leaf-shaped bug inhabits still pools, where it hunts other insects and small fish, trapping them with its **clasping front legs** and sucking out their body fluids. The long tube at the back of the body serves as a snorkel—every 30 minutes or so the water scorpion reverses up to the surface to replenish its air supply.

Treehoppers

Treehoppers first appeared on our planet about 50 million years ago. Entomologists (scientists who study insects) think there are up to 3,200 species that live in warmer regions worldwide, especially in tropical forests. Many of these insects have large, thorny projections on the thorax, which give them their alternative common name of thorn bug.

▼ THORNY THORAX
Even if the foul taste does not put them off, predators are bound to find attacking the thorny thorax a challenge.

FACT FILE

- **Number of species:** Around 3,200
- **Distribution:** Worldwide
- **Diet:** Treehoppers suck sap from plants. Any undigested sap passes through the treehopper's body as honeydew. Ants love honeydew and will stand guard over the insect to protect it.

▶ MASTER OF DISGUISE
From a distance, the distinctive thornlike projection on the thorax of the treehopper helps break up the shape of the insect. Predators might think that the treehopper is part of the plant upon which it is resting.

Thorn bug
Umbonia crassicornis

- **Length** Up to ½ in (1 cm)
- **Diet** Plant sap
- **Location** Central and South America and southern Florida

The **distinctive bump** on the back of the thorn bug is so sharp that it can pierce the sole of a shoe and puncture human skin. **This treehopper is a pest** in many parts of its range thanks to the damage it does to the plants on which it thrives.

◄ BUMPY ISSUES
Adult thorn bugs have just one bump on their backs, but the nymphs start off with three. The shape, size, and color varies widely between individuals.

Don't step on me!
Tread on the sharp thorax of the treehopper, and the resulting wound could easily become infected thanks to the tiny microorganisms that feed on the honeydew.

▲ CHEMICAL PROTECTION
Would-be predators usually steer clear of treehoppers and their nymphs (above) because the bodies of these distinctive bugs contain foul-tasting chemicals. The females even protect the eggs by coating them with a frothy substance that contains the same noxious chemicals.

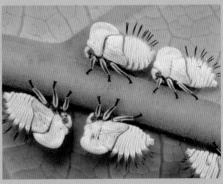

▲ NYMPHS
Female treehopper bugs lay hundreds of eggs and then guard them until they hatch about 20 days later. The female will then look after the brood. Treehoppers and their nymphs carpet the twigs and branches on which they live.

A *world* of beetles

More than a third of all insect species are beetles. They range in size from those just visible to the naked eye to giants that are 7½in (19cm) long. Beetles are found all over the world in every sort of habitat, on land and in fresh water. They have hard forewings called elytra, which close over the hindwings to protect them.

FACT FILE

? *Most beetles are not listed on the IUCN red list of endangered species. See pages 4–5 for more details.*

INVERTEBRATES

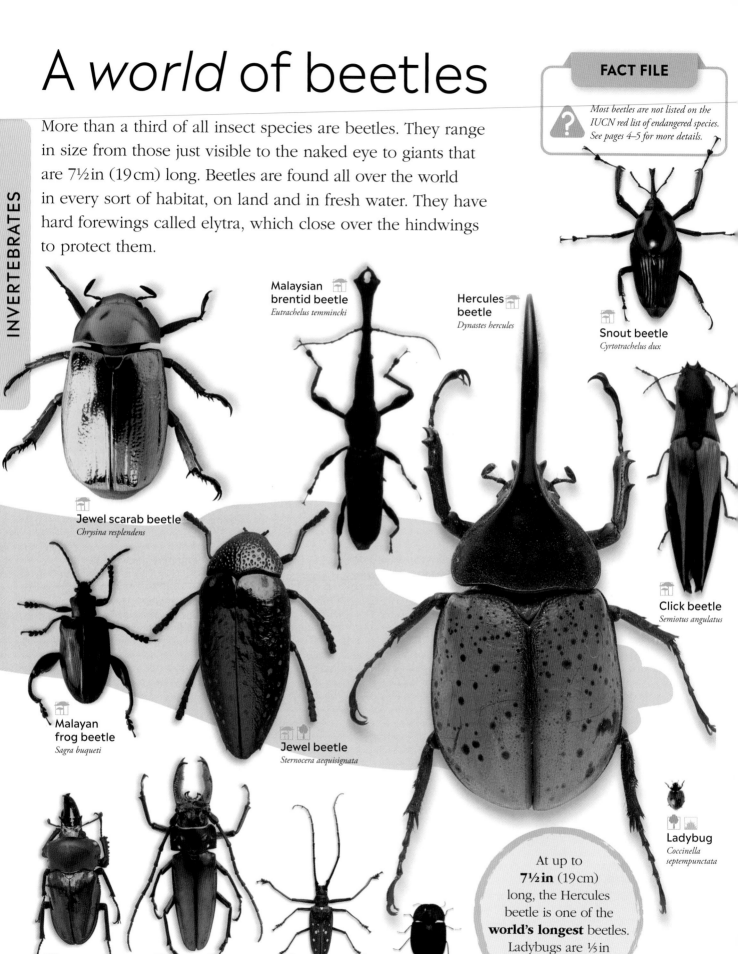

Snout beetle
Cyrtotrachelus dux

Malaysian brentid beetle
Eutrachelus temmincki

Hercules beetle
Dynastes hercules

Click beetle
Semiotus angulatus

Jewel scarab beetle
Chrysina resplendens

Malayan frog beetle
Sagra buqueti

Jewel beetle
Sternocera aequisignata

Ladybug
Coccinella septempunctata

King stag beetle
Phalacrognathus muelleri

Longhorn beetle
Callipogon barbatus

Longhorn beetle
Batocera rufomaculata

Pie-dish beetle
Helea subserratus

At up to **7½ in** (19cm) long, the Hercules beetle is one of the **world's longest** beetles. Ladybugs are ⅕in (5mm) long.

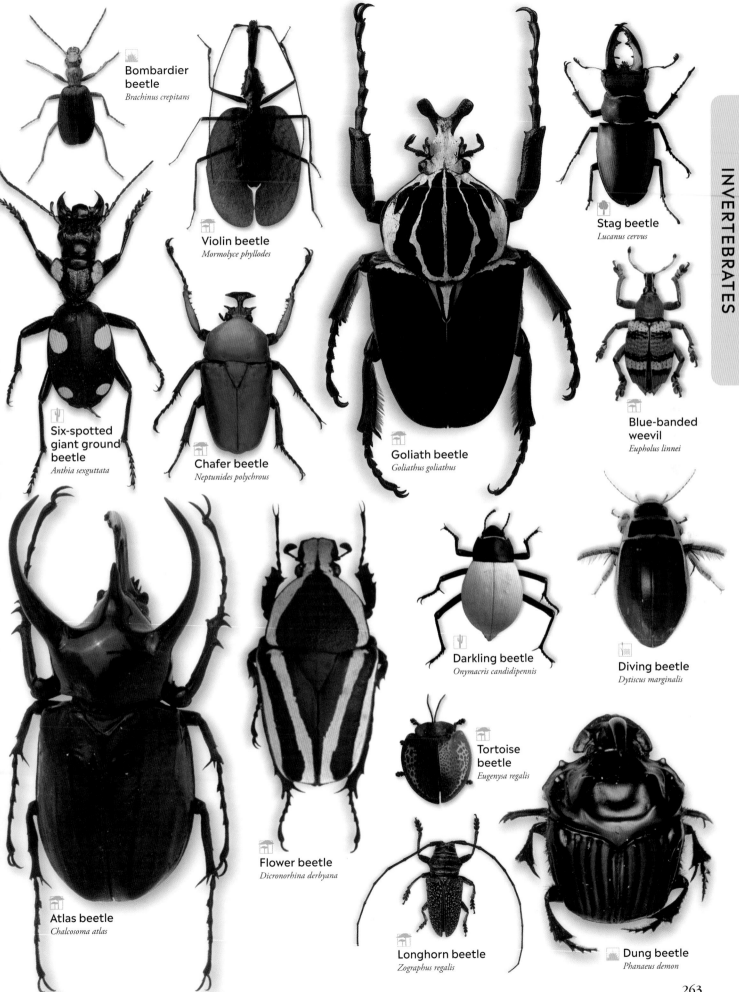

Bombardier beetle
Brachinus crepitans

Violin beetle
Mormolyce phyllodes

Stag beetle
Lucanus cervus

Six-spotted giant ground beetle
Anthia sexguttata

Chafer beetle
Neptunides polychrous

Goliath beetle
Goliathus goliathus

Blue-banded weevil
Eupholus linnei

Darkling beetle
Onymacris candidipennis

Diving beetle
Dytiscus marginalis

Tortoise beetle
Eugenysa regalis

Flower beetle
Dicronorhina derbyana

Atlas beetle
Chalcosoma atlas

Longhorn beetle
Zographus regalis

Dung beetle
Phanaeus demon

Wetas

The flightless wetas of New Zealand are some of the world's most ancient species still alive today. The different types vary in size, with the giant wetas being among the biggest insects on Earth. The word "weta" derives from the native Māori word *wetapunga*, meaning "God of Ugly Things."

MOUNTAIN STONE WETA
New Zealand offers a varied climate, and the mountain stone weta has adapted to this. During winter at high altitudes, the mountain stone weta can survive being frozen at temperatures of 14°F (−10°C).

Poor Knights weta

Deinacrida fallai

- **Length** 6–8 in (15–20 cm)
- **Status** Vulnerable
- **Location** Poor Knights Islands, New Zealand

Poor Knights wetas are one of 11 giant weta species. They split their time between the trees and ground, where they lay their eggs. **Nocturnal**, they **feed on fruit and fungi**, with insects forming a minor part of their diet. Though large, the crown of heaviest weta has gone to the wetapunga of Little Barrier Island, where a pregnant female weighed a staggering 2½ oz (70 g).

CONSERVATION

Giant wetas have become increasingly threatened. One main reason for this is the introduction of predators, such as rats and mice, into their natural habitats. Giant wetas are listed as vulnerable and conservationists have set up captive breeding programs around New Zealand.

Giant wetas aren't the only weta group in New Zealand. There are also about 10 species of tree weta which, as their name suggests, are mainly located crawling around in trees. More compact than the giant wetas, tree wetas live in small groups and can be found in the wooden burrows made by wood-boring beetle larvae. Watch out, though; they may be tiny, but tree wetas possess a nasty bite!

▲ THREATENING BEHAVIOR
The weta definitely puts the creepy into creepy-crawly. But it's not as scary as it looks and can feel threatened itself. To protect itself the male bush weta adopts a defensive posture. It stretches its large jaws, raises its spiny legs above its head, and hisses aggressively.

A mammal role for an insect
Millions of years ago, the New Zealand archipelago broke away from the main landmass. Because few mammal species made it onto the islands, the weta evolved behaviors usually associated with small rodents, such as burrowing and preying on smaller insects.

Ants

Ants are found on almost every land mass on the planet, except the frozen Antarctic. They live in highly organized colonies, usually with one queen or breeding female and an army of female workers. The workers build shelters, find food, and defend their nests.

Giant ant

Dinoponera gigantea

- **Length** 1⅖ in (36 mm)
- **Diet** Seeds, fruits, insects, and spiders
- **Location** South America

One of the biggest ants in the world, giant ants live in relatively **small colonies** of around 100 individuals. Their nests are found under mounds of soil. Inside are **networks of connecting tunnels**. The ants mostly forage for food at night, and feed on small, live animals.

KEEPING ON TOP

Giant ants do not have a queen—instead they have a breeding worker called a mother ant. If a rival challenges her position, she marks it with a chemical, then leaves it for her workers to kill and dispose of.

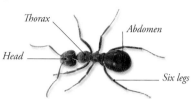
▼ GIANT ANTS *cut up large pieces of food using their serrated jaws, which are known as mandibles.*

Leaf-cutter ant
Atta cephalotes

- **Length** Queen 1⁴⁄₁₀ in (35 mm)
- **Diet** Fungus
- **Location** Central America and South America

These ants have **sharp jaws** that they use to cut parts of leaves from plants in their forest homes. They carry the leaf parts back to their nests where the pieces decay. Fungus grows on the decaying leaves, and the ants eat this fungus. **More than 5,000,000 ants may live in each nest**.

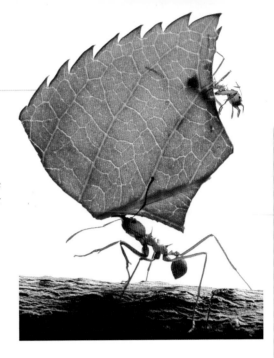

Honeypot ant
Myrmecocystus mimicus

- **Length** Queen ⁷⁄₂₀ in (9 mm); workers ⁶⁄₂₅ in (6 mm); repletes up to 1¹⁄₂₅ in (30 mm)
- **Diet** Insects and nectar
- **Location** Western US and Mexico

These ants **survive hot, dry habitats** by using workers as food storage pots. The workers, called "repletes," **gorge on nectar** until their abdomens are stuffed and swollen. They then act as living larders, feeding other ants in the colony. When two colonies meet, they put on "tournaments" of display fighting. The colony with the most ants wins. The losers run away.

Wood ant
Formica rufa

- **Length** ½ in (10 mm)
- **Diet** Aphids, flies, caterpillars, beetles, and honeydew
- **Location** Europe

An aggressive hunter, the wood ant **feeds on other insects**. It also "milks" aphids by stroking each individual until the aphid releases a droplet of sweet honeydew. Wood ants live in nests containing up to 1,000,000 inhabitants. If the nest is disturbed, the ants **swarm out and bite** the intruder.

Fire ant
Solenopsis invicta

- **Length** Queen ⁴⁄₁₀ in (8 mm)
- **Diet** Young plants, seeds, and insects
- **Location** South America, US, Australia, and New Zealand

This tiny, **stinging ant** lives in a soil nest, often on lawns, pastures, or roadsides. If disturbed, the ant releases a chemical that alerts other fire ants nearby. These then rush to attack. Their sting is extremely painful—similar to burning—and **can cause death** to people who are sensitive to the sting.

Weaver ant
Oecophylla smaragdina

- **Length** Queen ⁷⁄₁₀ in (15 mm); workers ½ in (11 mm)
- **Diet** Honeydew
- **Location** Asia and Australia

Weaver ants build their nests by pulling the leaves of trees together and **"weaving"** them with silk produced by the ants' larvae. A colony made up of 500,000 ants may stretch over 10 or more trees.

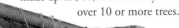

Bulldog ant
Myrmecia gulosa

- **Length** ⁹⁄₁₀ in (21 mm)
- **Diet** Honeydew, nectar, and small insects
- **Location** Australia

A bulldog ant has good eyesight, **large serrated jaws**, and a powerful sting. Bulldog ants remain perfectly still until prey comes into range, then **ambush** it. All the prey they catch is taken back to the nest where it is fed to the growing larvae.

Termites

Relatives of the cockroaches, some termites build huge mounds that dominate the landscape. They feed on plant matter. Termites are often considered pests, as they eat crops and infest houses, chewing through wooden walls and beams until the house is destroyed.

1,000,000 termites
live in this cathedral termite mound. They all work for the good of the colony and will protect it with their lives.

FACT FILE

- **Number of species:** 3,100
- **Key features:** Six legs. No obvious body divisions. Workers are usually small and pale colored. Soldiers are bigger, often with large jaws. Neither usually have eyes. All live in colonies.

Relative sizes

Queen

Worker   *Soldiers*   *King*

Magnetic mounds
In northern Australia, termites build mounds up to 13 ft (4 m) high. These are likened to magnetic compasses as the narrow sides face north and south and the wide sides face east and west. This ensures that only a small area of the mound faces the hottest midday sun.

Cathedral termite mounds
Cathedral termites of the genus *Macrotermes* build cement-hard mounds from soil and saliva. The mounds are ventilated by a network of tunnels and holes that can be opened to let in air, or blocked up with mud to stop heat escaping. The mounds protect the colony from predators such as ants, spiders, and lizards.

Cross section of a cathedral termite mound. Food stores and nurseries are mostly underground.

Ground level

Food stores

Fungus grown in gardens inside the nest

Nurseries containing eggs

King and queen's royal chamber

Cathedral mound termite

Macrotermes bellicosus

- **Length** Workers ½₅ in (4 mm); soldiers ³⁄₁₀ in (6 mm); queen 4⁹⁄₂₅ in (110 mm)
- **Diet** Fungus, wood, and dry plant matter
- **Location** Africa

Like all termites, cathedral mound termites are **social insects**. They live in highly organized colonies, like ants or bees. Their **main food is fungus**, which grows in chambers inside their nests. The fungus feeds on chewed-up wood that has passed through the termites' bodies.

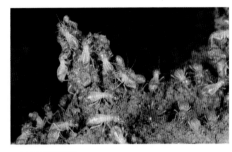

▲ WORKERS
Most termites in the colony are workers. Their job is to build and maintain the nest, find food, and care for the eggs.

▲ BECOMING QUEEN
The only termites capable of having young are the reproductives. Once a male and female mate, the female lays eggs and a new colony begins. The female is now a queen (above). Her mate is the king.

▲ THE QUEEN'S BODY
As the queen gets older, her abdomen expands and she is able to produce increasing numbers of eggs. A fully grown queen can produce more than 2,000 eggs in a day.

Bees and wasps

Alongside ants, bees and wasps form one of the most plentiful groups of animals on Earth. The honey bee and common wasp are a familiar sight on a summer's day and humans have become reliant on them for the predation of pests, pollination, and for honey production.

FACT FILE

- **Number of species:** There are 160,000 species of wasp and 20,000 species of bee.
- **Key features:** Both bees and wasps possess two pairs of wings and large compound eyes. Some species live in colonies, though most live a solitary life. Wasps are generally predatory and hairless, whereas bees are hairy and feed on pollen and nectar.

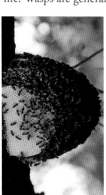

Honey bees' nest (at left and below)

FRIEND OR FOE

The bee is widely seen as the gardener's friend because of its role in pollination, though the wasp's role shouldn't be forgotten. As a predator, it acts as an efficient pest control agent. In fact, almost every pest insect has a species of wasp that preys on it.

Honey bee
Apis mellifera

- **Length** ⅖–⅘ in (10–20 mm)
- **Location** Originally Europe, western Asia, and Africa; now worldwide

Honey bees were first domesticated by the ancient Egyptians more than 4,500 years ago. This taste for honey hasn't waned and the art of bee-keeping, known as apiculture, is still practiced the world over. Wild honey bees live in colonies, which can be made up of more than **50,000 worker bees** and just **one fertile queen**. The queen can live up to two years, unlike the workers who only survive for about one month.

POLLEN COLLECTOR *Bees land on flowers to collect nectar, which is used to make honey, and pollen, which is used to feed the bee larvae. When they land on each flower, pollen sticks to their legs. It is stored in pollen baskets on their hind legs.*

Giant horn-tail wasp

Urocerus gigas

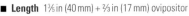

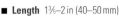

- **Length** 1⅗ in (40 mm) + ⅔ in (17 mm) ovipositor
- **Location** Europe

The name and appearance of the giant horn-tail conjures up a fearsome vision, though it is **quite harmless**. The stinger-like projection seen on a female is known as an ovipositor. It is actually part of her reproductive organ, and is used to **bore into trees**, so she can lay her eggs. The grubs that hatch will feed on the wood.

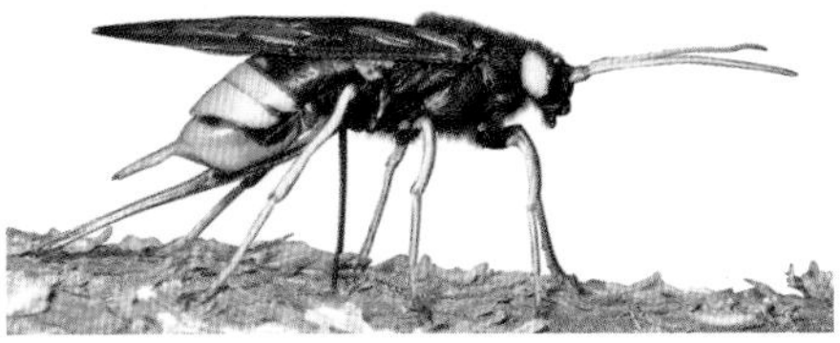

Tarantula hawk wasp

Pepsis formosa

- **Length** 1⅗–2 in (40–50 mm)
- **Location** US and Mexico

The tarantula hawk wasp is one of the biggest wasps in the world. It gets its name from its **ability to hunt down large tarantula spiders** and paralyze them with a powerful venom. It uses the spiders as food for its grubs. The tarantula hawk wasp possesses a ¼-in- (7-mm-) long stinger to inject its venom, which is said to give the **most painful sting** of any insect.

Buff-tailed bumblebee

Bombus terrestris

- **Length** ½–⅞ in (12–22 mm)
- **Location** Europe

The buff-tailed bumblebee is usually the first bumblebee to emerge after winter. The young, fertilized queens have **thick fur** to protect them during the cold months. They nest below ground.

Carpenter bee

Xylocopa violacea

- **Length** ⅘–1⅖ in (20–23 mm)
- **Location** Europe

These wood-working bees use their **powerful jaws** to bore tunnels in wood to make their nests. They don't eat the wood, they discard it or use it to create partitions. The male bees aggressively guard the nest, buzzing loudly and dive-bombing anything that comes near. It is all for show because they don't pose any real threat as the **males cannot sting**. The females can sting, but aren't aggressive.

Giant ichneumon wasp

Rhyssa persuasoria

- **Length** 1⅗ in (40 mm) + 1⅗ in (40 mm) ovipositor
- **Location** Mainly Europe

The giant ichneumon is a **parasitic wasp**. The female hunts down giant horn-tail wasp grubs by sensing the vibrations they make when chewing through wood. Using her long ovipositor, she drills through the wood and lays her eggs on the grubs. Her babies will grow, slowly **eating their grub host**.

European hornet

Vespa crabro

- **Length** ⅘–1⅖ in (20–35 mm)
- **Location** Europe, Asia, and North America

The hornet is a **social wasp and lives in a colony** of up to 500 insects. The hornet shoulders a bad reputation because of its imposing look and **aggressive-sounding buzz**. In truth, it rarely stings unless seriously provoked.

Potter wasp

Eumenes fraternus

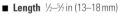

- **Length** ½–5⁄7 in (13–18 mm)
- **Location** North America

This crafty little wasp gets its name from the **pot-shaped nests** it builds out of mud and water. Inside, it lays a single egg and packs it full of food, usually paralyzed caterpillars. Adult potter wasps are **solitary** and feed on nectar.

Flies

Flies are a large group that covers common house flies to exotic mosquitoes. Flies have one pair of wings but they also have the shrunken remains of a second pair. These are called halteres and act as flight stabilizers, allowing these insects to fly with incredible skill and agility. Flies will eat almost anything, including flesh, blood, feces, urine, rotting plants, sweat, and nectar.

FACT FILE

- **Number of species:** 160,000
- **Key features:** Most have large compound eyes. Some have sharp mouths for piercing prey; others have fleshy mouths that suck food.
- **Size:** Ranges from tiny gnats to the South American *Gauromydas heros* with its 4-in (10-cm) wingspan.

Size comparison

Sucking mouthparts

Mosquitoes can be deadly. Females use syringe-like mouthparts to suck blood from other animals. Anopheles gambiae mosquitoes (below) bite humans, passing on the parasite that causes malaria.

Leaf-mining fly
From the Agromyzidae family

- **Length** 1/32–1/4 in (1–6 mm)
- **Diet** Plants, leaves, stems, seeds, and roots
- **Location** Worldwide

Many farmers consider these flies to be a **major pest**. Their larvae will munch their way through the leaves of any plants they happen to come across and can often destroy an entire crop in this way.

Malaria mosquito
Anopheles gambiae

Housefly

Musca domestica

- **Length** ⅕–¼ in (5–6 mm)
- **Diet** Organic waste, including leftover food, rotting flesh, and feces
- **Location** Worldwide

House flies are **found almost everywhere**, feeding on any food that humans and other animals leave lying around. They help **spread more than 100 diseases**, including cholera and typhoid. But without them, huge amounts of organic waste would not decompose and would just pile up.

Crane fly

Tipula paludosa

- **Length** ¾–1 in (18–25 mm)
- **Diet** Plant roots and nectar (adults)
- **Location** Worldwide

These **fragile flies** are sometimes known as daddy-long-legs. Despite their large wings, they are **poor fliers** and rarely get very far from the ground. The tough-looking, 1½-in- (40-mm-) long larvae are called leatherjackets. They live in rotting wood, bogs, and damp soil, where they eat plant roots, especially those of grass. Crane flies often make a tasty snack for passing birds.

Stalk-eyed fly

Cyrtodiopsis whitei

- **Length** ⅓–⅖ in (7–10 mm)
- **Diet** Fungi, bacteria, and rotting plants
- **Location** Southeast Asia

To prove who is the best and therefore most likely to attract a mate, male stalk-eyed flies literally **go eyeball-to-eyeball with each other**. The male with the longest eye stalks usually wins. The loser normally flies off unhurt to search for another male, hopefully smaller than himself, that he can challenge for the right to mate.

Tsetse fly

Glossina morsitans

- **Length** ⅓–⅔ in (7–15 mm)
- **Diet** Blood
- **Location** Africa and southern Arabian peninsula

Adult tsetse flies are **bloodsuckers**. They use their piercing mouthparts to suck blood from humans and other animals. They can drink up to three times their weight in blood in one sitting. By feeding in this way, tsetse flies **spread a fatal sleeping sickness** that affects people and cattle.

Abdomen swollen with blood after feeding

Before feeding

Blue bottle fly

Calliphora vomitoria

- **Length** ⅖–⅔ in (10–15 mm)
- **Diet** Rotting meat and plants, and feces
- **Location** Europe, North America, and northern Asia

These flies can **sniff out any rotting flesh or feces that is lying around**, even from as far away as 5 miles (8 km). Their **disgusting diet** means that blue bottles do an important job in helping to clear away a lot of undesirable organic waste. The female fly lays her eggs, up to 2,000, while she is feeding.

Hornet robber fly

Asilus crabroniformis

- **Length** ⅘–1 in (20–25 mm)
- **Diet** Insects and decaying organic matter
- **Location** Europe

Huge eyes; a long, thin body; and grasping, spined legs make this fly an **excellent aerial hunter**. Its daggerlike mouthparts inject paralyzing saliva into its prey, which it sucks up.

Bee fly

Bombylius major

- **Length** ½–⅔ in (12–15 mm)
- **Diet** Nectar and bee grubs
- **Location** Europe, North America, and northern Asia

With its stout, furry body and high-pitched whine, the bee fly does a good job of **mimicking a bee**. But the long, rigid proboscis (feeding tube) held out in front of its head gives the game away. A bee's proboscis curls up when not in use. Bee fly larvae live as parasites in the nests of solitary bees. Here they feed on stored nectar and bee grubs.

Proboscis

Haltere

Butterflies and moths

The marvellous patterns and brilliant colors of their wings mean that butterflies are a more welcome sight than most insects. But many members of the huge group of animals to which they belong are in fact tiny, hairy, brown moths. These delicate-looking creatures are also much tougher than they appear. Some can survive in deserts and even the freezing Arctic.

FACT FILE

- **Number of species:** 170,000
- **Key features:** Four wings and large compound eyes. Most have a long, coiled feeding tube (proboscis).
- **Size:** Largest moth: Atlas (*Attacus atlas*); smallest butterfly: Western pygmy blue (*Brephidium exilis*).

Size comparison

MONARCH BUTTERFLY *Every fall, tens of millions of these butterflies migrate from the cold of Canada and the eastern United States to the warm sunshine of Mexico and California. Some fly more than 2,500 miles (4,000 km).*

METAMORPHOSIS

When a butterfly's or moth's egg hatches, a caterpillar crawls out. A caterpillar's main job is to eat and grow until it is as big as it can be. Then it stops eating and a tough, leathery coat forms around it. It has turned into a pupa. Inside this protective coat, the caterpillar changes into a winged adult. When it is ready, the new moth or butterfly emerges and flies away.

Fully grown caterpillar

Pupa forms

New butterfly emerges

Ready for take-off

Atlas moth
Attacus atlas

- **Wingspan** 8–11 in (20–28 cm)
- **Location** Southern China and Southeast Asia

This giant is the **largest species of moth** in the world. But being so big does not seem to stop many other animals from attempting to hunt it down and make a meal of it. To help scare off predators, this moth's wings have **special protective markings** that look very similar to those found on a highly poisonous cobra snake. The atlas moth secretes a wool-like silk that is used for cloth in parts of China.

Postman butterfly
Heliconius melpomene

- **Wingspan** 3–4 in (8–10 cm)
- **Location** Central America and northern South America

This colorful butterfly lives for six months or more. Most moths and butterflies only live for a few weeks, and the **long life** of this species may be due to its highly nutritious diet. Like all butterflies and moths, it sucks up nectar from flowers using its **long proboscis**, or feeding tube. At the same time, it takes up large amounts of pollen, which is particularly rich in health-giving nutrients.

Indian leaf butterfly
Kallima inachus

- **Wingspan** 3¼–4¼ in (8.5–11 cm)
- **Location** South Asia from India to Japan

This butterfly is **difficult to see** when it is at rest. This is because the coloring on its underside makes it **look like a leaf**. But if it is disturbed, it rapidly opens its wings, flashing the bright blue and orange of its upper surface. This change confuses predators, giving the butterfly a few seconds to escape being eaten.

Peacock butterfly
Aglais io

- **Wingspan** 2–2½ in (5.5–6 cm)
- **Location** Europe and North Asia

Adult peacock butterflies **hibernate all winter** in sheltered spots, such as a hollow in a tree, a cavity in a building, or even a garden shed. On the first sunny days of spring, the females emerge and fly off to look for stinging nettles on which they lay their eggs. Each **female lays about 500 eggs**.

Death's head hawk-moth
Acherontia atropos

- **Wingspan** 3½–4¾ in (9–12 cm)
- **Location** Africa, Europe, and western Asia

This moth **loves honey** and breaks into beehives to get it. The bees sometimes attack, but usually they ignore it, possibly because this moth can give off a scent that makes it **smell like a bee**. It is also quite noisy. The caterpillar makes a clicking sound by grinding its jaws and the adult squeaks loudly.

Morpho butterfly
Morpho peleides

 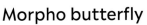

- **Wingspan** 5–7⅞ in (13–20 cm)
- **Location** Central and South America

The scales on this butterfly's wings are actually transparent, not blue, and act **like prisms**. The blue coloring is caused by the way these "prisms" split up sunlight falling on the wings into its component colors. The wings are so **bright** that they are visible from ⅝ mile (1 km) away.

Sunset moth
Chrysiridia croesus

- **Wingspan** 3½–4¼ in (9–11 cm)
- **Location** East Africa

This is one of the few moths that **flies during the day**. Like other day-flying moths, it is brightly colored. Like the morpho butterfly, its **dazzling colors** are not due to special pigments, but are caused by having prism-like scales on its wings. In this case, these scales split up the sunlight striking them into a rainbow of colors.

Orange-barred sulphur butterfly
Phoebis philea

- **Wingspan** 2¾–3¼ in (7–8.5 cm)
- **Location** Southern US and Central and South America

At the height of summer, thousands of these shimmering, golden-yellow butterflies **gather together** on the banks of dry riverbeds. They are there to **suck up the mud**, which has large quantities of nutritious minerals dissolved in it. This unusual activity is known as "mud puddling."

Moths and *butterflies*

There are about 170,000 species of butterflies and moths, and 90 percent of them are moths. It can be difficult to tell a moth from a butterfly. Most butterflies fly during the day and most moths fly at night. Moth antennae range from single strands to feathery branches. Butterflies have clubbed antennae.

Goat moth
Cossus cossus

MOTHS

Owl moth
Brahmaea wallichii

Provence burnet moth
Zygaena occitanica

African moon moth
Argema mimosae

Oak eggar
Lasiocampa quercus

Madagascan sunset moth
Chrysiridia rhipheus

Hoop pine moth
Milionia isodoxa

Buff-tip
Phalera bucephala

Hieroglyphic moth
Diphthera festiva

Garden tiger moth
Arctia caja

Magpie moth
Abraxas grossulariata

White witch moth
Thysania agrippina

Pale tussock
Calliteara pudibunda

Hornet moth
Sesia apiformis

Verdant sphinx hawk-moth
Euchloron megaera

BUTTERFLIES

Peacock butterfly
Aglais io

Underside view

Small copper
Lycaena phlaeas

Cocoa mort bleu
Caligo teucer

Queen Alexandra's bird-wing
Ornithoptera alexandrae

Checkered skipper
Carterocephalus palaemon

The Queen Alexandra's bird-wing is the **largest butterfly** with a wingspan of up to 11 in (28 cm). The small copper has a wingspan of 1 in (2.5 cm).

Lesser grass blue butterfly
Zizina otis

African giant swallowtail
Papilio antimachus

Japanese emperor
Sasakia charonda

Blue morpho
Morpho menelaus

Viceroy
Limenitis archippus

Cairns bird-wing
Ornithoptera priamus

Hewitson's blue hairstreak
Thecla coronata

Great spangled fritillary
Speyeria cybele

Great orange tip
Hebomoia glaucippe

Scorpions

The scorpion's thick armor plating makes it the arachnid equivalent of a battle tank. It has four pairs of legs; two strong pincers; and a long, curling tail. The tail carries a venomous sting. This is mainly a weapon of defense but can also be used to paralyze prey. The venom of some species is lethal to humans. Scorpions spend most of the day in the shade, coming out to hunt at night.

They think I'm a taxi service!

Scorpions give birth to live young. After they emerge, the female carries the whole brood on her back wherever she goes. Sometimes, there can be as many as a hundred babies holding on. Until a young scorpion develops its own hard shell and tail stinger, it needs its mother to protect it against predators.

PINCER MOVEMENT
Scorpions use their pincers to catch and hold on to prey. If the prey is small enough, the scorpion simply crushes it to death.

Giant desert hairy scorpion

Hadrurus arizonensis

- **Length** 4–7 in (10–18 cm)
- **Location** Southwestern North America

This is the largest native scorpion in North America. It gets its name from its size, and the brown hairs on its tail and legs. These **hairs detect air and ground vibrations** and are useful in finding prey. Usually, this scorpion lies in wait, ready to ambush a suitable victim. Although this scorpion's **eyesight is poor**, its senses of hearing and touch are excellent.

▲ DEFENSE TACTICS *When threatened, a scorpion lifts its two pincers and waves them aggressively at its attacker. If this doesn't work, it will bring its tail forward to sting the aggressor.*

▼ RANGE OF SIZE *The emperor scorpion is one of the largest species and grows to more than 8 in (20 cm) in length. Originally from Africa, these scorpions are sometimes kept as pets, despite their painful sting. Numbers are threatened by over-collection. The European scorpion is only about 1⅕ in (3 cm) long and shelters in wall crevices. Its sting is only mildly painful.*

EUROPEAN SCORPION

EMPEROR SCORPION

Spiders

Spiders creep about on eight long legs. Most of them have eight eyes as well. The size of a spider ranges from a few millimeters to 1 ft (30 cm). Spiders can be found in a wide variety of habitats. Many live in burrows in the ground. Others find their way into our homes.

▲ WATER SPIDER (Argyroneta aquatica) *This is the only species that lives under water. It survives by spinning an air-bell to live in. Females wrap their eggs in silk and spend most of their time inside the bell.*

▼ CRAB SPIDER *(Misumena vatia) This spider, often sitting like a crab, waits on flowers for its prey. It catches large meals, including butterflies and bees.*

SILK SPINNERS

Spiders have many different uses for the silk they make. Lots of spiders spin webs as a trap for their prey. Then they can sit and wait for their food to arrive. Silk cocoons are made to protect spiders' eggs. Spiders also use silk to line and seal their burrows.

▼ BABOON SPIDER *Like other tarantulas, the king baboon spider comes out at night to hunt. It feeds on a variety of animals including lizards, large insects, and mice.*

Female king baboon spider
Pelinobius muticus

FACT FILE

- **Number of species:** More than 45,000 species of spider.
- **Key features:** Predatory animals that have two body segments and eight legs. All spiders produce silk, but not all use it to trap their prey. Most have venom, though only 200 species possess a bite that is harmful to humans.

Size comparison of biggest species

Northern black widow

Latrodectus variolus

   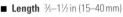

- **Length** ⅗–1½ in (15–40 mm)
- **Location** North America

Black widows possess a **potent neurotoxic venom.** The bright hourglass markings warn its predators not to bother it. The female is bigger, lives longer, and is more venomous than the male. Over a summer, a female will produce 4–9 sacs of eggs, each containing 100–400 eggs.

Brown huntsman spider

Heteropoda venatoria

- **Length** 3–5 in (75–125 mm)
- **Location** North America, Asia, and Australia

The brown huntsman gets its name from its **ability to hunt its prey using speed** and its powerful mouth parts. It does have the ability to spin a tangle web, but the web is only used to slow down prey. This spider **feeds on cockroaches**, which makes it a welcome visitor to households. It does have a **venomous bite**, though it isn't too powerful, and it is more likely to flee when disturbed.

King baboon spider

Pelinobius muticus

- **Length** 4¾–7⅘ in (120–200 mm)
- **Location** Eastern Africa

This is an **aggressive** spider. It will attack with little reason and inject venom through its long fangs. When threatened, it rears up to show its fangs and **hisses**. It is active at night, searching for prey and excavating its burrow, which can go down more than 6½ ft (2 m).

European cave spider

Meta menardi

- **Length** 1½–2 in (40–50 mm)
- **Location** Europe

The **adult cave spider is photophobic**, meaning it doesn't like light, and searches for caves, tunnels, and dark holes. In complete contrast, the baby cave spiders are attracted to light. This is thought to allow the species to spread beyond the home cave. Cave spiders **prey on smaller invertebrates**, especially slugs. They possess venom, but it isn't strong. This, coupled with their lack of aggression, has landed them the tag of "gentle giants."

Indian ornamental spider

Poecilotheria regalis

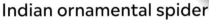

- **Length** 7–9 in (180–230 mm)
- **Location** India

The Indian ornamental spider belongs to the tarantula family. It usually lives high in trees, its **long legs** helping it climb. The female is a silver-gray and is larger than the brown male. In the wild, the Indian ornamental spider is **lightning fast** and has a strong venom. It preys on large insects, lizards, and birds.

Spiny-backed orb weaver

Gasteracantha cancriformis

- **Length** ¹⁄₁₃–⅓ in (2–9 mm)
- **Width** ⅓–½ in (9–13 mm)
- **Location** North and South America

The spiny-backed orb weaver is easily identified by its **brightly colored and pointy body**. The females are larger than the males, and they live a **solitary life** within their webs. The web can be 3¼–19½ feet (1–6 m) off the ground and is a series of loops and spirals. The webs have a catching area of up to 2 ft (60 cm), trapping flies, moths, and beetles.

Spider *silk*

Spiders are known for producing silk. The silk is made from protein and is produced by small organs called spinnerets. Many spiders use silk to catch prey, usually by building a web into which insects fly and get stuck. Other spiders use silk to transport themselves on the breeze.

▲ IN A SPIN *Orb-web spiders build webs that radiate out from a central hub. They then fill in the gaps between the strong framework strands with a long spiral of sticky silk thread.*

▲ DECORATION *The spider Cyclosa insulana decorates its web with bands of silk. No one is sure why it does this, but it may be to hide the spider from view, to strengthen the web, or to stop birds flying into it and breaking it.*

TARANTULAS Many tarantulas use silk to line their burrows. This may be to stop the burrows falling in and to keep them moist. Some tarantulas also produce sticky silk on their feet that helps them grip when climbing vertical surfaces.

◀ ZIGZAGS *The silver argiope spider (Argiope argentata) can be found from the US down to northern South America. It is known for the dense, zigzag-shaped webbing that it makes on plants. Usually these spiders sit in the middle of their web with their legs in the shape of an X.*

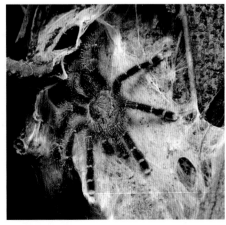

Crustaceans

This large group of arthropods includes a diverse range of creatures, from tiny, delicate water fleas to heavily armored lobsters. Nearly all live underwater, either in fresh waters or seas, though a few—including woodlice and land crabs—have joined us humans on land.

A PARASITIC LIFE

Some crustaceans live attached to other animals. These are known as parasites. Some parasitic crustaceans, such as sea lice, cling to the skin of fish, but can swim independently. Others, like the tongue worm, are more dependent on their hosts. They attach their tongue-shaped bodies to reptiles, birds, and mammals using five mouthlike appendages. Tongue worms rely on the host's blood supply to provide them with food to live and reproduce.

▼ FOLLOW THE LEADER
This mysterious single-file migration of the Caribbean spiny lobster is triggered by a drop in water temperature. The exact reason for the migration is unknown, but biologists believe it is to find warmer, calmer waters.

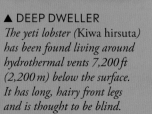

▲ DEEP DWELLER
The yeti lobster (Kiwa hirsuta) has been found living around hydrothermal vents 7,200 ft (2,200 m) below the surface. It has long, hairy front legs and is thought to be blind.

Caribbean spiny lobster
Panulirus argus

  15

- **Length** 8–18 in (20–45 cm)
- **Location** Western Atlantic Ocean

The Caribbean spiny lobster is a **shy**, **nocturnal crustacean** that hides in the coral reef during the day for protection. Unlike most lobsters, it doesn't have large front claws. It ventures out at night to search for mollusks and echinoderms to eat but it will also **scavenge for food**, feeding on the remains of dead sea creatures and sometimes dead plants it finds on the seabed.

Tadpole shrimp

Triops cancriformis

- **Length** Up to 4⅓ in (11 cm)
- **Location** Europe

Tadpole shrimp have hardly changed for 220 million years, and are considered **living fossils**. They are born survivors and multiply in huge numbers in perfect conditions, while their eggs can survive freezing temperatures and drought. They also get the award for the crustacean with the **most legs**, with 11 pairs on its thorax and up to six pairs on each rear segment.

Peacock mantis shrimp

Odontodactylus scyllarus

- **Length** 1¼–7 in (3–18 cm)
- **Location** Indo-Pacific

This rainbow-colored mantis shrimp may look pretty, but it harbors a **nasty surprise**. It loiters in its burrow using its supersensitive eyesight to locate lunch. It then **ambushes** at lightning speeds, smashing its prey with its powerful claws.

Water flea

Daphnia pulex

- **Length** 1/16–⅛ in (2–5 mm)
- **Location** Worldwide

These small freshwater crustaceans move around in a jerky fashion, using their antennae to propel themselves toward their lunch. They prey on smaller crustaceans, though they are generally **filter feeders**, sucking up single-celled organisms. Water fleas have to mate to reproduce, and the young fleas are **reared in a pouch** inside the adult's exoskeleton.

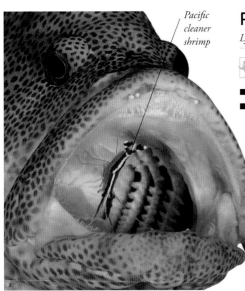

Pacific cleaner shrimp

Pacific cleaner shrimp

Lysmata amboinensis

- **Length** 2½–3 in (60–70 mm)
- **Location** Red Sea and Indo-Pacific

At first glance these helpful little shrimp look **very well trained** or possibly crazy. They gather together to provide **"cleaning stations"** on coral reefs, where they remove dead tissue and parasites from various fish (including some that are the shrimp's **natural predators**). Cleaner shrimp have a selfish motive, though— they are **scavengers**, and they naturally feed on the material they remove.

Robber crab

Birgus latro

- **Length** 40 in (100 cm) over outstretched legs
- **Location** Indian and western Pacific oceans

Robber crabs are the largest of the land crabs. **Living in burrows**, they have been found up to 2 miles (6 km) inland. They are also known as coconut crabs because they were once thought to eat coconuts. They have **powerful claws** that enable them to crack open nuts and seeds.

Common woodlouse

Oniscus asellus

- **Length** ⅖–⅗ in (10–16 mm)
- **Location** Western and northern Europe

This is one of the biggest woodlice in Europe. It thrives in damp, dark environments, and happily **eats dead plants** and rotting animals. Common woodlice are known as decomposers, and **they help to decay and recycle vast amounts of organic waste**.

Goose-necked barnacle

Pollicipes polymerus

- **Length** 4–6 in (10–15 cm)
- **Location** Northern and eastern Pacific

The name "goose-necked" comes from the fleshy, **leathery stalk** that the barnacle uses to cling to rocks. It is a **filter feeder** and catches smaller crustaceans and plankton. In the Middle Ages, people thought these barnacles were young geese trapped on the riverbed.

Spider crabs are instantly recognizable by their triangular shell, or carapace, and their long, thin legs. They pick up sponges, seaweed, anemones, and even bits of wood, which they attach to hairs on their body and legs to act as a disguise. They will swap their decorations to match new surroundings.

Japanese spider crab

Macrocheira kaempferi

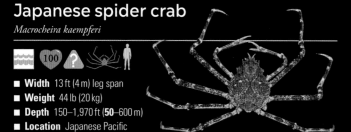

- **Width** 13 ft (4 m) leg span
- **Weight** 44 lb (20 kg)
- **Depth** 150–1,970 ft (**50**–600 m)
- **Location** Japanese Pacific

These crabs are the largest crustaceans and the biggest living arthropods. They usually have a **knobbly orange body** and legs with **white spots**. The biggest specimens have a body 15 in (37 cm) wide, with each leg measuring up to 6½ ft (2 m) long.

▶ NASTY NIPPERS
Male Japanese spider crabs are bigger than females, and their front legs grow longer. Both sexes have a pair of pincers that are capable of prizing open mollusk shells. The crab's other eight legs end in spikes that it uses to dig into the sea floor.

It gets chilly down here!

With a body the size of a large dinner plate, and its long, extendable legs, the Japanese spider crab walks slowly across the sea floor like an enormous mechanical spider as it scavenges for food. It lurks in the deep, cold ocean waters around Japan.

A TASTY LUNCH

Although the Japanese spider crab is the biggest crustacean in the ocean, it is still preyed upon by even larger predators, such as the giant octopus. It is also caught and eaten by humans.

PICKY EATERS

Despite their long limbs, these leggy crustaceans don't break any speed records. Often too slow to catch speedy live prey, they pick away across the seabed looking for dead animals or slow invertebrates. Some have been seen to eat various seaweeds. The front claws are used to pick their lunch to pieces and pass it into the mouth.

◀ **PORTLY SPIDER CRAB**
(Libinia emarginata)
The portly spider crab is a species of crab found in coastal waters. This crab grows a "garden" of sponges and seaweed across its back. The carapace is shiny and covered with short hairs. These trap microscopic sea creatures that then set up home here. The portly spider crab is slow-moving and eats what it can find.

Centipedes and millipedes

Despite looking similar, centipedes and millipedes have evolved in very different directions. Millipedes have become slow-moving, heavily armored herbivores, while centipedes are fast, lightweight predators. Another major difference is in the number of legs—millipedes have two pairs on each segment, centipedes only one.

Giant African millipede
Archispirostreptus gigas

PILL MILLIPEDE

■ **At first glance, the pill millipede** looks similar to a land crustacean called a woodlouse. However, the millipede has a large, shield-like plate behind its head, more legs, and a glossy black appearance.

Pill millipedes have 13 smooth body segments. A woodlouse has 11 rough segments.

If attacked by a predator, the pill millipede can roll itself into an armor-plated ball.

My feet really hurt ...

The front pair of legs in all centipedes has evolved into hollow fangs through which they inject venom into their victim. The walking legs of the giant desert centipede are also tipped with sharp claws that can cut human skin and drip venom into the wound.

Flat-backed cyanide millipede

Harpaphe haydeniana

- **Length** 1½–2 in (30–51 mm)
- **Location** North America

With its black and yellow **warning colors**, this millipede has few predators. If it is threatened, it secretes pungent-smelling, highly toxic hydrogen cyanide through pores in its sides. So far only one ground beetle has been discovered that can deal with this **defense mechanism**. Females have 31 pairs of legs, while males have only 30 pairs of legs.

Giant desert centipede

Scolopendra heros

- **Length** 5–7⅞ in (130–200 mm)
- **Location** Southern US

Giant desert centipedes are extremely efficient predators. They are **capable of sprinting** at speeds of up to 1½ ft (0.5 m) per second and use all of their 21 pairs of legs to ensnare their prey before delivering a **paralyzing bite**. Centipedes can kill large prey such as lizards and mice. Females will protect their eggs and watch over juveniles until they can fend for themselves.

Claw-tipped leg

Segmented body

Garden centipede

Lithobius forficatus

- **Length** ¾–1½ in (20–30 mm)
- **Location** Europe

This **common species** is found in yards. **At night, they hunt** for small invertebrates that hide under rocks and fallen logs. In gardens, the underside of a plant pot makes a good place for them to **go in search of food**. If they are uncovered, they will quickly run for **shelter**.

Cave centipede

Scutigera coleoptrata

- **Length** ⅖–2½ in (10–60 mm) including legs
- **Location** Europe, Asia, and North America

Perfectly evolved for life in caves, this centipede has **long legs and antennae** that allow it to feel for its prey in the dark. Once the prey is located, the centipede swiftly pounces and injects a **potent venom** to kill it. They are also found in the basements and cellars of houses, where they feed on spiders, ants, cockroaches, and other pests.

Shocking pink dragon millipede

Desmoxytes purpurosea

- **Length** 1¼ in (3 cm)
- **Location** Thailand

Not many animals would contemplate eating this spiky little millipede—its **vivid pink color** warns attackers that it is extremely poisonous, as well as **difficult to swallow**. Armed with this protection, it wanders freely across open ground and among the vegetation of the Thai forest where it lives.

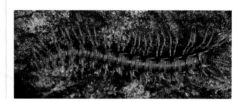

Amazonian giant centipede

Scolopendra gigantea

- **Length** 10¼–13½ in (260–350 mm)
- **Location** South America

Few animals will tackle a fully grown giant centipede. However, if another creature does try to make a meal of one of these it will have to deal with its **venomous** bite, 46 powerful clawed legs, and a pair of **needle-tipped appendages** at the rear end.

▼ ON THE ATTACK *Giant centipedes have been known to attack prey that is almost as big as themselves, including mice and bats.*

Echinoderms

Echinoderms are found in seas and oceans all over the world. They include starfish, sea urchins, brittle stars, sea cucumbers, and sea lilies and feather stars. Many are vividly colored. This is because of special pigment cells in the skin. In some species, these cells are sensitive to light and the animal changes color as night falls.

FACT FILE

- **Number of species:** 7,000
- **Key features:** Echinoderms have a wide range of body shapes. Some have arms and some are spherical or cylindrical. A central cavity may be enclosed by a tough skeleton, known as a "test." A unique internal system of water-filled canals is used to move, feed, and breathe.

▶ **HYDRAULIC ANIMAL**
The system of water-filled canals links up to "tube feet" that stick out of gaps in the test. Echinoderms can crawl along the seabed by pumping water into these sucker-like feet.

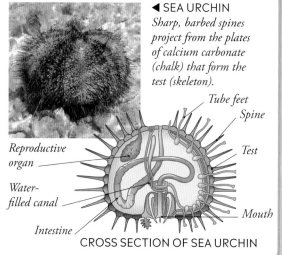

◀ **SEA URCHIN**
Sharp, barbed spines project from the plates of calcium carbonate (chalk) that form the test (skeleton).

Reproductive organ

Water-filled canal

Intestine

Tube feet

Spine

Test

Mouth

CROSS SECTION OF SEA URCHIN

Brittle star
Ophiura ophiura

- **Size** 3–4 in (8–10 cm) arm span
- **Diet** Crustaceans, plankton, and decaying organic matter
- **Location** Northeast Atlantic Ocean

Like all brittle stars, of which there are 2,000 species, this one has five long, **flexible arms** that radiate out from a disklike body. It uses these snakelike limbs to "row" itself across the sea floor. Brittle stars often feed on decaying matter, but this one is also an **active predator**. To snare its prey, it loops its long arms around its victim. Then it swiftly leaps on top and begins to devour its meal.

Violet sea apple
Pseudocolochirus violaceus

- **Length** 6–6½ in (15–17 cm)
- **Diet** Decaying organic matter and plankton
- **Location** Eastern Indian Ocean and western Pacific Ocean

This is a type of sea cucumber. Its soft body can be a variety of different colors, although its feet are always yellow and the area around its mouth is usually blue or violet. It feeds by extending the ring of **feathery tentacles** that surround its mouth, using them to trap bits of food and tiny organisms that are flowing past in the sea current. It then pulls the tentacles into its mouth, drawing in its catch. If a violet sea apple is injured or disturbed, it often reacts by **releasing a poison** that can kill many small fish and other small sea animals.

Blue starfish

Linckia laevigata

 10

- **Size** 8–12 in (20–30 cm) arm span
- **Diet** Decaying organic matter, plankton
- **Location** Indian Ocean and western and central Pacific Ocean

Its **striking color** makes this starfish one of the most eye-catching inhabitants of the coral reef. Some individuals are also bright orange. Like many echinoderms, the blue starfish can **regrow any lost limbs**. But the ability of this species to do this is particularly impressive. If the animal is pulled apart by a predator, any arms that do not get eaten can grow into a completely new starfish.

Cotton-spinning sea cucumber

Holothuria forskali

  8

- **Length** 8–10 in (20–25 cm)
- **Diet** Decaying organic matter
- **Location** Northeast Atlantic Ocean

If this sea cucumber is attacked, it has an extraordinary defense mechanism. It **expels its internal organs**, including its entire digestive, respiratory, and reproductive systems. This sticky mass not only confuses a predator, but can trap and entangle it as well. Over time, **new replacement organs** grow back inside the sea cucumber's body.

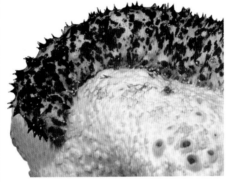

Common starfish

Asterias rubens

 10

- **Size** 8–20 in (20–50 cm) arm span
- **Diet** Mollusks and crustaceans
- **Location** Northeast Atlantic Ocean

Huge groups of common starfish are often found in places where the feeding is good. Sometimes as many as 800 can be seen packed together in a few square yards. Starfish enjoy eating bivalve mollusks, such as mussels and clams. The starfish grabs its prey and uses its tube feet to prize open the bivalve's shell. Then it **pushes its stomach out of its body** and into the shell, where it digests the now defenseless animal.

Feather star

Antedon petasus

  5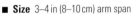

- **Size** 3–4 in (8–10 cm) arm span
- **Diet** Decaying organic matter and plankton
- **Location** North Sea

This feather star has **10 arms** and likes to make its home in sheltered places, half-hidden by rocks, or in a wreck. All feather stars spend the first months of their lives attached by a stalk to a pebble, or seaweed. They **break free and swim off** as soon as their arms have developed fully.

Crown-of-thorns starfish

Acanthaster planci

  8

- **Size** Up to 27½ in (70 cm) arm span
- **Diet** Corals, mollusks, sea urchins, and algae
- **Location** Red Sea, Indian Ocean, and Pacific Ocean

This is one of the world's **largest starfish**. For protection, it has a dense coat of thorny spines. If it is touched or stepped on, these **spines release a toxin** that can cause severe pain, nausea, and vomiting. Corals are this starfish's favorite food. Its voracious appetite has **damaged many coral reefs**, including the vast Great Barrier Reef off the coast of Australia.

Glossary

Aerial Relating to air.

Agile Able to move quickly and easily.

Amphibian A type of cold-blooded vertebrate, such as a frog or newt. Most amphibians develop from larvae that live in water and breathe through gills, and become land-dwelling adults that breathe air through lungs.

Anal Of fins, near the tail.

Antenna Movable sense organ on the head of animals such as insects and crustaceans.

Antler Bony growth, often branched, on a deer's head. Unlike horns, antlers usually grow and are later shed every year.

Aquatic Living or growing in or near water.

Arachnid A type of animal, such as a spider or scorpion, that has a two-part body and four pairs of legs.

Arboreal Living in or connected with trees.

Artery A vessel that carries blood away from the heart.

Arthropod An animal with a segmented body; jointed limbs; and a hard, outer covering.

Australasia A term used to describe the area that includes Australia, New Zealand, Papua New Guinea, and neighboring islands in the Pacific Ocean.

Baleen Brushlike fringe that some whales have instead of teeth to strain food from the water.

Beak A set of narrow, protruding jaws, usually without teeth.

Blowhole Nostril on top of the head of whales, dolphins, and porpoises; hole in the ice that aquatic mammals breathe through.

Blubber The thick layer of fat that protects some animals (such as whales and seals) from the cold.

Bovid A mammal related to cattle with hooves divided in two (cloven hooves).

Breed To produce young.

Bristles Short, stiff, coarse hairs.

Buoyancy The tendency of a body or an object to float in water.

Burrow A hole in the ground that some animals (such as rabbits) live in.

Camouflage Colors or patterns on an animal's skin or fur that allow it to blend with its surroundings.

Carnivorous Often used to describe animals that eat meat, but also refers to animals in the order Carnivora, such as bears and cats, all of which have long, sharp teeth.

Carrion The remains of dead animals.

Cartilage Firm, flexible tissue that is part of the skeleton of vertebrates. In fish such as sharks, the entire skeleton is made of cartilage.

Cell The smallest existing unit of living matter.

Claw Pointed, horny nail on an animal's foot.

Cnidarian A type of simple aquatic animal such as a sea anemone.

Colony A group of animals (such as penguins) that live together.

Comb Fleshy crest on a bird's head.

Coniferous Referring to a tree with scaly cones that contain seeds.

Courtship The process by which animals attract their mates.

Crèche A group formed by the chicks of some birds such as flamingos, terns, and ostriches.

Crustacean A type of arthropod, mainly aquatic, that has a hard shell.

Dabbling The action of a waterbird when it upends to reach food deep down in the water with its beak.

Deciduous Referring to a tree that sheds its leaves in the fall and grows new ones in the spring.

Den A safe resting place for an animal.

Diurnal Active during the day.

Echinoderm A type of symmetrical marine animal such as a starfish.

Echolocation Locating distant or invisible objects by bouncing sound waves off them.

Environment The natural world all around us, including land, air, and living things.

Exotic Dramatically unusual; introduced from another country.

Extinct No longer existing on Earth.

Falconry The sport of training falcons or using them to catch game.

Fang A sharp tooth, or a hollow tooth used to inject venom.

Flank The side of an animal between the ribs and the hip.

Flipper An aquatic mammal's paddle-shaped limb.

Flock A group of birds or mammals assembled together.

Fluke A rubbery tail flipper on whales and similar creatures.

Forage To actively seek out food.

Forelimb/forefoot A limb or foot at the front of an animal's body.

Gam A large group of whales that travel together.

Gills Feathery structures on the side of a fish's head that extract oxygen from the water.

Gnaw To bite or nibble continuously.

Graze To feed on growing grass and other green plants.

Grooming Describes an animal's behavior when it cleans itself or another animal.

Habitat The place, or type of place, where a plant or animal lives naturally.

Harem Often used to describe a group of female animals under the protection of one male.

Hatch To emerge from an egg or a pupa; to keep an egg warm so it will hatch.

Hatchling Recently hatched young (for example, a turtle).

Heath A large area of uncultivated land, usually with peaty soil; see moor.

Herd A large group of animals that feed and travel together.

Hibernate To go into a deep sleeplike state during the winter.

Hind limb/hind foot A limb or foot at the rear of an animal's body.

Hooves The horny feet that animals such as horses and reindeer have.

Horn A hard, pointed growth on some mammals' heads.

Immune Having a high level of resistance to one or more diseases.

Incisor In mammals, a flat tooth at the front of the jaw used for slicing or gnawing.

Insectivores Animals that eat insects.

Invertebrate An animal without a backbone.

Keratin A tough protein found in hair, nails, claws, hooves, and horns.

Lair A home or resting place of a wild animal.

Larva A young stage in the life of an animal, in which it looks completely different to the adult; for example, a caterpillar or tadpole.

Litter A group of young animals born to the same mother at the same time.

Lodge The den or lair of a group of animals such as beavers.

Luminous Giving off light; bright.

Mammal A warm-blooded animal that feeds its young on milk produced by the female.

Mane The long, thick hair that grows on the neck of some animals, such as horses and male lions.

Marine Connected with the sea.

Marsupial A type of mammal with a pouch on the female's abdomen to hold developing young.

Migration Moving from one place to another according to the seasons, usually to find food or to breed.

Mollusk A type of invertebrate that has a soft body without segments, and—usually but not always—a shell.

Monotreme An egg-laying mammal such as a platypus.

Monsoon Seasonal wind accompanied by heavy rain.

Moor A large area of uncultivated land, usually with peaty soil; see heath.

Mudflat Muddy area of ground exposed at low tide, but under water at high tide.

Muscle A type of living tissue that contracts and relaxes to produce movement.

Mustelid One of a family of predatory mammals such as weasels, ferrets, or badgers.

Necking A mating ritual of male giraffes in which they lock necks and sometimes clash heads.

Nectar Sweet liquid, produced by flowers; some birds and insects feed on nectar.

Nest A structure built by animals, usually to lay eggs in.

Nocturnal Active at night.

Nursing Referring to a female mammal feeding her young on her milk.

Offspring The young of a person, animal, or plant.

Operculum The body flap that covers a fish's gills.

Organism An individual member of a biological species.

Ossicone Small horn covered with skin.

Pacing A distinctive walk in which both legs on the same side move together, then both legs move together on the opposite side; seen in camels and their relatives.

Pack A group of animals that join together for activities such as hunting.

Passerine A perching songbird such as a warbler or a thrush.

Patagium A skin flap, such as a bat's wing, used for flying or gliding through the air.

Pectoral Of fins, behind the head.

Pelvic Of fins, on the underside.

Perch To settle or rest, often briefly.

Photophore A light-emitting organ, especially one of the luminous spots on some marine fish.

Pigment A substance that colors other materials.

Pinniped One of a group of mammals, such as seals and walruses, that have flippers instead of feet.

Placenta The organ inside the womb of a female mammal that nourishes the developing young.

Plankton The mass of tiny algae and animals that float around in the sea and provide food for marine animals.

Plumage A bird's feathers.

Predator An animal that hunts, kills, and eats other animals.

Preening When a bird cleans and smooths its feathers with its beak.

Prehensile Adapted for seizing or grasping; often used to describe a tail.

Prey An animal that is hunted, killed, and eaten by a predator.

Pride A group of lions.

Primate An animal that has hands or feet that can grasp, and a relatively large brain.

Pronking Behavior seen in some antelopes in which they bounce up and down on stiff legs when they are frightened or excited.

Protected (species) A type of animal whose life or habitat is safeguarded by law to save it from extinction.

Pupil The round, dark opening in the eye that gets bigger and smaller to control the amount of light that enters.

Pygmy A very small example of its kind, such as a pygmy shark.

Quill The hollow, horny center of a feather.

Rainforest Dense, tropical woodland that gets very heavy rainfall.

Raptor A bird of prey.

Regurgitate Bring back food that is not completely digested from the stomach to the mouth.

Reptile A class of vertebrates that breathe air and are usually cold blooded, such as snakes and lizards.

Reservation An area of land set aside for the protection of particular animals or habitats.

Rodent Gnawing mammals such as mice and rats.

Roost To settle down for rest or sleep, or to perch.

Ruminate To regurgitate food and chew it again—sometimes called "chewing the cud."

Scales Small, overlapping plates that protect the skin of some animals such as fish and reptiles.

Scavenge To feed on the carcasses of other animals.

School A large group of fish swimming close together.

Sett The burrow of a badger.

Sheath A close-fitting covering.

Shoal A large group of fish swimming together in a loose formation.

Sirenian A member of an order of mammals, including the dugong, that has a flat tail, paddlelike front limbs, and no hind limbs.

Skeleton The rigid framework (usually bone or cartilage) of an animal's body.

Snout A long, projecting nose.

Social Involving interaction with other animals.

Solitary Likely to live alone.

Sonar The process of detecting an underwater object, such as prey or a fellow creature, by using sound waves.

Spawn To produce or deposit eggs; used of aquatic animals.

Spherical In the shape of a sphere or round ball.

Spine An animal's supporting column or backbone.

Stoop The action of a bird when it dives down very quickly, usually to attack prey.

Suckle To feed milk to young from a teat or breast.

Talon The sharp claw on a bird of prey.

Temperate Moderate, not extreme.

Tentacle A long, bendy, armlike body part that aquatic animals such as squid and cuttlefish use for touching and grasping.

Terrestrial Relating to land.

Territory An area occupied and defended by an animal, or a group of animals.

Toxic Relating to a poison or a toxin.

Troop A gathering of one kind of primate, such as monkeys.

Tropical Relating to hot, humid regions.

Tusk An enlarged, hornlike tooth. Elephants and walruses have tusks.

Vein A vessel that carries blood toward the heart.

Venom Poisonous liquid produced by some animals such as snakes and scorpions.

Vertebrate An animal with a backbone.

Wetland Tidal flat or swamp where the soil is permanently wet.

Whiskers Long, sticking-out hairs or bristles that grow near an animal's mouth.

Wingspan The measurement from the tip of one wing to the tip of the other when the wings are outstretched.

Index

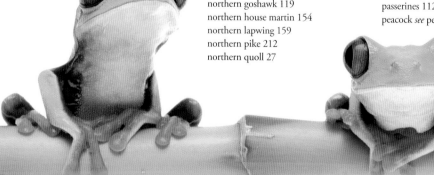

INDEX

Acknowledgments

The publisher would like to thank the following people for their help with making the book: Anastasia Baliyan for design assistance; Bipasha Roy, Chhavi Nagpal, Rupa Rao, and Manjari Thakur for editorial assistance; Saloni Singh for the jacket; Caroline Stamps for proofreading; and Helen Peters for indexing.

Smithsonian Enterprises

Avery Naughton, Licensing Coordinator, Licensed Publishing
Paige Towler, Editorial Lead, Licensed Publishing
Jill Corcoran, Senior Director, Licensed Publishing
Brigid Ferraro, Vice President, Consumer and Education Products
Carol LeBlanc, President

Smithsonian Institution consultants:
National Museum of Natural History

Don E. Wilson, Curator Emeritus, Vertebrate Zoology;
Carla J. Dove, Ph.D., Feather Identification Laboratory;
Lynne R. Parenti, Curator of Fishes and Research Scientist;
Jeremy Jacobs, Collections Manager, Division of Amphibians and Reptiles;
Gary F. Hevel, Research Collaborator, Department of Entomology;
Stephen Cairns, Research Scientist, Invertebrate Zoology;
Jerry Harasewych, Research Scientist, Invertebrate Zoology;
Kristian Fauchald, Research Scientist, Invertebrate Zoology
Chris Mah, Research Associate, Invertebrate Zoology

National Marine Fisheries Service

Allen Collins, Research Scientist;
Martha Nizinski, Research Scientist.

Contributors to the first edition:

Amy-Jane Beer, Alex Cox, Leon Gray, Natalie Godwin, Emma Forge, Tom Forge, Sophie Pelham, Vicky Wharton, Romaine Werblow, Lee Wilson, Kevin Royal, and Chris Bernstein.

The publisher would like to thank the following for their kind permission to reproduce their photographs:

(Key: a-above; b-below/bottom; c-center; f-far; l-left; r-right; t-top)

Valerie Abbott: 17cl; **Alamy Images:** Ch'ien Lee / Minden Pictures 44tr; Michael Quinton / Minden Pictures 51cra; imageBROKER.com GmbH & Co. KG / Nigel Dennis 123bl, Damon Coulter 154bl; imageBROKER / Daniel Heuclin 174b; Robert Wyatt 180b; Roberto Nistri 208cl, David Fleetham 209cla; Mike Veitch 210–211; Birgitte Wilms / Minden Pictures 216br; Avalon.red / Oceans Image 216c, Science History Images / Photo Researchers 236b, Avalon.red / Anthony Bannister 269tr, Nature Picture Library / Ingo Arndt 269cra; Enrique R. Aguirre Aves 139tr; AfriPics.com 109tr; Alaska Stock LLC 223br; Bryan & Cherry Alexander 131tr; AndyLim.com 235cl; Heather Angel 19cr; Arco Images 14b, 145tc, 177bl, 178b, 283tr; Auscape International 181tr; Bill Bachmann 117br; Peter Barritt 133bl; Glenn Bartley / All Canada Photos 154cr; Blickwinkel 124cl, 163clb, 163cr, 177bc, 179r, 185c, 185r, 198 (Malabar), 200l, 202l, 206l, 208l, 210l, 212l, 214l, 216l, 218l, 220l, 222l, 246cr, 257cr, 271cr; Steve Bloom 11br, 109cra, 129tl, 144b; Rick & Nora Bowers 166tr, 191c; John Cancalosi 125br; Nigel Cattlin/Holt Studios International Ltd. 227br, 257c; Brandon Cole Marine Photography 231tl, 290bl; Bruce Coleman Inc. 179c; Mark Conlin 304; Andrew Darrington 185l; Danita Delimont 117tr, 121br; Thomas Dobner 249cl; Matthew Doggett 161cl; Redmond Durrell 300, 301; Karin Duthie 181cl; Florida Images 169cr; FotoNatura 127bl; Stephen Frink Collection 235cr, 285cl, 291br; Johan Furusjö 129bl; Tim Gainey 274b; Guillen Photography 287br; Blaine Harrington III 124b; Mike Hill 149br; Bjorn Holland 286b; Friedrich von Horsten 91cr;

Chris Howes/Wild Places Photography 232c; Iconotec 239cr; imagebroker 43br; INTERFOTO Pressebildagentur 167tr; Jonathan Samuel Gregg Irwin 162c; Andre Jenny 125bl; Steven J. Kazlowski 7tl, 120bl, 120–121; Kevin Schafer 127tr, 130–131, 163bl, 187tr; Holt Studios International Ltd 259cr; Juniors Bildarchiv 179bl, 182–183, 186t, 259bl; Kuttig - Animals 183tr; LMR Group 129tr; John E. Marriott 15tl; Chris Mattison 171c, 197bl; Mediacolor's 246tr; Melba Photo Agency 49br; Louise Murray 264–265; N:id 281bl; Eyal Nahmias 275br; NaturePics 259tl; David Noble Photography 19c; Rolf Nussbaumer 139bc; Papillo 170, 198 (Emerald), 227clb; Jacky Parker 157cr, 157tr; Robert C. Paulson 249tr; Wolfgang Polzer 181br; Premaphotos 181c; Adam Seward 10c; Martin Shields 179cl, 189c; Marco Simoni 133cl; Terry Sohl 142cr; tbkmedia. de 107br; David Tipling 136–137; Tom Uhlman 50–51; Duncan Usher 12c; Ariadne Van Zandbergen 21crb; John van Decker 135bl; Travis VanDenBerg 235tr; Visions of America, LLC 120cla; Visual & Written SL 25br, 247br, 284; David Wall 18–19c; John Warburton-Lee Photography 213tc; Dave Watts 148l; Petra Wegner 227tr; Maximilian Weinzierl 12–13c; Whitehead Images 289cr; Wildlife GmbH 18l, 196t, 210crb, 211cr, 211cra; Anna Yu 43c; Jim Zuckerman 7tc, 176bl, 176–177t; **Ardea:** Kathie Atkinson 195br; Ian Beames 45bl; Hans & Judy Beste 27cl; Leslie Brown 140–141; Julie Bruton-Seal 85tc; Piers Cavendish 25cr; Bill Coster 119br; Johan De Meester 66; Steve Downer 32br; Jean-Paul Ferrero 42t; Kenneth W Fink 33cl, 137tr; François Grohier 23r, 46tr, 102bl, 102cl, 126b, 271tr; Greg Harold 198 (Turtle); John Cancalosi 17cla, 39cl, 123cr; Ken Lucas 39br, 189t, 289tr; Geoff Moon 21cr; Hayden Oake 75cb; Pat Morris 44bc, 193br, 193c, 199tr, 229br; Jadgeep Raiput 88; Sid Roberts 149c; Geoff Trinder 45br; David & Katie Urry 229tr; M Watson 11tl, 25tr, 132b;

M. Watson 40–41, 41br, 94br, 101cr; Doc White 10tl; Jim Zipp 118l; Andrey Zvoznikov 30tl; **Kevin Arvin:** 271br; **GK Bhat:** 186cl; **Bill Blevins:** 199 (Woodhouse); **BluePlanetArchive.com:** Ingrid Visser 2crb (Dolphin), Dave Forcucci 5tc, Ingrid Visser 20–21c, 23l, Ingrid Visser 52, 200–201, 201cr, Rudie Kuiter 203bc, 203bl, David B. Fleetham 203br, James D. Watt 208b, 208tl, Dan Burton 209br, 209tl, Doug Perrine 214–215, Doug Perrine 215cra, 215tr, Espen Rekdal 216bl, 216c, John C. Lewis 216cr, 216tr, Dan Burton 217bl, Doug Perrine 217br, Clay Bryce 217clb, Steve Drogin 217cla, Masa Ushioda 217tr, 217tl, e-Photo / Nobuo Kitagawa 219cra, David Kearnes 219crb, 219br, 219tr, Dave Forcucci 220, Doc White 220–221bs, 221bl, e-Photo / Makoto Kubo 221br, Doc White 221c, Doc White 221clb, 221cl, Rudie Kuiter 221crb, 221cr, Doc White 221tl, Gregory Ochocki 221tr, Andrew J. Martinez 231tr, Franco Banfi 239tr, e-Photo / Makoto Hirose 286bc, 286bl; **Lia Brand Photography Inc.:** 19tr; **Meng Foo Choo:** 19cra; **Corbis:** Remi Benali 18bc; Niall Benvie 153bl; Jonathan Blair 164bl; Brandon D Cole 52l, 231cl; Kevin Fleming 76b; Michael & Patricia Fogden 260cl; Martin Harvey 143tr; Frank Lane Picture Agency 291cr; Frans Lanting 111c; Danny Lehman 21c; Joe McDonald 11crb; Arthur Morris 142tr; Joel W Rogers 223cr; Jeffrey L Rotman 286br; Galen Rowell 11c; Josef Scaylea 137br; Kevin Schafer 133tr, 174ca; Paul A Souders 4–5b, 183bck, 296–297; Herbert Spichtinger 148r; Kennan Ward 105cb; **Tammyjo Dallas:** 8 (snake); **Dr Melanie Dammhahn:** 37cl; © **Tim Davenport/ WCS:** 39tc; **Christoph Diewald:** 16b; **DK Images:** American Museum of Natural History 180cl; Peter Chadwick/Courtesy of the Natural History Museum, London 148bc, 151crb; Malcolm Coulson 129tc; Philip Dowell 129cr; Dudley Edmonson 62crb; Exmoor Zoo, Devon 135tl; Chris Gomersall Photography 127tl; Frank

ACKNOWLEDGMENTS

Greenaway/Courtesy of the Natural History Museum, London 127cr, 257br, 275bl, 275c, 275crb, 276cl; Rowan Greenwood 129br; Colin Keates/Courtesy of the Natural History Museum, London 275tc; Mike Linley 196c; Maslowski Photo 151cl; National Birds of Prey Centre, Gloucestershire 118br, 119bl, 119cr; Natural History Museum, London 113c, 113tl; Stephen Oliver 113tr, 151bl; David Peart 20cl, 167cl; Barrie Watts 16–17; Jerry Young 62cr, 274t, 275cra; **James Eaton, Birdtour Asia:** 155bc; **Dreamstime.com:** Kateryna Kon 9tl (Archaea); Smitty411 43cla; Vaclav Matous 145cr; Joe888 241crb, Irina Pislari 291cr; Mauro Rodrigues 271cl; **Tolis Flioukas:** 9 (hermit crab); **FLPA:** Michael & Patricia Fogden/Minden 146–147; J W Alker 228r; Terry Andrewartha 105bl; Fred Bavendam 242bl, 242–243t; Matthias Breiter 51cr; Richard Brooks 123br; Wendy Dennis 149cl; Reinard Dirscherl 240b; Richard Du Toit/Minden Pictures 62b, 100–101; Michael Durham 34br; Gerry Ellis/Minden Pictures 69cra; Peter Entwistle 249cr; Yossi Eshbol 31tl; Katherine Feng/Globio/Minden Pictures 69br, 69cr; Foto Natura Stock 93b, 93cl; Tony Hamblin 118tr, 142bl; David Hosking 265br; Mitsuhiko Imamori 269br; Jurgen & Christine Sohns 30br, 42b, 43bl, 176br; Gerard Lacz 63cl; Frans Lanting 6–7, 31br, 37br, 81t, 160–161, 292–293; Hans Leijense 60–61, 93cr; S & D & K Maslowski 28bl, 28c; Chris Mattison 198 (Monte); Phil McLean 139tl; Claus Meyer/Minden Pictures 279–279; Michio Hoshino/Minden Pictures 38br, 64–65, 104–105t; Minden Pictures/ZSSD 65br; Patricio Robles Gil/Sierra Madre/Minden Pictures 86–87; Mark Moffett/Minden Pictures 197br, 256b, 267bl; Yva Momatiuk/John Eastcott/Minden Pictures 76–77; Piotr Naskrecki 253t; Chris Newbert/Minden Pictures 229tl; Flip Nicklin 54–55; Pete Oxford 71cr; Panda Photo 189br; Fritz Polking 109br; Michael Quinton/Minden 105cr; Len Robinson 155br; Walter Rohdich 162bl; Cyril Ruoso/Minden Pictures 68–69; Malcolm Schuyl 33bc, 33tl; Chris & Tilde Stuart 102–103; Roger Tidman 67br; Jan Vermeer/Foto Natura 78b; Larry West 190tr, 281tl; Terry Whittaker 32bc, 77b, 139c; D P Wilson 140bl; Martin B Withers 2 (Dingo), 62tl; Norbert Wu 2tl, 26r, 229cr, 235bl;

Zhinong Xi 107cr; **Neil Furey:** 33ca; **Getty Images:** Education Images / Universal Images Group 131crb, AFP 156–157, **200–201 Getty Images:** Stone / Georgette Douwma, Wild Horizons / Universal Images Group 203bc(Jawfish), 233bc; Ingo Arndt 133cr; Pete Atkinson 151tl; Gary Bell 169tl; Gary Benson 94t; Walter Bibikow 17c; Emanuele Biggi 273br; DAJ 5tl, Flip De Nooyer/FotoNatura 127br; Roger Deha Harpe 165br; Georgette Douwma 201c; Michael Dunning 180tr; Nicole Duplaix 173cr; Michael Durham 190b; Danny Ellinger 135tr; Tim Flach 267tr; Larry Gatz 3 (hammerheads), 201l, 206–207; George Grall 197c; Gavin Hellier 1; Kevin Horan 116–117; Gavriel Jecan 275tr; Rene Krekels 7tr, 188; Tim Laman 254–255; Timothy Laman 28tl, 191tr; Patrick Landmann 261cr; Cliff Leight 86t; Michael Melford 222–223; Michael Nichols 22–23, 89br; Patricio Robles Gil/Sierra Madre/Minden Pictures 89bl; Mark Moffett 196b; Piotr Naskrecki 261br; Paul Nicklen 86b; Michael & Patricia Fogden 194–195; Michael Redmen 184–185; Tui De Roy 133bc, 133tl, 149tl; SA Team/Foto Natura 167c; Kevin Schafer 59crb; Chris Schenk 126tr; Yomiuri Shimbun 232–233; Tom Stoddart 91br; Ben Van Den Brink 270bl; Wim van Egmond 285tr; Tom Vezo 63br; Birgitte Wilms/Minden Pictures 216br; Norbert Wu 213bc, 218–219; Minden Pictures/ZSSD 110–111; **Jack Goldfarb/Design Pics Inc.:** 199 (Couch's spadefoot); **Andreas Graemiger:** 11cra; **Thor Håkonsen:** 255tr; **Mark Hamblin:** 133 cr; **Chod A. Hedinger:** 15tr; **imagequestmarine.com:** Jim Greenfield 291c; Takaji Ochi 290–291; Peter Parks 239c; **Getty Images / iStock:** Omar Ariff 215br; Bostb 186br; Marshall Bruce 10bl; Michel De Nijs 17cra; Alan Drummond 10br; Mike Golay 15bl; Hazlan Abdul Hakim 10bc; Andrew Howe 153cr, 154bc; Frank Leung 111cr; Jurie Maree 18ca; Peter Miller 10tr; Phil Morley 12cra; Dawn Nichols 125tr; Katrina Outland 285br; Lorenzo Pastore 91t; Matej Pribelsky 112l; Achim Prill 192; Proxyminder 270b; Ryan Saul 208cr; Steve Snyder 273cr; Jan Will 17crb; Mark Wilson 10fbr; **Stephen Kelly:** 16c; **Ray Macey:** 257cl; **Earl F. Martinelli:** 19tl; **Ric McArthur:** 11cla; **Sean McCann:** 257bl; **Taco Meeuwsen:** 153c; **Cheryl Moorehead:** 227ftl; **National Geographic**

Image Collection: Darlyne A. Murawski 282–283; **Natural Visions:** 69tr, 104bl; **naturepl.com:** Pete Oxford 37cra, Tui De Roy 145br, Ingo Arndt 38l; Peter Blackwell 72br, 171br; Brandon Cole 169tr; Bruce Davidson 97br, 280–281b; Doug Perrine 92–93, 93t, 167br, 230–231b; Jurgen Freund 165bl, 235br, 238t; Nick Garbutt 31cl; Tony Heald 98t; Kim Taylor 34cr, 256t; Eliot Lyons 83b; Tom Mangelsen 106br; Luiz Claudio Marigo 251cr, 283br; George McCarthy 67tl; Rolf Nussbaumer 138; William Osborn 153br; Pete Oxford 37bl, 57b, 79br, 97cr; Pete Cairns 79cr, 106–107; Constantinos Petrinos 285tc; Tony Phelps 279t; David Pike 41tr; Premaphotos 251br, 283cr; Peter Reese 265tr; Jeff Rotman 238–239tc; Jose B Ruiz 155tc; Andy Sands 273bl; Phil Savoie 154c, 273cl; Peter Scoones 234; Anup Shah 36, 98b, 99tl, 164br; Igor Shpilenok 31cr; Sinclair Stammers 280t; Lynn M. Stone 70–71, 80–81, 173bc; David Tipling 85tr; Jeff Vanuga 105cl; Tom Vezo 288b; Doc White 81b; Staffan Widstrand 99br, 122b; Mike Wilkes 101br; Simon Williams 268–269; Solvin Zankl 239tc; **NHPA/Photoshot:** Bryan & Cherry Alexander 85cr; ANT Photo Library 28–29; Daryl Balfour 72–73t, 73bl; Anthony Bannister 30tr, 175bl, 269cr; Bill Coster 135br, 155cl; Laurie Campbell 135cl; Lee Dalton 115cb; Stephen Dalton 112t, 249tl, 260–261, 279br, 279cb; Nigel J Dennis 143br; Nick Garbutt 23c, 83tr, 97tr, 147cr; Ken Griffiths 267br; Adrian Hepworth 147br; Daniel Heulin 143c, 191br, 199c; James Warwick 96–97, 97ftl, 150–151; B. Jones & M. Shimlock 228l; Rich Kirchner 51br; Stephen Krasemann 70l, 137cr; Martin Harvey 183cr, 268b; Dr Eckart Pott 129c; Cede Prudente 173br; Steve Robinson 82b, 97tl; Andy Rouse 44l, 108–109; Jonathan & Angela Scott 109crb; Taketomo Shiratori 84c; Gerrit Vyn 125c; M. I. Walker 229bl; Dave Watts 27br; Martin Wendler 169br; **Photolibrary:** Animals/Earth Scenes 174tr; Kathie Atkinson 26cl, 257tr; David Courtenay 81c; Daniel Cox 79bl; David M. Dennis 237tc; IFA–Bilderteam GmbH 61r; Juniors Bildarchiv 46b; London Scientific Films 227bl; Oxford Scientific Films 147tr; Werner Pfunder 104br; Mary Plage/OSF 99c; Survival Anglia 155r; Konrad Wothe 25crb; **Stuart Plummer:** 19bc; **Guido & Philippe Poppe—www.poppe-images.com:** 231cr; **Stefano**

Prigione: 14tl; **Press Association Images:** AP 284bl; **PunchStock:** Design Pics 193tr; Digital Vision 173bl; Digital Vision/Caroline Warren 164–165l; Jupiter 239br; **Raymond Racaza:** 19cl; **Dr Gil Rilov:** 233bl; **Mel José Rivera Rodriguez:** 179tc; **Mike Robles:** 9 (blue starfish); **rspb-images.com:** Chris Knights 114tc, 154tl; **Science Photo Library:** Charles Angelo 235tl; Nigel Cattlin 258; John Devries 134b; Eye of Science 12br; Pascal Goetgheluck 266; Richard R. Hansen 250–251, 251tr; Gary Meszaros 259tc; Sinclair Stammers 9tr; Merlin D. Tuttle 32t; Jean-Philippe Varin 267tl; Jerome Wexler 12bl; **Shutterstock.com:** Kitch Bain 4tl; lego 19861111 58–59b; Joe Barbarite 226bl; Lara Barrett 226cl; Mircea Bezergheanu 226clb; Stephen Bonk 3 (Newt); Sandra Caldwell 2 (Echidna); Ivan Cholakov 3 (Iguana); EcoPrint 226cl; Richard Fitzer 225br; Josiah J. Garber 227cr; Mark Grenier 4tc; Peter Hansen 3 (Snake); Lavigne Herve 227cl; Eric Isselée 298–299; Ivanov 290cl; Mawroidis Kamila 224bc; Cathy Keifer 3 (Mantis); Kelpfish 3 (Starfish), 226–227b; K. L. Kohn 3 (Frog); D. J. Mattaar 3tr, 4tr, 224bl, 302–303; Mayskyphoto 3 (Parrot); David Mckee 2 (Ape); Mishella 4ftl; rsfatt 174cl; Vishal Shah 294–295; Johan Swanepoel 18cb; Morozova Tatyana 234b; Florin Tirlea 224–225; Alan Ward 5tr; Richard Williamson 3 (Anemon); **Chandan Singh:** 11tr; **Frank Steinmann:** 197ca; **Still Pictures:** John Cancalosi 172bl; Martin Harvey 73br, 90–91; **Kayla Swart:** 19clb; © **Uthai Treesucon/www.arkive.org:** 49cr; **www.uwp.no:** Erling Svenson 291bl; **Brian Valentine:** 248–249, 272, 272t; **Eric Vanderduys:** 191cr; **Nikki van Veelen:** 9 (sponge); **Gernot Vogel:** 173cb; **Warren Photographic:** 84tl, 85bl, 246b, 253cl; Jane Burton 109bl; Kim Taylor 252, 289c, 289cl; **Tom Weilenmann:** 19cla; **Wikimedia Commons:** Holger Gröschl 271tl; Rowland Shelly, PhD, North Carolina State Museum of Natural Sciences 289tl; **Sergey Yeliseer:** 154tr.

All other images © Dorling Kindersley